REDESIGNING THE FUTURE

REDESIGNING THE FUTURE

A SYSTEMS APPROACH TO SOCIETAL PROBLEMS

RUSSELL L. ACKOFF

University of Pennsylvania

A WILEY-INTERSCIENCE PUBLICATION

JOHN WILEY & SONS   New York · London · Sydney · Toronto

Library of Congress Cataloging in Publication Data:

Ackoff, Russell Lincoln, 1919-
  Redesigning the future.

  "A Wiley-Interscience publication."
  Bibliography: p.
  1. United States—Social conditions—1960-
2. Social problems. 3. Social change. 4. System
theory. I. Title.

HN65.A6   309.1 '73 '092   74-10627
ISBN 0-471-00296-8

Printed in the United States of America

10 9   8   7   6   5   4   3   2   1

To

Herman Wrice,

William Ellison,

and

August A. Busch III,

who have the courage, capability,
and commitment

_____

PREFACE

If you read the newspapers and are still satisfied with the state of the world, put this book down; it is not for you. My objective is not to convert those who are satisfied — even though I believe they need conversion — but to give those who are dissatisfied cause for hope and something to do about it.

To many of those to whom the world seems to be out of control, there appears to be little that can be done about it. But as long as there is even a little that can be done about it, we ought to be doing it. What can an individual — a smaller and smaller part of a larger and larger society — do about the state of that society? The distinguished and dissatisfied Spanish philosopher José Ortega y Gasset offered an answer, *produce a mobilizing idea:*

> ... man has been able to grow enthusiastic over his vision of ... unconvincing enterprises. He has put himself to work for the sake of an idea, seeking by magnificent exertions to arrive at the incredible. And in the end, he has arrived there. Beyond all doubt it is one of the vital sources of man's power, to be thus able to kindle enthusiasm from the mere glimmer of something improbable, difficult, remote.

An idea can mobilize individuals into a social crusade in search of an ideal. It can induce them to undo and redo what they have done wittingly or unwittingly, and to regain control over the whole of which they are part and, more importantly, of themselves.

Collective action directed at redeveloping society can arise only out of desperation and hope. Desperation, in turn, arises out of deprivation and frustration; hope out of ideas that hold promise. There is no lack of deprivation and frustration, but there is a lack of ideas that can mobilize the disillusioned, the disappointed, and the deprived into collective action. This book tries to provide some, but to claim that it succeeds would be pretentious. I can only hope that I have shown that such ideas are possible and how they might be developed.

An idea is a combination of a conception of what might be done and a hypothesis about the consequences of doing so. What ideas one has are the products of his point of view. But even those with the same point of view may have different ideas. Therefore, this book begins with four chapters that are largely devoted to developing a new point from which to view the world. In the remaining chapters I examine a sample of the more important crises confronting society and attempt to generate ideas about how these could be treated more effectively than they are currently.

I do not claim authorship of any of the ideas presented. I am sure others have had each of the ideas I treat as my own, even where I am unaware of it. No idea can mobilize a large number of individuals into action unless most of them can treat it as their own. My hope, therefore, is that in this work I articulate what many others have thought and desire to claim as their own.

My effort to do so has been stimulated by continuous exposure to university students who have taught me more than I know and who have provided the base on which my hopes for tomorrow rest. Among these I would particularly like to thank Burt Cohen, Bob Cort, Pete Davis, Jim Emshoff, Bill Finnie, John Hall, Francisco Sagasti, and Jorge Stein. In addition there have been many friends with whom in conversation and correspondence many of the ideas in this book first came into my consciousness. These include Stafford Beer, C. West Churchman, Thomas A. Cowan, Fred E. Emery, Gerald R. Galbo, Sir Charles Goodeve, Britton Harris, Burr McCloskey, Hasan Ozbekhan, Leon Pritzker, Patrick Rivett, Eric Trist, and the three to whom this book is dedicated.

I am also grateful for all the help received from Jeanne Gibstein in preparing this manuscript.

RUSSELL L. ACKOFF

Philadelphia, Pennsylvania
May 1974

CONTENTS

REDESIGNING THE FUTURE

PART ONE

IN GENERAL

CHAPTER ONE

———————

THE REVOLUTION
WE ARE IN

Revolution, *a total or radical change of circum-*
stances or of system.
Crisis, *a serious or decisive state of things, or the*
point of time when an affair must soon terminate
or suffer a material change, a turning point, a criti-
cal juncture.

WEBSTER'S UNIVERSAL DICTIONARY, 1936

The presence, if not prevalence, of crises is normal in most societies. Ours is
not an exception. It does not follow, however, that our society must decline
and face doom. Decline and doom are not inevitable; they can be avoided, but
they may not be. Survival is not inevitable either.

Like Rome most earlier societies that rose subsequently fell, at least
partway. Not too long ago Spain was the richest and most powerful nation on
earth. Later both France and England won and lost this distinctive position.
Before Spain's dominance Syria, Egypt, Greece, and many other societies
traveled through history like shooting stars, appearing on one horizon and
disappearing on the other. Survival—let alone "thrival"—of a society is not
assured by any historical law. If anything, history seems to indicate that the
fall of an elevated society is inevitable. But the future is not completely
contained in the past; much of it has yet to be written.

Some think it is too late to do anything about the future. For example, Jacques Ellul, the French religious mystic, argues that our social order is determined by its technology, that this technology is changing in a self-determined way, and, therefore, that society is no longer controlled by man. As the eminent Dutch historian of science and technology, R. J. Forbes, put it: "Ellul seems to endow *La Technique* [the technological order] not only with anthropomorphic but with demonological attributes."

Most of us react to Ellul's thesis as Forbes did: "Technology does *not* have such internal dynamism and is wholly incapable of setting its own rules on the basis of its own logic within a completely closed circle." However, even if we maintain that technology is still susceptible to our control, it does not follow that we are controlling it. Alvin Toffler, in his widely read *Future Shock*, observed: "The horrifying truth is that, so far as technology is concerned, no one is in charge." It may not be controlling us, but we certainly are not controlling it.

If we are to design the future and improve the quality of life, we must determine how the state of our affairs differs from that of earlier societies. Because of an increasing rate of technological change, social and environmental crises are generated and come to a head more rapidly today than at any previous time. Therefore, they require societal responses that are quicker and surer than were required in the past. But our society does not provide them. Its structure and functioning does not facilitate rapid response. Its lack of responsiveness to crises generates discontent among a growing number of its members, discontent that manifests itself in disruptive protest, civil disobedience, or alienation from society. Our society responds more rapidly to disruptions than it does to the crises that produce them, and it often does so with repressive measures. These, in turn, stimulate further protest and disobedience. The cycle—protest, repression, protest—either intensifies or dissipates in indifference. Either outcome leads to social disintegration. Consider this cycle in more detail.

"The rate of social and technological change is greater today than it has been at any time in the past." This much-repeated statement is true but it does not differentiate our moment in history from others; it has been equally true at most times in the past. What does differentiate our time from previous ones is a qualitative change brought about by the rate of change we have achieved. Sir Charles P. Snow identified it in his famous lecture on *The Two Cultures:* "During all human history until this century, the rate of social change has been very slow. So slow, that it could pass unnoticed in one person's lifetime. That is no longer so. The rate of change has increased so much that our imagination can't keep up." Sir Goeffrey Vickers, the eminent British social philosopher, put it another way: "The rate of change increases at an accelerating speed, with a corresponding acceleration in the rate at which further responses can be made; and this brings us nearer the threshold beyond which control is lost."

Accelerating technological change is widely recognized. It is the principal theme of Alvin Toffler's *Future Shock*. Toffler's central thesis is that our society's inability to adapt to the increasing rate of change—not to its content or direction—is the most critical problem of our times.

In my lifetime there has been a greater increase in the speed of travel than there was in all of history up to my birth. The rates at which information can be communicated, energy can be generated, and products can be manufactured have gone through similar accelerating increases. Such changes mean that in your lifetime and mine society has had to face larger changes than civilization as a whole has had to face from its inception up to our births. And the rate of change continues to accelerate.

Technological change has produced more wealth and affluence, more consumption, more education, more communication, and more travel in our century than was produced in all preceding centuries. It has also changed society in fundamental ways and produced such crises as are examined in Part II of this book. Society does not yet know how to respond rapidly and effectively to these crises and it may not learn how to do so in time. Therefore, there is an urgent need to change our society in ways that increase its ability to learn and adapt.

Increases in the rate of change of technology have decreased the effectiveness of experience as a teacher. It is too slow. Trial and error require more time than is currently available between changes that require response. The lag between stimulus and response brought about by reliance on experience permits crises to develop to a point at which we are forced to respond to them with little relevant knowledge. An increasing portion of society's responses are made out of desperation, not out of deliberation. Antipoverty, antidiscrimination, anticrime, and antinarcotics measures recently taken in the United States are examples.

Donald Schon, an American authority on innovation, reflecting on our decreasing ability to solve social problems, observed: "The times required for diagnosis, for design of demonstration, or for extension to the next instance, are long enough . . . to include changes which invalidate conclusions once they are reached."

Because of the rapid and extensive distribution of news that has been made possible by advances in communication technology, the world is approaching what Marshall McCluhan called a "global village." In this village public issues and pressures build up rapidly, requiring governments to respond more quickly than they ever have in the past.

Furthermore, the highly developed societies of today are the first dominantly urban societies in history. Most of their members live in environments that are more man-made than natural. Mismanagement of these "artificial" environments has significantly increased the rate of deterioration of the natural environment. The life-supporting capabilities of the natural environment are being reduced at an increasing rate.

But contemporary man is not restricted to use of slow means of self-destruction. He has the ability to eliminate most, if not all, of his species with one fell swoop. The destructive forces that he commands can virtually remove a possibility always previously available to society, that of making a comeback. The possibility of complete self-destruction has deep psychological effects on all of us, but particularly on the young who were born and bred in the presence of the specter it produces. These effects include widespread indifference to, alienation from, and hostility toward our society. Little wonder that George Wald, professor of biology at Harvard University and a Nobel Prize winner, believes that what is bothering students is that they are by no means sure they have a future.

Because the new instruments of destruction are so complex and expensive they are completely in the hands of a few governments. This enables these governments to prevent their being forcefully overthrown by any group in society other than the military. The possibility of popular political revolution has been virtually eliminated in many countries. Therefore, today's malcontents are restricted to disobedience, protest, harassment, and disruption. As a result, the methods of societal obstruction have been developed to a fine art. The larger, more affluent, and more complex a society the harder it is to overthrow its government, but the easier it is to disrupt. In poorly developed societies, for example, it is difficult to disrupt communication and transportation. Witness the efforts of the United States to do so in North Viet Nam. Not so in well-developed countries in which a few well-placed bombs, aircraft hijackings, and kidnappings can create widespread inconveniences and require costly and time-consuming countermeasures.

New tactics of protest have made it possible for a little activity by a few to have a large effect on many. According to Alvin Toffler: "As interdependency grows, smaller and smaller groups within society achieve greater and greater power for disruption. However, as the rate of change speeds up, the length of time in which they can be ignored shrinks to near nothingness."

Concentration of power in the hands of an unresponsive or ineffective government fertilizes the seeds of civil discontent and disobedience. Such disobedience, in turn, usually evokes repressive measures by government, which stimulates more discontent. The result is an increase in law and a decrease in order.

In the past it was possible for those who were dissatisfied with their society to go to an unsettled area and start a new one. Today, however, our planet is so occupied and organized as to make such escape impossible. There are no unclaimed lands. New societies can only be formed within old ones and even this has become more difficult. The effect of this inability "to get away from it all" is reflected in a statement by one of the characters in George C. Chesbro's story, "Short Circuit":

> Men have lost a very special kind of freedom. . .and it can never be replaced. That freedom was the ability to go places no man had ever been, and see things no one else had. It was the freedom to *leave* a certain kind of life and know there was something else, something different. There was room to escape. . .
>
> Freedom, real freedom, requires *room* to exercise it in. There isn't any more room. It's all been used up. And some of us are dying because of it.

Now, more than ever before, those who want to try new societal structures and functions are locked into societies that resist even minor change. Emigration, where permitted, makes escape possible but not the creation of a new society. Large-scale social experimentation is almost impossible.

On the other hand, no previous age has ever been as well equipped as ours is to deal with its problems. Whether we use these capabilities on the right problems in the right way is still a matter of social choice, but that choice will have to be made soon because the opportunity to make it diminishes with the passage of time.

Almost every aspect of our society appears to be in the state of crisis and to be undergoing revolutionary change. The 1967 National Conference on Public Administration identified five contemporary revolutions: the social, the technological, the political, the economic, and the administrative. One can add the revolution of the young, the sexual revolution, the colonial revolution, the educational revolution, the urban revolution, and many others.

The revolutions through which our society is going are not independent of one another. They reflect some very basic cultural changes: interrelated changes in man, his environment, and how and what he thinks about both. Although we give a great deal of attention to changes in the state and behavior of man, we tend to englect changes in the way he views and thinks about these changes. Changes of our point of view and way of thinking not only give rise to new interpretations of what is happening but also to new ideas as to what can be done about it.

A person's ability to manage his or his society's affairs depends more on his understanding of, and attitudes toward, the world that contains him than on his problem-solving methods. Put another way, his success depends more on his view of the world and the philosophy he lives by than it does on his science and technology. The reasons for this are neither complex nor obscure.

Successful problem solving requires finding the right solution to the right problem. We fail more often because we solve the wrong problem than because we get the wrong solution to the right problem. The present worldwide concern with readjusting personal and social priorities reflects a greater and more pervasive concern with the problems we have failed to face than with those we have faced unsuccessfully.

The problems we select for solution and the way we formulate them depends more on our philosophy and world view than on our science and technology. How we go about solving them obviously depends on our science and technology, but our ability to use them effectively also depends on our philosophy and world view. These, in turn, depend on the concepts and ideas we use and how we use them to organize our perceptions of the world. Fundamental changes in these organizing concepts and ideas and the way they are used move societies from one age to another.

I believe, and will try to show, that our society is now in the early stages of a change of age that results from a radical change in our point of view, our way of thinking, and the kind of technology they are producing. We are going through an intellectual revolution that is as fundamental as that which occurred in the Renaissance. The Renaissance ushered in the Machine Age which produced the Industrial Revolution. The currently emerging intellectual revolution is bringing with it a new era that can be called the *Systems Age* which is producing the *Postindustrial Revolution.* I believe these changes give rise to most of the crises we face and simultaneously offer whatever hope there is for dealing with them effectively.

In the remainder of this chapter I described the new point of view and way of thinking that are emerging and bringing the Systems Age with them. In the following three chapters I try to show how this way of thinking raises three very general "organizing problems" of which the many problems and crises that confront us are manifestations. In the remaining chapters I try to show how the systems point of view and way of thinking can be applied to these problems and crises so as to develop more effective ways of dealing with them.

THE MACHINE AGE

Machine Age thinking was *analytical* and based on the doctrines of *reductionism* and *mechanism.*

Reductionism is a doctrine that maintains that all objects and events, their properties, and our experience and knowledge of them are made up of ultimate elements, indivisible parts. For example, the physical sciences, which ruled the scientific roost during the Machine Age, maintained that everything was ultimately made up of indivisible particles of matter called *atoms.* Although the concept of the atom is generally believed to have been first suggested by the ancient Greek philosopher Democritus (about 420 B.C.), it languished for almost two thousand years. It was revived in the Renaissance by such important thinkers as Bruno, Francis Bacon, Descartes, and Newton; but it was revived as a philophical rather than a scientific idea. It did not emerge as an important scientific concept until the latter part of the eighteenth century. Since then the concept of the atom, which no one has ever observed directly, has undergone progressive development; for example, it was later taken to be made up of particles of energy. But it remained the ultimate particle of matter. Today some believe the atom itself has parts called "quarks" or "partons," but they do not deny the existence of some kind of ultimate particle of matter.

Atoms were taken to possess energy, and energy was conceived as the power of doing work. Work, in turn, was defined as the production of an effect on matter; for example, moving or transforming it.

Chemists reduced the different kinds of matter to different kinds of elementary substances. Biologists accepted the cell as the ultimate element of life. Liebniz (1646–1716), a major German philosopher and mathematician, postulated the existence of psychic elements, *monads.* John Locke (1632–1704), an equally distinguished British philosopher and prepsychologist, argued for the existence of ultimately simple elements of experience and knowledge, "simple ideas." Much later Sigmund Freud, the founder of psychoanalysis, reduced personality to the interaction between three ultimate elements: the *id, ego,* and *superego.* In addition, he and most psychologists postulated the existence of such indivisible elements of psychic energy as instincts, drives, motives, and needs.

Every science sought ultimate elements. But these elements were ranked in order of complexity. Because it was believed that what we experience directly are physical things and their properties, ultimate reality was taken to be physical. Therefore, physics was considered to be the basic experiential science. Even the basic concepts used in other sciences were taken to be derivable from those used in physics. Chemistry was taken to be based on physics, biology on chemistry, psychology on biology, and the social sciences on psychology. These dependencies were believed to be one-directional. Nature was believed to be organized hierarchically as science was.

Analytical thinking is a natural complement to the doctrine of reductionism. It is the mental process by which anything to be explained, hence understood, is broken down into its parts. Explanations of the behavior and properties of wholes were extracted from explanations of the behavior and properties of their parts. The temperature of a body, for example, was explained as a function of the velocity of the particles of matter of which it was composed. An automobile's behavior was explained by identifying its parts and explaining the behavior of each and the relationships between them.

Analysis was also central to problem solving. Problems to be solved were first "cut down to size"; that is, reduced by analysis to a set of simpler problems. The simpler problems were then solved and their solutions were assembled into a solution of the whole. If the problem to be solved could be reduced to a set of independent subproblems, then the solution to the whole was nothing more than the sum of the solution to its parts. For example, the problem of running a city was broken down into running transportation, housing, health, education, police, and so on. It was believed that if each of these functions were managed properly, even if independently of one another, then the city as a whole would be run properly.

When the whole to be explained could not be disassembled into independent parts, the relationships between them had to be understood in order to understand the whole. Consistent with reductionism, it was believed that all interactions between objects, events, and their properties could be reduced by analysis to one fundamental relationship, *cause-effect*. One thing was said to be the cause of another, its effect, if the first was both *necessary* and *sufficient* for the other. An effect could not have occurred unless its cause had, and it had to occur if its cause had. For example, if striking a bell is considered necessary and sufficient for it to make a sound, then the strike is taken to be the cause and the sound to be its effect.

Because a cause was taken to be sufficient for its effect nothing was required to explain the effect other than the cause. Consequently, the quest for causes was *environment free*. It employed what is now called "closed-system" thinking. Laws—like that of *freely* falling bodies — were formulated so as to exclude environmental effects. (The vacuum in which free falling can occur is a *non*environment.) Specifically designed nonenvironments, *laboratories*, were used to exclude environmental effects on phenomena under study.

Environment-free causal laws permit no exceptions. Effects are completely determined by causes. Hence the prevailing view of the world was *deterministic:* everything that occurred in it was believed to be completely determined by something that preceded it. And since it was believed that everything and every event could be reduced to particles of matter and their motion, every phenomenon was believed to be explainable in principle by the laws that governed matter and motion. This belief applied to animate things as well as inanimate. Animate bodies were thus viewed as machines differing in no essential way from inanimate bodies. Hence the physical sciences were believed to be all that is required to explain life. Such a view was called *mechanism.*

Those who held the mechanistic view found no need for teleological concepts — functions, goals, purposes, choice, and free will—in explaining natural phenomena. Such concepts were considered to be either meaningless, illusory, or unnecessary in science. Philosophers were left to deal with the dilemmas their exclusion produced.

Carried to its limit reductionistic causal thinking yielded a conception of the *universe as a machine.* It was believed to be like a hermetically sealed clock, an environment-free self-contained mechanism whose behavior was completely determined by its own structure and the causal laws that applied to it. The major question raised by this conception was: Is the universe a self-winding clock or does it require a winder, God? The prevailing belief was that God was required. The world was thus conceived as a machine created by God to serve his purposes, a machine for doing His work. Additionally, man was believed to have been created in the image of God. Hence it was quite natural for men to attempt to develop machines that would serve their purposes, that would do their work.

THE INDUSTRIAL REVOLUTION

Machines, not surprisingly, were thought to be reducible to three basic mechanical elements: the wheel and axle, the lever, and the inclined plane. Work was similarly analyzed and reduced to ultimately simple work elements. The process of doing so came to be known as "work study." Machines were developed to perform as many of these basic tasks as were technologically feasible. Men performed those that could not be mechanized. Men and machines were organized into processing networks the apotheosis of which is the mass production and assembly line.

Mechanization—the replacement of man by machine as a source of physical work—affected the nature of the tasks left for man to perform. Men no longer did all the things required to make a product; rather they repeatedly performed simple operations that were a small part of the production process. Consequently, the more machines were used as substitutes for men, the more men were made to behave like machines. Mechanization led to the dehumanization of man's work. This was the irony of the Industrial Revolution. It is not surprising that a society that thought of the world as a machine came to think of man as one also.

THE SYSTEMS AGE

Although eras do not have precise beginnings or ends, the 1940s can be said to have contained the beginning of the Systems Age. The new age is attached to an intellectual framework that is built over and around the one it replaces. The old framework has not been destroyed or discarded; it has been adapted and extended. The new age is a remodeled version of the old. What was "all" in the past has become a "part" of the present. The doctrines of reductionism and mechanism, and the analytical mode of thought are being supplemented and partially replaced by the doctrines of *expansionism* and *teleology*, and a new *synthetic* (or systems) mode of thought.

Expansionism is a doctrine that maintains that all objects, events, and experiences of them are parts of larger wholes. It does not deny that they have parts but it focuses on the wholes of which they are part. Expansionism is another way of viewing things, a way that is different from, but compatible with, reductionism. It turns attention from ultimate elements to wholes with interrelated parts, to *systems*. Preoccupation with systems emerged during the 1940s. A few of the highlights of this process are worth noting.

In 1942 the American philosopher Suzanne Langer argued that over the preceding two decades philosophy had shifted its attention from elementary particles, events, and their properties to a different kind of element, the *symbol*. A symbol is an element that produces a response to something other than itself. Its physical properties are of no essential importance. In 1946 Charles W. Morris, another American philosopher, built on Langer's work a framework for the scientific study of symbols and the *wholes* of which they were part, *languages*. The works of Langer and Morris were accompanied by the growing importance given to semiotic, the sciences of signs and symbols, and to linguistics, the science of language. It was natural for many to maintain that what we know about reality is reflected in the signs with which we represent its content and in the language of which these signs are part. But some went further and claimed that what we know of reality is conditioned by what language we use; hence the nature of reality is to be found in the analysis of language.

In 1949 Claude Shannon, a mathematician at Bell Laboratories, turned attention to a larger process of which language was a part, *communication*. He provided a theory that formed the basis for what came to be known as the communication sciences. Almost simultaneously another mathematician, Norbert Wiener, of the Massachusetts Institute of Technology, placed communication into a still larger conceptual context, *control*. In so doing he founded *cybernetics*, the science of control through communication.

Note that this progression from symbol through language, communication, and control was one from elements to larger wholes. It was expansionistic, not reductionistic. This expansion did not end with Wiener's work. One more step was taken. In the early 1950s science went through an "aha" experience and came to realize what it had been up to in the preceding decade: it was becoming preoccupied with *systems*. Attention was drawn to this concept by the work of biologist Ludwig von Bertalanffy who predicted that it would become a fulcrum in modern scientific thought. He saw this concept as a wedge which could open science's reductionistic and mechanistic view of the world so that it could deal more effectively with problems of living nature—with biological, behavioral, and social phenomena—for which he believed application of physical science was not sufficient and, in some cases, not even possible. The concept of "system" has since played an increasingly large role in organizing both our lay and scientific view of the world. The concept is not new but its organizing role is. Its assumption of this role is a major factor in our "change of age."

A system is a set of two or more interrelated elements of any kind; for example, concepts (as in the number system), objects as in a telephone system or human body), or people (as in a social system). Therefore, it is *not* an ultimate indivisible element but a whole that can be divided into parts. The elements of the set and the set of elements that form a system have the following three properties.

1.   The properties or behavior of each element of the set has an effect on the properties or behavior of the set taken as a whole. For example, every organ in an animal's body affects its overall performance.

2.   The properties and behavior of each element, and the way they affect the whole, depend on the properties and behavior of at least one other element in the set. Therefore, no part has an independent effect on the whole and each is affected by at least one other part. For example, the behavior of the heart and the effect it has on the body depend on the behavior of the lungs.

3.   Every possible subgroup of elements in the set has the first two properties: each has a nonindependent effect on the whole. Therefore, the whole cannot be decomposed into independent subsets. A system cannot be subdivided into independent subsystems. For example, all the subsystems in an animal's body-such as the nervous, respiratory, digestive, and motor subsystems—interact, and each affects the performance of the whole.

Because of these three properties a set of elements that forms a system always has some characteristics, or can display some behavior, that none of its parts or subgroups can. *A system is more than the sum of its parts.* A human being, for example, can write or run, but none of its parts can. Furthermore, membership in the system either increases or decreases the capabilities of each element; it does not leave them unaffected. For example, a brain that is not part of a living body or some substitute cannot function. An individual who is part of a nation or a corporation is thereby precluded from doing some things he could otherwise do, and he is enabled to do others he could not otherwise do.

Viewed structurally, a system is a divisible whole; but viewed functionally it is an *indivisible whole* in the sense that some of its essential properties are lost when it is taken apart. The parts of a system may themselves be systems and every system may itself be a part of a larger system. For example, a state contains cities and it part of a nation; all are systems.

In the Systems Age we tend to look at things as part of larger wholes rather than as wholes to be taken apart. This the the doctrine of *expansionism.*

Expansionism brings with it the *synthetic mode of thought* much as reductionism brought with it the analytic mode. In analysis an explanation of the whole is derived from explanations of its parts. In synthetic thinking something to be explained is viewed as part of a larger system and is explained in terms of its role in that larger system. For example, universities are explained by their role in the educational system of which they are part rather than by the behavior of their parts, colleges and departments.

The Systems Age is more interested in putting things together than in taking them apart. Neither way of thinking negates the value of the other but by synthetic thinking we can gain understanding of individual and collective human behavior that cannot be obtained by analysis alone.

The synthetic mode of thought, when applied to systems problems, is called the *systems approach.* In this approach a problem is not solved by taking it apart but by viewing it as a part of a larger problem. This approach is based on the observation that when each part of a system performs as well as possible relative to the criteria applied to it, the system as a whole seldom performs as well as possible relative to the criteria applied to it. This follows from the fact that the sum of the criteria applied to performance of the parts is seldom equal to the criteria applied to that of the whole. The following illustration makes this clear.

Suppose we collect one each of every available type of automobile and then ask some expert automotive engineers to determine which of these cars has the best carburetor. When they have done so we note the result. Then we ask them to do the same for transmissions, fuel pumps, distributors, and so on through every part required to make an automobile. When this is completed we ask them to remove the parts noted and assemble them into an automobile each of the parts of which would be the best available. They would not be able to do so because the parts would not *fit together.* Even if the parts could be assembled, in all likelihood they would not *work together well.*

An all-star football team is seldom as good as the best team in the set from which the players are drawn. But, you might say, if the all-stars were to play together for a while they might become the best team. Yes, but when they do, some, if not most, of them would no longer be selected as all-stars.

System performance depends critically on how well the parts fit and work together, not merely on how well each performs when considered independently.

Furthermore, a system's performance depends on how it relates to its environment—the larger system of which it part—and to the other systems is that environment. For example, an automobile's performance depends on the roads over which it is driven and on the presence and driving of other automobiles on those roads. Therefore, in systems thinking an attempt is made to evaluate performance of a system as a part of the larger system that contains it. A corporation, for example, is not evaluated by how well it performs relative to its own objectives but rather relative to the objectives of the society of which it is part.

One important consequence of this type of thinking is that science itself has come to be reconceptualized as a system whose parts, the disciplines, are interdependent. This contradicts the hierarchical notion of science in which there is only a one-directional dependence among disciplines and in which physics is taken to be independent of all other empirical disciplines. Scientific disciplines are no longer thought of as dealing with different aspects of Nature, nor is Nature believed to be organized in the same way science is. The disciplines are increasingly thought of as *points of view* most of which are applicable to the study of most phenomena and problems. For example, no discipline is irrelevant in efforts to solve ecological problems. Therefore, the environmental sciences include all the sciences.

In the Systems Age science is developing by assembling its parts into an expanding variety of increasingly comprehensive wholes. The new developments—such as cybernetics; operations research; the behavioral, communication, management, and policy sciences; and systems engineering—are *interdisciplinary*, not disciplinary. Even the interdisciplines are seen as parts of a still larger whole, the systems sciences which, note, form a system of sciences.

In the past a complex problem was usually decomposed into simpler problems suitable for different disciplines. Then each discipline would solve its part of the problem and these solutions would be assembled into a solution of the whole. But contemporary interdisciplines do not work this way; a variety of disciplines work together on the problem as a whole. For example, experts in health, housing, transportation, education, and other aspects of urban life work together on a city's problem taken as a whole rather than divide it into parts suitable for each to work on separately.

Unlike traditional scientific disciplines which seek to distinguish themselves from each other and to spin off new disciplines when new areas of interest develop within them, the new interdisciplines seek to extend themselves and merge with each other, to increase the number of disciplines they incorporate, and to enlarge the class of phenomena with which they are concerned. They strive for more comprehensive syntheses of knowledge and therefore thrive on interaction with each other. Systems Age scientists are not bound by loyalty to any one discipline or interdiscipline but move easily from one to another.

It will be recalled that in the Machine Age cause-effect was the central relationship in terms of which all actions and interactions were explained. At the turn of this century the distinguished American philosopher of science, E. A. Singer, Jr., noted that cause-effect was used in two different senses. First, it was used in the sense already discussed: a cause is a necessary and sufficient condition for its effect. Second, it was also used when one thing was taken to be necessary but *not* sufficient for the other. To use Singer's example, an acorn is necessary but not sufficient for an oak; various soil and weather conditions are also necessary. Similarly, a parent is necessary but not sufficient for his or her child. Singer referred to this second type of cause-effect as *producer-product*. It has also been referred to since as probabilistic or nondeterministic cause-effect.

Because a producer is not sufficient for its product, other producers (coproducers) are also necessary. Taken collectively these constitute the producer's environment. Hence, the producer-product relationship yields environment-full (open-system), not environment-free (closed-system), thinking.

Singer went on to show why studies that use the producer-product relationship were compatible with, but richer than, studies that used only deterministic cause-effect. Furthermore, he showed that a theory of explanation based on producer-product permitted objective study of functional, goal-seeking, and purposeful behavior. The concepts *free will* and *choice* were no longer incompatible with mechanism; hence they need no longer be exiled from science.

Later the University of Cambridge biologist G. Sommerhoff independently came to the same conclusions Singer had. In the meantime, Arturo Rosenblueth, Norbert Wiener, and J. H. Bigelow, who collaboratively laid the foundations for cybernetics, showed the great value of conceptualizing the new self-controlling machines developed during World War II as functioning, goal-seeking, and purposeful entities. In effect, they showed that, whereas it had been fruitful in the past to study man as though he were a machine, it was becoming at least as fruitful to study self-controlling machines as if they were men. Thus, in the 1950s, *teleology*—the study of goal-seeking and purposeful behavior—was brought into science and began to dominate our conception of the world.

In mechanistic thinking behavior is explained by identifying what caused it, never by its effect. In teleological thinking behavior can be explained either by what produced it or by what it produces or is intended to produce. For example, a boy's going to the store can be explained either by his being sent there by his mother, or by his wanting to buy ice cream. Study of the functions, goals, and purposes of individuals and groups—not to mention some types of machine—has yielded a greater ability to evaluate and improve their performance than did the study of them as purposeless mechanisms.

THE POSTINDUSTRIAL REVOLUTION

The doctrines of expansionism and teleology and the synthetic mode of thought are both the producers and the products of the Postindustrial Revolution. But this revolution is also based on three technologies the first two of which were developed during the (First) Industrial Revolution. One of these emerged with the invention of the telegraph in the first half of the nineteenth century. It was followed by the telephone in 1876 due to Alexander Graham Bell and the wireless by Marconi in 1895. Radio and television followed in this century. Such devices mechanized *communication*, the *transmission of symbols*. Since symbols are not made of matter, their movement through space does not constitute physical work. The significance of this fact was not appreciated until recently.

The second technology emerged with the development of devices that can *observe* and *record* the properties of objects and events. Such machines *generate and remember symbols* that we call *data*. The thermometer, odometer, speedometer, and voltmeter are familiar examples of observing machines, instruments. In 1937 there was a major advance in the technology of mechanized observation when it "went electronic" with the invention of radar and sonar in England.

Instruments can observe what humans cannot without mechanical aids. But observation, like communication, is not physical work.

The third and key technology appeared in the 1940s with the development of the electronic digital computer. This machine can *manipulate symbols logically*. It is able to process raw data in such a way as to convert them into usable form, into *information* and to convert information into *instruction*. Thus it is both a *data-processing* (information-producing) and a *decision making* (instruction-producing) machine.

The technologies of symbol generation, storage, transmission, and manipulation made it possible to mechanize *mental work*, to *automate*. Automation is what the Postindustrial Revolution is all about.

Development and utilization of automation technology requires an understanding of the mental processes that are involved in it. Since 1940 many interdisciplines have been developed to generate and apply understanding of these mental processes and their role in control. These interdisciplines include those previously mentioned: cybernetics; operations research; the behavioral, communication, management, and policy sciences; and systems engineering. Such interdisciplines provide the "software" of the Postindustrial Revolution just as industrial engineering provided much of it for the First.

Neither the hardware nor the software of the Postindustrial Revolution provides panaceas for our problems. They can be used either to create or to solve problems, and they can solve them either well or badly. The net effect of this revolution will depend on how well we use its technology and the ends for which we do so. The revolution can become retrogressive if we do not control it. It is controllable, but we may not control it or we may control it badly.

The future depends greatly on what problems we decide to work on and how well we use Systems Age technology to solve them.

THE ORGANIZING PROBLEMS OF THE SYSTEMS AGE

Because the Systems Age is teleologically oriented it is preoccupied with systems that are purposeful; that is, with systems that can display choice of both means and ends. Most of what interest remains in purely mechanical systems derives from their use as tools by purposeful systems. Furthermore, Systems Age man is most concerned with those purposeful systems whose parts are also purposeful, with *groups*—in particular, with those groups whose parts perform different functions, *organizations.*

All groups and organizations are parts of larger purposeful systems. Hence all of them are purposeful systems whose parts are purposeful systems and which themselves are part of a larger purposeful system. All the organizations and institutions that are part of society, and society itself, are part of such three-level hierarchical systems.

Therefore, there are three central problems that arise in the management and control of purposeful systems: how to increase the effectiveness with which they serve their own purposes, the purposes of their parts, and the purposes of the systems of which they are part. These are, respectively, the *self-control*, the *humanization,* and the *environmentalization* problems.

The self-control problem consists of designing and managing systems so that they can cope effectively with increasingly complex and rapidly emerging sets of interacting problems in an increasingly complex and dynamic environment. The humanization problem consists of finding ways to serve the purposes of the parts of a system more effectively and to do so in such a way as to better serve the purposes of the system itself. Finally, the environmentalization problem consists of finding ways of serving the purposes of environmental systems more effectively and to do so in such a way as to better serve the purposes of the system itself.

Each of the organizing problems of the Systems Age is examined in detail in the following three chapters.

CHAPTER TWO

THE SELF-CONTROL
PROBLEM

*It may well be that our present chaos will engulf
and drag us down as a nation which achieved the
miraculous in technology but was unable to adapt
itself to the new world man created. The United
States may well collapse and bring down most,
if not all, of humanity. We do have the means
to destroy ourselves; it is naive to assume that
the use of these means is beyond the realm of
possibility.*

*We also have within our grasp the means to
deal with our problems in an effective manner. . .*

PHILIP M. HAUSER

When one purposeful system controls another of which it is part, the first
manages the second. Management involves *decision making* and decision
making involves *problem solving* whenever the decision maker is in doubt
about the choice to make. Therefore, problem solving has traditionally been
taken to be an essential function of management. Through systems thinking,
however, we have come to doubt the existence of problems and solutions to
them. This doubt, and the sense in which "existence" is a part of it, requires
explanation.

In the Machine Age problems were thought of as "out there," as purely
objective states of affairs. But John Dewey, the great American philosopher,

challenged this notion and argued that decision makers have to extract problems from the situations in which they find themselves. They do so, he said, by *analyzing* the situation. Hence problems are products of thought acting on environments; they are elements of problematic situations that are abstracted from these situations by analysis. What we experience, therefore, are problematic situations, not problems which, like atoms and cells, are conceptual constructs.

We have also come to realize that no problem ever exists in complete isolation. Every problem interacts with other problems and is therefore part of a set of interrelated problems, a *system of problems*. For example, the race problem, the poverty problem, the urban problem, and the crime problem, to mention but a few, are clearly interrelated. Furthermore, solutions to most problems produce other problems; for example, buying a car may solve a transportation problem but it may also create a need for a garage, a financial problem, a maintenance problem, and conflict among family members for its use.

English does not contain a suitable word for "system of problems." Therefore, I have had to coin one. I choose to call such a system a *mess*. This concept is as central in this book as is that of a "system." This book is about messes. This chapter is about "mess management."

A mess is a system of external conditions that produces dissatisfaction. It can be conceptualized as a system of problems in the same sense in which a physical body can be conceptualized as a system of atoms. Therefore, problems that can be decomposed to simpler problems are really messes. Ultimately simple problems, like any ultimate elements, are abstract subjective concepts. Such elements cannot be observed because we cannot conceive of anything that can be observed but not taken apart. For example, we cannot see geometric points; they are abstractions. What we see and call points are small areas. Therefore, even what appears to us as a simple problem is really a "minimess."

In the Machine Age messy problematic situations were approached analytically. They were broken down into simpler discrete problems that were often believed to be capable of being solved independently of one another. We are learning that such a procedure not only usually fails to solve the individual problems that are involved, but often intensifies the mess. The solution to a mess can seldom be obtained by independently solving each of the problems of which it is composed. This appears to be the case, for example, in our current handling of the urban mess. Efforts to deal separately with such aspects of urban life as transportation, health, crime, and education seem to aggravate the total situation.

The attempt to deal holistically with a system of problems is what *planning*, in contrast to problem solving, should be all about. In the Machine

Age a great deal of effort went into the development of effective methods of problem solving but little thought was given to planning. In the Systems Age more attention is being given to development of effective methods of planning.

PLANNING

For many years social and organizational planning was ignored and held in disrepute in the United States and other Western Nations because of its association with communism. The communists believe in strongly centralized planning. Hence it was incorrectly assumed by many Americans that planning necessarily implies a strong central government or management. It was only after noncommunist France successfully planned its recovery from World War II and did so without either centralized planning or concentration of power at the top, that we began to understand that planning can serve any political or organizational philosophy, just as problem solving can. It can increase the effectiveness of either a decentralized democracy or a centralized autocracy.

There are many managers and administrators who still do not believe in planning. Attitudes toward it vary a great deal but they can be grouped into four general types: *inactive, reactive, preactive,* and *interactive.* These attitudes are mixed in varying proportions in each individual and organization and the mixture may change from time to time or from situation to situation. Furthermore, a wide variety of attitudes toward planning may be found in any one organization at any one time. Nevertheless, one of these attitudes usually dominates the others in both individuals and organizations. In a sense, these four attitudes are like primary colors; they can be mixed in many different ways to provide a wide range of secondary attitudes and these change under different "lighting" conditions. Despite the variety of mixtures in which they are found, the pure forms are easily recognizable.

After I have described the "pure" attitudes in what is obviously a biased way, I nevertheless argue that under different conditions each may be best. Therefore, as will also be apparent, my bias derives from what I believe our current condition is.

Inactivism

Inactivists are satisfied with the way things are and the way they are going. Hence they believe that any intervention in the course of events is unlikely to improve them and is very likely to make them worse. Inactivists take a do-nothing posture; they try to "ride with the tide" without "rocking the boat." Their management philosophy is conservative. They seek stability and survival. They are willing to let well-enough alone and hence are what have come to be known as "satisficers."

Inactivists believe that most apparent social and environmental changes are either illusory, superficial, or temporary. They typically see those who cry "Crisis!" as panic mongers and prophets of doom. Inactivists recall the pervasiveness of such cries and crises throughout their society's or organization's history and point to the evasiveness of the dooms foreseen. Because their society or organization has survived all of their previous crises, inactivists argue, there is no reason to believe they will not continue to do so.

Inactive organizations require a great deal of activity to keep changes from being made. They accomplish nothing in a variety of ways. First, they require that all important decisions be made at "the top." The route to the top is deliberately designed like an obstacle course. This keeps most recommendations for change from ever getting there. Those that do are likely to have been delayed enough to make them irrelevant when they reach their destination. Those proposals that reach the top are likely to be further delayed, often by being sent back down or out for modification or evaluation. The organization thus behaves like a sponge and is about as active.

Inactivists take a position on an issue only when forced to. "Forced to" means doing so is the only way left to keep changes from being made. Wherever possible, words are used in place of action. Inactivists are prolific producers of policy statements, white papers, strategy documents, position papers, reports, memoranda, and any other kind of document that can substitute for action.

Another prevalent means by which inactivity is achieved consists of setting up committees, councils, commissions, study groups, task forces, and what-have-you at the drop of an issue. The responsibilities of such groups are deliberately left vague so that they can spend most of their time in defining their functions and in jurisdictional disputes.

When one of them manages to generate a recommendation, those who were not respresented in the group can object to their lack of representation and have another group formed to take them into account. This process can go on indefinitely, particularly if augmented by occasional personnel changes.

On those rare occasions when an inactive organization takes action it is almost certain to be understaffed and underfinanced. This minimizes any possible impact it might have.

Feasibility is the principal criterion used by inactivists in selecting means. Ends are more likely to be fitted to means than conversely. As A. O. Hirschman and C. E. Lindblom, perhaps the best known spokesmen for this position, suggest in their proposed strategies for decision making: "Instead of simply adjusting means to ends, ends are chosen that are appropriate to nearly available means." Inactivists tend to want what they can get rather than try to get what they want.

When inactivists intervene in the course of events they do so as little as possible. In the words of Hirschman and Lindblom: "Attempts at understanding are limited to policies that differ only incrementally from existing policy." Little wonder they call their overall strategy "disjointed incrementaliism."

Inactivists have a greater fear of doing something that does not have to be done (errors of commission) than of not doing something that should be done (errors of omission). Hence they tend to react only to serious threats, not opportunities. By so doing they practice what has come to be known as "crisis management."

In general the only organizations that can survive inactive management are those that are protected from their environments by subsidies that assure their survival independently of what they accomplish. The most conspicuous examples of such organizations in our society are universities, government agencies, and publicly protected private monopolies such as utility companies.

Needless to say, inactivists do not believe in planning. They do not even believe in problem solving.

Reactivism

Reactivists prefer a previous state to the one they are in and they believe things are going from bad to worse. Hence they not only resist change but they try to unmake previous changes and return to where they once were. They are generally nostalgic about "the good old days." Their propensity to return to the past makes their management philosophy reactionary.

Reactivists are moved more by their hates than by their loves. Their orientation is remedial, not aspirational. They try to avoid the undesirable rather than attain the desirable. They see very little new in anything proposed and still less that is worthwhile in what they accept as new. Their reaction to most proposed changes is: "We tried it and it doesn't work." For example, a railroad executive once told me after I had proposed using linear programming to solve a problem he had that he had tried it on the problem about ten years ago and it had not worked. At the time linear programming was considerably less than ten years old.

Because technological change is so conspicuous and because the past has always had less technology than the present, technology is the reactivists' principal scapegoat for whatever ills they perceive. They prefer art to science: the art of muddling through to the science of management. In dealing with problems they rely on common sense, intuition, and judgment based on long experience. The longer the experience, the better. They believe experience is the best teacher and the best school is the school of hard knocks. For this reason they place high value on seniority, immobility, and age and allocate status and responsibility proportionately thereto.

Reactivists dislike complexity and try to avoid dealing with it. They reduce complex messes to simple problems that have simple solutions—solutions that are "tried and true." They are panacea-prone problem solvers, not planners. They try to recreate the past by undoing the mess they believe the planning of others has wrought.

Unlike inactivists, reactivists do not ride with the tide; they try to swim against it back to a familiar shore. It is not surprising, therefore, that once successful but now declining institutions and organizations are particularly susceptible to this point of view.

Preactivism

Preactivists are not willing to settle for things as they are or once were. They believe that the future will be better than the present or the past, how much better depending on how well they get ready for it. Thus they attempt to *predict and prepare*. They want more than survival; they want to grow—to become better, larger, more affluent, more powerful, more many things. They want to do better than well enough; they want to do as well as possible, to *optimize*.

Preactivists are not only concerned about doing something wrong (errors of commission) but also about *not* doing something right (errors of omission). Consequently, they are as occupied with potential opportunities as they are with actual and potential threats. They attempt to identify and deal with problems before they become serious and, if possible, before they arise. For this reason they are preoccupied with forecasts, projections, and every other way of obtaining glimpses of the future. They believe the future is essentially uncontrollable but that they can accelerate its coming and control its effects on them. Therefore, they plan *for* the future; they do not plan the future itself.

Preactive planning and problem solving is based more on logic, science, and experimentation than on common sense, intuition, and judgment. Unlike reactivists, preactivists tend to credit science and technology for most of the progress we have enjoyed and to blame current problems and crises on their misuse or abuse. They seek to solve problems and exploit opportunities more through research and development than by individual and institutional change. They are hardware, rather than software, oriented; thing, rather than people, oriented. When they must deal with people they prefer to deal with them collectively, impersonally, rather than individually, because they believe collective behavior is more predictable.

Preactive decision makers and planners tend to think of the system to be managed in terms of the resources over which it has direct control. They are preoccupied with allocation and use of these resources within the system. They do not try to influence other systems in the environment; they tend to perceive the environment as constraining rather than as enabling. Hence they are competitive rather than cooperative when other systems are involved.

If the management philosophy of the reactivist is reactionary, of the inactivist, conservative, then the preactivist's is liberal. Preactivists seek change *within* the system, but not change *of* the system or its environment. They are reformers, not revolutionaries. They seek neither to ride with the tide nor to buck it, but to ride in front of it and get to where it is going before it does. In this way, they believe, they can take advantage of new opportunities before others get to them.

Preactive planners take their function to consist of producing plans and presenting them to those empowered to act, but not involvement in implementing approved plans. Preactivists see planning as a sequence of discrete steps which terminate with acceptance or rejection of their plans. What happens to their plans is the responsibility of others.

Interactivism

Interactivists are not willing to settle for the current state of their affairs or the way they are going, and they are not willing to return to the past. They want to design a desirable future and invent ways of brining it about. They believe we are capable of controlling a significant part of the future as well as its effects on us. They try to *prevent,* not merely prepare for, threats, and to *create,* not merely exploit, opportunities.

Preactivists, according to interactivists, spend too much time trying to forecast the future. The future, they argue, depends more on what we do between now and then than it does on what has happened up until now. The major obstacle between man and the future he desires is man himself.

Interactivists are not willing to settle for survival or growth. They seek self-development, self-realization, and self-control: an increased ability to design and control their own destinies. They are neither satisficers nor optimizers; they are *idealizers.* They plan to do better in the future than the best that presently appears to be possible. They pursue ideals that they know can never be attained but that can be continuously approached. Thus to them the formulation of ideals and the design of idealized futures are not empty exercises in utopianism, but necessary steps in setting long-range directions for continuous development.

They treat ideals as relative absolutes: ultimate objectives whose formulation depends on our current knowledge and understanding of ourselves and our environment. Therefore, they require continuous reformulation in light of what we learn from approaching them.

Because of the accelerating rates of technological and social change, interactivists try to design the systems they control so as to increase their ability to learn and adapt rapidly. They maintain that experience is no longer the best teacher; it is too slow, too ambiguous, and too imprecise. Therefore, they attempt to replace experience by experimentation wherever possible. They try to design the implementation of every decision as an experiment that tests its effectiveness and that of the process by which it was reached.

No aspect of a system is precluded from change. Interactivists are willing to modify a system's structure, functioning, organization, and personnel as well as its allocation and use of resources.

Unlike preactivists, interactivists try to induce cooperative changes in environing systems, changes that are as fundamental as those they seek for the systems they can control directly. They consider the world, not merely their neighborhood, to be their arena.

Interactivists consider technology to be neither good nor bad in itself, but to have a potential for either. Its effects, they believe, depend on how people use it. Thus they view behavior and technology as interrelated aspects of *sociotechnical systems.* They treat science and the humanities as two aspects of one culture, not as two cultures. Like the head and tail of a coin these aspects can be discussed or viewed separately, but they cannot be separated.

According to interactivists science is the search for similarities among things that are apparently different, and the humanities are the search for differences among things that are apparently similar. Scientists seek the general and humanists seek the unique. To deal effectively with a problematic situation one must be able to determine both what it has in common with previously experienced situations and how it differs from them. Awareness of similarities enables us to use what we already know; awareness of differences enables us to determine what must still be learned if the situation is to be dealt with effectively. The humanities furnish us with the problems, science and technology with means for solving them.

Interactivists are radicals; they try to change the foundations as well as the superstructure of society and its institutions and organizations. They desire neither to resist, ride with, nor ride ahead of the tide; they try to redirect it.

Despite the obvious bias in my characterization of these four postures there are circumstances in which each is most appropriate. Put simply, if the internal and external dynamics of a system (the tide) is taking one where one wants to go and is doing so quickly enough, inactivism is appropriate. If the direction of change is right but the movement is too slow, preactivism is appropriate. If the change is taking one where one does not want to go and one prefers to stay where one is or was, reactivism is appropriate. However, if one is not willing to settle for the past, the present, or the future that appears likely now, interactivism is appropriate. My bias for interactivism derives from my belief that our society can be much improved and that it is not tending to improvement. Our intervention is therefore required.

Inactivists and reactivists at best treat planning as a ritual or prayer that may bring the intervention of a superior force in the course of events. They do not view it as a process which directs one's own intervention.

Preactive planners try to accelerate the future and control its effects on the system they plan for, but they do not try to redirect it. Interactive planners do. Preactive planning deals with products rather than producers. For example, a preactive urban transportation planner tends to assume continued growth of demand for automotive transportation and no significant change in the nature of the automobile. These, he assumes, are out of his control. Therefore, he tries to reduce projected future congestion by increasing the number and size of streets and roads and by expanding other modes of travel. The interactive planner, on the other hand, considers such things as changing the automobile and the city so that the demand for transportation and roadways is modified. He attempts to manipulate the producers of problems as well as their effects.

The short-to-medium range future receives the attention of the preactivist. The interactivist gives more attention to the long range because he believes that short-run gains are frequently paid for by larger long-run losses, and long-run gains are often preceded by short-run losses. Therefore, he believes it is essential to seek a proper balance between long- and short-run consequences of current behavior. The ability to perceive and be governed by long-run consequences is the essence of *wisdom*. Knowledge may be enough for effective problem solving but it is not enough for effective planning. Planning also requires wisdom and wisdom is as much a product of the humanities as it is of science.

Interactivists have extracted four principles of planning practice from their experience.

1.   *Participative planning.* The principal benefits of planning are not derived from consuming its product (plans), but from engaging in their production. In planning, process is the most important product. Hence, effective planning cannot be done *to* or *for* an organization; it must be done *by* it. The proper role of the professional planner is not to plan for others but to facilitate their planning for themselves; that is, to provide everyone who can be affected by planning with an opportunity to participate in it, and to provide them with the information, instruction, and motivation that will enable them to carry it out effectively.

2. *Coordinated planning.* All aspects of a system should be planned for simultaneously and interdependently. No part or aspect of an organization can be planned for effectively if planned for independently of any other part or aspect. For example, planning to reduce crime should involve all aspects of the criminal justice system and more: education, housing, employment, health services, welfare, and so on. All societal functions should be dealt with. In planning, breadth is more important than depth and interactions are more important than actions.

3. *Integrated planning.* In multilevel organizations like governments or corporations planning is required at every level and planning at each level should be integrated with planning at every other level. In organizations whose objectives dominate those of its members, such as corporations, strategic planning (selection of ends) tends to flow from the top down, and tactical planning (selection of means) tends to flow from the bottom up. This flow is usually reversed in a system whose primary function is to serve its members. Strategy and tactics are two aspects of behavior. Strategy is concerned with long-range objectives and ways of pursuing them that affect the system as a whole; tactics are concerned with shorter-run goals and means for reaching them that generally affect only a part of the organization. Although they cannot be separated in principle, they often are in practice. This means that one or the other type of planning is not carried out consciously and, hence is not made explicit. Both types should be done interdependently, consciously, and explicitly.

4. *Continuous planning.* Because purposeful systems and their environments are changing continuously, no plan retains its value over time. Therefore, plans should be updated, extended, and corrected frequently, if not continuously. Continuous planning is necessary if a system is to learn and adapt effectively. A plan's actual performance should be compared frequently with explicitly stated expectations. Where they deviate from each other significantly, the producers of the deviation should be identified and appropriate corrective action taken.

Interactive planning is a system of activities; hence its five phases are interdependent. They are as follows.

1. *Ends planning.* Determining what is wanted: the design of a desired future. This requires specifying goals, objectives, and ideals; short-run, intermediate, and ultimate ends.

2. *Means planning.* Determining how to get there. This requires selecting or inventing courses of action, practices, programs, and policies.

3. *Resource planning.* Determining what types of resources—for example, men, machines, materials, and money—and how much of each will be required, how they are to be acquired or generated, and how they are to be allocated to activities once they are available.

    4.   *Organizational planning.* Determining organizational requirements and designing organizational arrangements and the management system that will make it possible to follow the prescribed means effectively.

    5.   *Implementation and control planning.* Determining how to implement decisions and control them: maintaining and improving the plan under changing internal and external conditions.

The interactive planner initiates ends planning by designing an *idealized future* for the system being planned for. This is a design of the future that begins "from scratch." All constraints other than technological feasibility are removed. One would not assume, for example, direct transfer of the content of one mind to another without communication of symbols. Such a constraint does not preclude consideration of technological innovations but these are restricted to what is believed to be possible. On the other hand, all financial and political constraints are removed. Therefore, the design is an explicit formulation of the planners' conception of the system they would create if they were free to create any system they wanted.

    Most system planning is retrospective: preoccupied with identifying and removing deficiencies in the past performance of system components. Retrospective planning moves *from* what one does not want rather than *toward* what one wants. It is like driving a train from its caboose. One who walks into the future facing the past has no control over where he is going. Idealization rotates planners from a retrospective to a *prospective* posture.

    The process of designing an idealized future for a public or private system usually brings about the following five important results.

    First, it facilitates the direct involvement of a large number of those who participate or hold a stake in the relevant system. No special skills are required and the process is fun. Playing God always is. People with no previous planning experience quickly become deeply involved. It enables them to criticize the existing system in a completely constructive way.

    Second, in this context agreement tends to emerge from apparently antagonistic participants and stakeholders. Most disagreements arise with respect to means, not ends. Idealization is concerned with ends, not means. Awareness of consensus relative to ends usually brings about subsequent cooperation relative to means among those who would not otherwise be so inclined.

    Third, the idealization process forces those engaged in it to formulate explicitly their conception of organizational objectives. This opens their conception to examination by others and thus facilitates progressive reformulation of the objectives and development of consensus.

    Fourth, idealization leads those engaged in it to become conscious of self-imposed constraints and hence makes it easier to remove them. It also forces reexamination of externally imposed constraits that are usually accepted passively. Ways of removing or "getting around" them are then explored, often with success.

Finally, idealization reveals that system designs and plans, all of whose elements appear to be unfeasible when considered separately, are either feasible or nearly so when considered as a whole. Therefore, it leads to subsequent design and planning that is not preoccupied with doing what appears to be possible, but with making possible what initially appears to be impossible.

For example, in the recently completed idealized design of Paris carried out under the supervision of my colleague, Professor Hasan Ozbekhan, representatives of each of the many political parties in France participated and came to agreement. The design which they approved has been submitted to the French public in which it is being widely discussed at the time of this writing. The cabinet of France and the representative body of stakeholders who served as reviewers agreed on the desirability of making Paris a global rather than a French city, an informal capital of the world. Having agreed on this end they subsequently accepted means that they would have rejected summarily had they been proposed separately or out of this context. For example, they have agreed to move the capital of France from Paris, and to make Paris an open and multilingual city.

Once an idealized design has been prepared on which consensus has been obtained it is possible to begin planning the approach to that ideal. The output of such planning should be treated as tentative, subject to continuous revision in light of experience with it. The system for making such revisions—the planning-control system—must itself be planned. The concept of continuous control has only recently come into prominence.

CONTROL

In the Machine Age, the world was viewed as a closed system to be understood through analysis. Therefore, ultimate and final solutions to problems were believed to be obtainable. It was an era which John Dewey characterized by its "quest for certainty." In the Systems Age, systems are conceptualized as open and dynamic. Therefore, problems and solutions are conceptualized as snapshots of a moving process. Problems and solutions are in constant flux; hence *problems do not stay solved*. Purposeful systems and their environments are constantly changing. Solutions to problems become obsolete even if the problems to which they are addressed do not. For example, insects develop immunity to pesticides, people to desegregation programs, and societies to such laws as those which prohibit the use of alcohol or narcotics.

For these reasons purposeful systems not only need to deal with problem-systems, but they also need to maintain and improve solution-systems, plans, under changing conditions. Hence problem solving and planning have come to be conceptualized as continuous processes directed at approachable but unattainable ideals. Absolute truth and perfect efficiency are never obtained but we can always move closer to them.

Because of the increasing rate of social and technological change, control systems should be capable of responding frequently and rapidly to changes that are often different from those previously experienced. Therefore, control systems must adapt quickly when a change occurs and learn quickly between changes. Such systems cannot rely on normally paced experience for reasons considered earlier.

Any system whose function is to control another system must either be part of that system or, together with it, be part of the same larger system. Hence a control system can always be viewed as a subsystem. It may also contain its own subsystems.

A controlled system can only adapt and learn effectively if the subsystem that controls it can adapt and learn effectively. To be able to do so the controlling (management) subsystem must be able to perform four functions quickly and efficiently: (1) identify problems, (including threats and opportunities) and the relationships between them, (2) make decisions and plan, (3) implement and control the decisions and plans made, and (4) provide the information required to perform each of the first three functions.

In the Appendix the state of the art and science of management with respect to each of these functions is described. It is sufficient for my purposes here to point out that many of these functions can now be automated, but we are a long way from being able to automate them completely. Those management and mangement-support processes that can be automated most easily are those which are simplest, most routine, and most repeated. Automation can humanize management and management-support systems by relieving man of dull dronelike jobs thereby enabling him to take on more complex and challenging tasks that are often neglected for lack of time. We almost always do the familiar and simplest things first.

Of equal importance is the fact that by automating parts of management and its supporting activities, and by using recent developments in control theory, (1) responses to actual or potential threats and opportunities—adaptation—can be accelerated, and (2) by responding and evaluating the consequences of responses more rapidly, learning can also be accelerated.

CONCLUSION

I have argued that we must treat problem situations as a whole and not break them into parts which are treated independently of one another; that problem solving should be made an integral part of planning. Planning provides us with a way of acting *now* that can make the kind of future we want more likely. But planning is still an unwelcome process in many quarters. How it is treated depends on which of four attitudes toward the future dominates: reactive, inactive, preactive, or interactive. Of these only the last is consistent with the systems point of view and way of thinking. Interactive planning is committed to creating a future that approximates an explicitly formulated ideal as closely as possible, and that allows for continuous revision of that ideal. Such planning is necessarily participative, coordinated, integrated, and continuous.

Problems are conceptual constructs abstracted from complex situations that are systems of problems, messes. Solutions are also abstractions. No problems is ever finally put to rest. Therefore, solutions require control: continuous maintenance and improvement.

I have identified the characteristics that a management system must have if the managed system is to learn and adapt effectively. It must incorporate a problem-identification system, a decision-making and planning system, an implementation and control system, and an information system. Systems Age science and technology can increase the effectiveness of these subsystems considerably, and the relevant science and technology are developing rapidly. Hence, systems planners, designers, and managers must also learn how to learn and adapt more effectively if they are to exploit the opportunities that technological developments present. They must learn and adapt at least as effectively as the systems they design, manage, and plan for.

CHAPTER THREE

THE HUMANIZATION PROBLEM

Plan or be planned for.

MANTUA COMMUNITY PLANNERS

During the Machine Age organizations were thought of as though they were machines. A machine has no purpose of its own, nor do any of its parts. It is an instrument used by external entities to serve their purposes. Therefore, a corporation was thought of as an instrument of its owners; its function was taken to be that of providing them with a return on their investments. It was realized, of course, that the components of a corporation were human and had purposes of their own, but these were taken to be irrelevant to management of corporate affairs. Employment involved an implicit agreement to the effect that, in return for wages, an employee did not expect his employer to be concerned with his personal goals and objectives. Hence he could be, and he was, treated as though he were a replaceable part of a machine.

This was as true for managers as it was for laborers. According to Professor E. E. Jennings of Michigan State University: "Private life [of managers] ceased to exist apart from company life. The higher a man went, the more responsibility and, hence, less freedom to live privately.... Family life became just another cog in the corporate machine." Notice the figure of speech: "cog in the corporate machine."

As ownership of corporations became more dispersed and detached from their management, they began to be thought of as organisms—as entities that had a purpose of their own but whose parts did not. Following the biological analogy, survival and growth were taken to be the principal purposes of organizations. Managers took themselves to be the brains of the firm. They increased their control over it and began to treat themselves more humanely, but their attitudes toward workers were modified only slightly.

Workers were thought of as organs, parts of an organism rather than parts of a machine. They were treated as functioning but purposeless parts of a purposeful system. Their health and safety became a concern of management. More attention was given to creating conditions in which they could function more effectively relative to corporate, but not their own, purposes. Monetary incentives were used to stimulate desired responses. The worker was assumed to be drawn to money as inevitably as plants are drawn to light.

Such treatment of workers created no serious problems as long as they were educationally and economically deprived. They were willing to settle for almost any kind of work that facilitated their survival and that they could survive. The Protestant Ethic was used to make men believe that the more they suffered at work the better it was for their souls. The workplace was accepted as an earthly purgatory.

In the first half of this century, however, workers were better educated and their fear of economic destitution was reduced by the emergence of the welfare state. Hence they began to react against their work and the organizations in which they did it. They formed unions and demanded greater compensation for work, less work to do, and better working conditions. But work itself was not their major target. Unions, like management, accepted the mechanistic or organismic conception of the corporation.

Since World War II workers have increasingly made work itself the target of their attacks. The expectations, attitudes, and moods of those deprived of satisfying work have been changing. Workers are placing a higher value on themselves and think increasingly of corporations as instruments for serving their needs, rather than of themselves as instruments for serving corporate needs.

There is abundant evidence of widespread disenchantment with work at the present time. For example, in 1971 *Newsweek* reported "a distrubingly high rate of absenteeism" despite a recession and a high unemployment rate in the United States. There is an increasing number of young people, including many with higher education, who seek alternatives to work or to delay it as long as possible. The alleged fact that many adults prefer welfare to work is not evidence of the attractiveness of welfare but of the repulsiveness of the work available to them.

Commenting on a study recently issued by the Department of Health, Education, and Welfare entitled *Work in America*, a reporter for *The New*

York Times wrote: "A changing American work force is becoming pervasively dissatisfied with dull, unchallenging and repetitive jobs, and this discontent is sapping the economic and social strength of the nation."

As automation progresses, the technical content of many jobs increases and more skilled workers are required. The more specialized a worker's skill becomes, the harder it is for his boss to tell him how to do his job. Few managers, for example, can tell computer programmers and operators how to do their work; they can only tell them what results they want. Hence some freedom of choice is inherent in the increasing technology of work. A taste of freedom has a way of stimulating a craving for it.

The more skilled a worker is, the less inclined he is to give blind loyalty to an organization. He comes to think of himself as a professional. Therefore, his personal and professional interests become increasingly relevant to organizations seeking his skill. This, as Professor Jennings observed, is particularly true of managers:

> Then came World War II. . .and innovation was needed at all levels; no one person could possible know enough to maintain corporate viability.
>
> Corporations began placing their chips on young men not yet mesmerized by the loyalty ethic. . .
>
> Young executives grew self-confident that they could manage their own careers. . . When they saw upward mobility arrested, they opted for opportunities elsewhere. . . .
>
> The most mobile had the best chance to achieve and acquire experience; mobility bred competency that in turn bred mobility. Rapid executive turnover became a fact of life.

The current young, competent, and mobile generation, most of whose members were raised in predominantly permissive families, is sometimes referred to as the "Spock Generation"; they were Spocked rather than spanked in their childhood. Most of the older generation spent a part of their youth in the Great Depression during which permissive rearing of children was a luxury that few could afford. In addition, the 1920s and 1930s were too close to the Victorian era to have completely broken with the authoritarian concept of the family. The family was a small autonomous kingdom ruled by the father.

The products of permissiveness are not about to accept dictation from others, individually or collectively; hence the widespread desire, particularly among the young, for more participative democracy. Throughout the world the oppressed, frequently led by the young, are raising their voices to demand participation in decisions that affect them now and that will affect them in the future.

In the United States the young recently won the right to vote. They also want to have a part in running their schools, and insist on having a say as to which wars they will or will not fight. Similarly, the racially, economically, and sexually disadvantaged want to develop themselves and not be developed by others. Workers increasingly want to extract more satisfaction from their work and, through it, to realize more of their potential.

Still another aspect of the past is contributing to this emerging demand for participation. Consider the development of governmental structure. When the United States attained its independence and formed its own government it had a population of about three million. Its government had three levels: local, state, and federal. Because the basic unit of government was small, significant participation in its decision making by the citizenry was possible. Ramsey Clark, former Attorney General of the United States, noted:

> In 1787 New York City, then, as now, our largest metropolis, has 33,000 people, and Philadelphia, second largest. . . .had 20,000. Barely two dozen settlements had more than 2,500 people, and fewer than one of twenty of the total population lived in them.

Several cities and almost half of our states now have a population that exceeds that of the whole country in 1776. But the structure of our government has not changed significantly despite the tremendous growth in population and basic unit size.

People who live in large jurisdictions, as most Americans do, can participate little in their government. They cannot accept government's claim to be for and by the people. It can be argued, however, that not everyone can reasonably expect to participate directly in the government of a large democracy, but they can participate indirectly through their representatives on legislative bodies. Then how explain the underrepresentation in government of large segments of the population such as blacks and women? In 1972 there were only thirteen of each in Congress, and the young and many other segments of the population, including scientists, are not represented at all. Bella Abzug, congresswoman from New York City, is quoted by *Look* as having said that Congress is "a middle-aged, middle-class, white male power structure; no wonder it's been so totally unresponsive to the needs of the country for so long."

Corporations and governments are not unique in their failure to provide their members with opportunities for meaningful participation. Schools at all levels, professional sports teams, government agencies such as police and fire departments, military organizations, professional societies, hospitals, prisons, and most other types of organization have failed equally.

To summarize, in the Machine Age it was assumed, and usually correctly, that humans would adjust their objectives to those of organizations and institutions of which they were part. This assumption was realistic in a period in which economic insecurity and ignorance were pervasive. With increased education and economic security, attitudes toward organizations began to change. There is a growing demand that organizational objectives be adjusted to those of individuals, that they give their members a voice in their management, and that work be designed to fit human capabilities rather than that people be designed to fit mechanistically conceived jobs.

Therefore, a central problem of the Systems Age is how to humanize organizations and institutions; how to design them so that they better serve the purposes of their members and still effectively pursue their own purposes. To do so usually requires a change in both their form and functioning.

THE FORM AND FUNCTIONING OF ORGANIZATIONS

In the Machine Age most organizations were thought of as necessarily being *single headed* and *whole oriented*. Let me make the meaning of these terms clear.

A single-headed organization has an ultimate decision maker who can act for the whole and resolve any disputes that occur below him. Thus such organizations are pyramidal in structure with authority pushed up and responsibility pushed down. Freedom to decide increases with elevation in single-headed organizations; there is practically none at the bottom.

A whole-oriented organization is one in which the interests of the individual members are subordinated to those of the organization taken as a whole. Members of the organization must serve it more than it serves them. In an army, for example, survival of the organization takes precedence over survival of its individual members. Whole-oriented organizations demand loyalty and self-sacrifice from their members.

In the Systems Age our ideas about organization are beginning to change. We are coming to think that most organizations, public or private, should be *multiheaded* and *part oriented*.

A multiheaded organization is one in which there is no single ultimate authority, hence organizational decisions require agreement between two or more equals. A completely multiheaded organization is one in which every member has an equal voice in organizational choice. Many professional, social, and recreational clubs have this characteristic. Democratic organizations are supposed to be completely multiheaded. Autocracies are single headed.

A part-oriented organization is one whose objective is to serve the interests of its members however varied they may be. It has no purpose of its own. It is an instrument of its members. Some professional societies have this characteristic, at least in principle. Hospitals and other types of welfare institutions are also examples.

"Headedness" is a property of the procedures by which organizations select *means*, and "orientation" is a property of the procedures by which they select *ends*.

Pure organizational types are rare. Most organizations have mixed characteristics. For example, an autocratic corporation may contain a democratic research unit. Nevertheless, organizations tend to have dominant characteristics.

Many industrial organizations, most armies, and all fascist states are single headed and whole oriented. An ideally democratic community would be multiheaded and part oriented. Orphanages, nursing homes, hospitals, and schools are usually single headed and part oriented; that is, devoted to the interests of those they serve, but someone has authority over how they are served. Guerrilla bands and political parties are sometimes multiheaded and whole oriented; decisions are made democratically but the members' objectives are subordinated to those of the group.

A single-headed whole-oriented organization restricts its members' choices of both means and ends and thus reduces the variety of their behavior. It tends to impose machinelike behavior on them. In contrast, multiheaded part-oriented organizations tend to increase the choices available to their members and are thus variety increasing. They enable their members to behave more like human beings; they are humanized organizations.

Ideally, democracies are supposed to be multiheaded and part oriented; in practice, however, most of them fall far short of the ideal. Efforts to make them better approximate the ideal are humanizing efforts. Such efforts are by no means restricted to so-called democratic societies, nor to societies as a whole. They are also focused on social institutions and private organizations within societies, particularly on corporations.

The objective of humanization is *not* to turn all organizations into instruments whose *sole* purpose is to satisfy their members. To do so might easily put many organizations "out of business" because they also have a responsibility to the larger system of which they are part. This responsibility gives rise to the environmentalization problem that is the subject of the next chapter. The humanization and environmentalization problems are interactive, hence require joint solution.

Humanization has two aspects: satisfaction and participation. Satisfaction is a measure of the extent to which the purposes of the parts are well served by the whole. Participation involves the extent to which individuals take part in making decisions that affect their satisfaction. In an organizational context participation involves either self-control or control over those who control. Participation is itself a source of satisfaction, but satisfaction of a participant depends on other things as well: on the amount of conflict he is in, the nature of the activity he engages in, the environment in which he engages in it, the consequences of his activity (output or compensation), and the effect of his current activity on his future. I consider each of these aspects of group membership in the discussion that follows.

HUMANIZATION OF GOVERNMENT

The deficiencies of democratic governments—viewed humanistically—are of three interacting types. First, the legislative (decision-making) bodies are not sufficiently representative. Second, they do not address themselves to many critical issues and thus are less than perfectly responsive to the needs and desires of the governed. Finally, the quality of candidates for public office is frequently so low as to deprive the electorate of responsible and effective representation and meaningful choice. Consider each of these deficiencies in turn.

Why are most governmental decision-making bodies whose members are elected not as representative as many would like them to be and what can be done about it? To a large extent the answer to this question lies in geography.

The United States and other democracies are divided into geographically defined districts residents of which elect representatives to serve in legislative bodies. Therefore, elected legislators represent aggregations of citizens geographically defined, but these are not necessarily homogeneous communities whose members have similar interests, needs, and desires. During the Machine Age, interactions across geographic boundaries were more limited than they are today. In the past, needs, interests, and desires tended to derive from the vicinity in which one lived. This is no longer true. With instantaneous multimedia worldwide communication and rapid and inexpensive transportation, common-interest groups are more likely to be geographically dispersed than concentrated in one area. Furthermore, as the population of voting districts increases, their members become more varied and communication between them decreases. Members of contemporary common-interest groups—such as those concerned with womens' liberation, racial equality, the youth movement, ecology, and the problems of the aged—are widely dispersed. Such interest groups seldom constitute a majority in any voting district. As a result they are usually either un- or underrepresented.

This can be made clear by a simple example. Suppose that 90 percent of the population of a nation are As and 10 percent are Bs. Suppose further that these groups are evenly distributed so that the same percentages of As and Bs appear in each voting district. Under these conditions the Bs are not likely to elect any representatives. To obtain representation they must move together into homogeneous voting districts. This is what the blacks are doing, but not entirely by choice. The racial segregation that results breeds discrimination and discrimination reduces participation.

The time in which "majority rule" was an accepted justification of our voting system is passed. As Lord Wilfred Brown, a prominent British industrialist and student of management, pointed out:

> ...the simple rule of "the greatest good for the greatest happiness of the greatest number"...entails the imposition of change by the majority on the minority. We are now much more concerned with the rights of minorities. . . .
>
> It is not therefore only that people subject to authority want change but also that even when majorities have "democratically" agreed on change, minorities are increasingly ill content to tolerate such changes.

Minorities are "ill content" in part because they do not have adequate representation in critical decision-making bodies.

Proposed changes in the system of electing representatives, however rational, are not easy to bring about. (Witness the efforts to modify the obsolete electoral college in the United States.) The power of those currently in power is usually threatened by such proposals, and their approval is required. If anything can induce such approval it is a buildup of public pressure, but such pressure is not likely to develop until there is available a redesign of the election system that clearly would better serve public interests.

The design of an election system that I present here makes no pretense at being politically feasible; it is an idealized design that is intended to encourage others to design their own election systems and to stimulate public discussion of their output.

My design has three objectives. First, to make it possible for any interest group above a specified minimal size, however dispersed it is geographically, to obtain proportional representation *if it so desires*. But the design incorporates recognition of the fact that interests and issues change over time. Therefore, it creates constituencies that are as flexible and adaptive as possible. Second, to enable the public to determine which issues shall be discussed during and after campaigns. Third, to assure it of at least one candidate considered to be *good enough* by a plurality of *eligible* voters. Now to the design itself.

1. The number of representatives to be elected would be divided into the voting population to determine the average size of a constituency. The maximum and minimum sizes of a constituency are then specified; for example, no less than 90 percent or more than 110 percent of the average size.

2.   Platforms (not candidates) would be "nominated" by circulation of petitions for them. A platform could contain any number of planks, even as few as one. A political party could put up its platform and any other group could do so as well. Signatures of a specified number of eligible voters would be required to place a platform on the primary ballot.

3.   Information on the nominated platforms would be widely disseminated. In the primary each voter would identify his preferred platform and his preference ordering over as many additional platforms as he or she desires. If a voter finds no satisfactory platform he would vote for an *Open Platform*. If more people place their votes on the *Open Platform* than on all others combined, then the primary must be rerun at public expense. This process would be repeated until the nominated platforms collectively receive more votes than does the *Open Platform*.

4.   Only those constituencies that obtain the required minimal number of votes or more would be included in the final election. If sufficient people vote for a constituency (including the Open one) to form two or more constituencies of the required size, these would be formed by grouping the members geographically. Those who preferred a constituency that does not survive the primary would be placed into their highest ranked alternative that does survive. If none do, they would be placed in the *Open Constituency*. (See Note.)

5.   Candidates would then be nominated *within* each constituency by petition. They could be put up by political parties or any other group with *publicly registered* membership. All candidates running within a constituency would have to agree to support that constituency's platform, but they would be encouraged to disagree on other issues.

6.   On each ballot there would appear an entry of "No Candidate." To vote for No Candidate is to protest against the set of candidates offered. If No Candidate receives a plurality of votes, then new candidates must be selected and the election rerun. The cost of the rerun would be equally shared by the parties or groups who had nominated candidates defeated by No Candidate.

It would be the obligation of an elected representative to submit and support legislation that promotes the platform on which his constituency was based.

I have only sketched the essential characteristics of an alternative to our current system of elections. My sketch leaves unanswered a number of questions, particularly about implementation. The system I have described could be implemented by use of available communication and data-processing technology. (I have more to say below on the use of this technology to bring about increased participation in government.) Voting would require much more preparation by the voter, but this is unavoidable if voting is to be made more meaningful.

The proposed system would enable voters to express themselves on issues as well as candidates, thereby providing representatives and officials with information about public interests and priorities.

Constituencies might well be different in local, state, and national elections; and they might change from election to election. This would enable the system to learn and adapt.

Officials—for example, governors, mayors, and district attorneys—would be elected differently. Primaries would be conducted as now except for the presence of No Candidate on each ballot. In the runoff, candidates would be expected to express themselves on the issues raised by the platforms that have been nominated. No Candidate would also be listed on the final ballot.

Many variations of the design I have presented are possible, some with very attractive features; for example, the ability of a voter to allocate portions of his vote to different platforms and, subsequently, to candidates from different constituencies. The various possibilities require exploration and widespread public discussion.

Let me repeat that I do not argue for the political feasibility of the design I have proposed. The point of presenting it is to show that more representative democracy is conceivable, not to show that it is easy to come by. Hopefully, by showing that improvements are conceivable, the likelihood that the system will be improved is increased.

The issue of participation in government is not completely dispelled once the issue of representation has been taken care of. Increased participation also requires consideration of the size of governmental units and the relationships between them. As pointed out earlier, the number of layers of government in the United States has not changed since the nation's formation despite the multiplication of its population by a factor of about seventy.

The city, in which an increasing portion of the population lives, is too large a unit to permit significant participation in its government. Furthermore, since the differences between different parts of cities have been increasing, so have the differences in their problems. For this reason there is a clear need for government at a lower level than the city—for a governmental unit small enough to permit direct involvement in government of those who desire it. The *neighborhood* appears to be an appropriate unit for this purpose. It is already emerging as a self-organizing entity dedicated to promotion of its own welfare and development. (See the discussion of Mantua in Chapter 7.)

Neighborhood governments should be given responsibility for as many governmental functions as can be carried out effectively and efficiently at that level. These functions can be identified by comparative studies of small and large independent communities.

But even current city, state, and federal governments can be made more participative than they are now by using modern communication and data-processing technology. Hazel Henderson, a member of the Board of Directors of the Council on Economic Priorities, reported a number of ways in which such technology has been used experimentally to provide the "littleman" with a "chance to be heard." For example, she described a computerized system, developed by MIT's Operations Research Center, for handling complaints, suggestions, and other material sent to the Governor of Massachusetts. The system expedites the handling of such submissions and signals problem areas to the appropriate administrators. Such projects, Ms. Henderson observed:

> ... are the tip of an iceberg signaling a quiet revolution in public realization that computers and mass communications technology need not be a monolithic and centralizing force. People are discovering that these machines can just as easily be adapted to more humanized, organic and decentralized applications—wiring individual "cells" in our body-politic into the central nervous system.

The city cannot tackle metropolitan-area problems. They involve many local governments and often several states. Most cities cannot even solve their internal problems without cooperation from surrounding communities in the metropolitan area. Therefore, some type of regional government or intergovernment is clearly required. This requirement was extensively documented in a report of the Advisory Commission on Intergovernmental Relations (1965) which was established by the 86th Congress and approved by the President in 1959. Without some regionalization the range of choices available to a city is too restricted to permit it to solve its problems effectively. Hence even direct participation in its government is often frustrating if not futile.

In summary, humanization of government requires the addition of at least two levels of government: neighborhood, in metropolitan areas, and regional.

Individual government agencies, as well as governments as wholes, are faced with humanization problems. But intraagency humanization problems are similar to those of private organizations, of corporations in particular.

HUMANIZATION OF CORPORATIONS

Most organizations tend to promote intraorganizational conflicts, however unintentionally, and such conflicts tend to reduce satisfaction derived from work.

An organization's or institution's objectives are usually imposed on its members by use of incentives or disincentives based on measurements of their performance. For example, many factory workers are paid for the number of units they turn out. Such compensation imposes on the production worker the corporation's objective of maximizing output per unit time. If his compensation is reduced for defective work, lateness, or absence, corresponding corporate objectives are similarly imposed on him. In the public domain, income-tax deductions for charitable contributions reflect the government's desire to have charitable institutions supported.

Humanization of an organization requires making its objectives compatible with those of its individual members so that they are mutually reinforcing. When an individual is paid for the number of pieces he produces, it is assumed that one of his important objectives is to maximize his earnings. If this is true, such payment brings corporate and individual objectives into consonance. But the worker may have other objectives of equal or greater importance than maximizing his income, objectives that are poorly served by piece-payment. If this is so—and there is a great deal of evidence that it is—then incentive payments can increase conflict between the corporation and its employees. Consider the following example.

A company that produces a very large number of a small precision-made parts employs a large number of women as inspectors of its finished product. The average number of items correctly inspected per woman was decreasing and the average number incorrectly inspected was increasing. The women were paid a daily rate that was independent of their output. Hopeful of increasing their output, the company proposed a piece-rate compensation plan that would make it possible for the women to increase their earnings significantly. The women rejected the proposal without qualification. The company's puzzled managers called for help from a university-based research group.

The researchers found that the husbands of most of the women—and almost all were married—were employed and earning enough to provide their families with necessities. The women were working in order to increase the amount of money available to the family for *discretionary* goods and services, things they wanted but did not really need. But the women did not want to earn as much as their husbands because this might threaten their husbands' role as family breadwinner. Therefore, the women were not anxious to earn more than they already were. Furthermore, working carelessly at a leisurely pace enabled them to socialize with coworkers while doing their job and thus get some relief from a very dull and repetitive task.

More importantly, the researchers discovered that most of the women had children in school and that they felt guilty about not being at home when their children returned from school. The women either had to leave their children to care for themselves, which was a source of anxiety, or they arranged for others to take care of them, which they felt to be an imposition on these others. In either case the women felt guilty and blamed the company for the situation.

When the researchers learned this, they designed a new incentive system. A "fair day's work"—the number of items correctly inspected—was specified. This number was greater than the average daily output. The women were permitted to leave work and return home whenever the specified number was completed, or they could continue to work on a piece-rate basis for as much additional time as they cared to, production requirements permitting. They accepted this proposal enthusiastically and their output rate more than doubled. Errors decreased and satisfaction increased. They were able to meet their children when they returned from school.

The right incentive can bring the whole and its parts together, but the wrong one can take them apart. For example, consider the way most companies pay their advertising agencies. They receive a fixed percentage of the amount the company spends on advertising. Little wonder that there is so much and such redundant advertising. It is not surprising that many companies have trouble with their agencies and change them frequently. Imagine a corporation paying its tax consultant a percentage of the amount he determines the corporation must pay the government!

Use of incentives is not the only way of imposing organizational objectives on workers. Objectives can also be imposed by the measures used to evaluate individual performance. This can have a dehumanizing effect when the objectives imposed are incompatible, and they frequently are. Those who are subject to such conflicts are seldom provided with a way of trading off between the objectives. In many cases a gain relative to one objective can only be made if there is a loss relative to another. For example, it may not be possible to improve both the quantity and quality of production simultaneously. Product inspectors are sometimes told to simultaneously minimize the number of defective items accepted and the number of acceptable items rejected. In many cases one can be decreased only by increasing the other. Home-appliance repairmen working for one company were told to maximize the number of house calls successfully completed per day and also to minimize the number of spare parts they carried with them. This is like telling a child to have a good time *and* to be good. The fewer parts they carried, the more often they had to return to the warehouse for parts. The more often they made this trip, the fewer house calls they could make.

At the very best, conflicting objectives restrict choice. At the worst, they produce anxiety and frustration.

Objectives imposed from above are frequently not operationally defined; that is, specified in a way that enables those subject to them to determine objectively the extent to which the objectives are met. This leaves evaluation of performance a matter of a superior's judgment and such judgment often appears arbitrary and capricious to those subjected to it. For example, managers who are told to improve "community relations" or "employee morale" are often in this position. Workers who are told to improve the quality of their work without being told how quality is determined or being allowed to determine it themselves are in a similar position. Students subject to subjective grading by professors are familiar with the anxiety and frustration produced by trying to cope with lack of definition of quality.

Objectives imposed on interacting units of the same organization are also frequently incompatible. This produces conflict between the units, hence between their managers and those subordinates who identify with them. For example, a marketing department that is instructed to sell as much as possible wants as wide a range of products as possible. A production department that is simultaneously instructed to maximize production and minimize unit costs wants as small a product line as possible so that it can have long unbroken production runs. These departments and personnel within them are bound to conflict. Interunit conflicts of this type can be a major source of anxiety and frustration to both managers and workers.

There is a growing tendency for organizations to let managers (and sometimes workers) participate in setting the objectives by which their performance will be measured. Such involvement is called "management by objectives." There is no doubt that this type of participation increases a manager's commitment to the resulting objectives, but too frequently it does not eliminate conflict between objectives of different units because many managers do not comprehend the way in which objectives of different managers interact. Such comprehension is usually impossible without extensive research, but few managers have the human and financial resources necessary for conducting such research.

The Work Itself

A worker's attitude toward his employer is not solely a product of the incentives and objectives to which he is subjected. It also depends on the nature of the work he does, the environment in which he does it, the compensation he receives for it, the opportunity for participation in the design of his work and the work environment, and his prospects for advancement.

In most corporations all employees but the top executives are constrained by higher authorities not only with respect to what they can do (ends) but also with respect to how they do it (means). They usually wallow in a sea of prescriptions. But there has been a slowly increasing number of efforts to provide workers with more opportunity to participate in decision making that affects both what they do and how they do it. Such efforts are referred to alternatively as "job enrichment," "job enlargement," and "industrial democracy." Paul Blumberg, professor of sociology at Queens College, reviewed a significant portion of what he referred to as the "participative literature" and summarized his findings as follows:

> There is hardly a study in the entire literature which fails to demonstrate that satisfaction in work is enhanced or that other generally acknowledged beneficial consequences accrue, from a general increase in workers' decision making power. Such consistency of findings, I submit, is rare in social research.

Not all efforts at worker participation have been as successful as this summary suggests; for example, *work structuring* as it has been practiced by Philips in Holland. In this procedure groups of workers are told what is to be done and how, but they can determine who is to do what part of it and when, and they can modify the environment in which it is done. In Philips' report of this effort the following candid observation was made: ". . .it can be stated that efforts in this direction do not go far beyond an improvement of the 'atmosphere' in a group or department. In all probability these points are incidental in relation to the long-term attractiveness of the factory on the labour-market."

Work structuring appears to be a little like taking a prisoner out of solitary confinement and putting him in a high-security cell shared by others. The group is free to do whatever it wants within the cell, but not to leave it. This is some improvement, but not much. As the Philips' report observed: ". . .it is possible to draw the conclusion that the approach chosen left a great deal to be desired."

A less constrained version of job enrichment consists of creating tasks that involve a greater number of operations and sometimes all those required to make a product. For example, *Nation's Business* reported on such a humanizing effort at Motorola:

> . . .the men and women who make the tiny PAGEBOY II [an FM radio paging receiver] are not only totally responsible for their work, they even include a signed note to the customer which says, "I built this receiver in its entirety and I'm proud of it. I hope it serves you well—please tell me if it doesn't."

The company claims a better product and happier and more productive workers. One of its vice presidents, Mort Cooper, commented: "Everybody wins—it's got to be right."

Such redesigns can help in the short run but repetition of routine, no matter how complex, eventually becomes a bore. Therefore, an increasingly used alternative involves letting workers perform a large variety of jobs. For example, *The New York Times* reported that in the Topeka (Kansas) pet-food plant of General Foods all workers "get a chance to do every major job in the plant from unloading with a forklift truck to making complex tests in the quality-control laboratory. And they have unusual latitude in deciding—free of supervisors—how to spend their time." The general manager of the plant was reported as estimating "that the plant. . .is up to 30 per cent more productive than a comparable one. Its absenteeism averages 1 per cent and turnover is about 5 per cent a year, considerably lower than at other plants."

The ability to do different things at different times reduces, if not eliminates, boredom. The ability to learn how to do new things does more: it makes self-improvement possible. But if self-improvement is not accompanied by increased responsibility, it produces even more frustration than repetitive machinelike work. Therefore, opportunity for advancement and the chance to plan for it—career planning—are essential aspects of humanizing work. A person must be able to get ahead, know what is required to do so, and have access to the means of fulfilling these requirements. Thus every worker should have the opportunity to prepare a plan for his own future, and, additionally, he should be able to revise this plan in light of subsequent experience. Planning is not for organizations alone; it is equally relevant to individuals who want to control their own futures.

More freedom of choice usually implies more responsibility, and more responsibility, as *Fortune* pointed out, can produce another type of problem: "The most common theme of complaint heard in job-enrichment plants is that there should be, but often is not, more pay for more responsibility and more production."

Participation

If a large complex organization is to be viable, some type of hierarchical structure is required. This requirement appears to be incompatible with increasing participation of workers. Some companies, particularly those abroad, have tried to deal with this dilemma by giving workers representation on their boards of directors. The results are usually disappointing as Paul Blumberg observed: the "diverse forms of 'industrial democracy at the top' have been failures from the point of view of the workers."

Lord Wilfred Brown, who spent twenty-five years on corporate boards that have had workers' representatives on them, commented: ". . .'more participation'. . .was narrowed down by employees' representatives to the taking of 'full part' in the formulation of those policies which bear directly on working conditions." F. E. Emery and Einar Thorsund, distinguished Australian and Norwegian social psychologists, observed: "If democratic participation is to become a reality, it seems inevitable that it must be started at a level where a large proportion of employees are both *able and willing to participate.*"

How can workers at every level of an organization be given the opportunity to participate in decisions that directly affect them? And how can this be done in such a way as not to undermine the hierarchy required wherever there is a division of complex labor? One way it can be done is by use of what I call a *circular* organization.

A Circular Organization

A circular organization is intended to maximize opportunities for relevant participation by its members, to maximize the extent to which the organization serves the purposes of its members and, by so doing, better serves its own purposes. To grasp the essentials of such an organization it is necessary to consider only a simplified three-level organization which, if conventionally organized, can be represented by the chart shown in Figure 3.1. Each box in this chart represents an organizational unit headed by a manager. For example, A_3, B_3, and C_3 might be departments; A_2, B_2, and C_2, divisions; and A_1, the corporate headquarters. Or they might be a university's

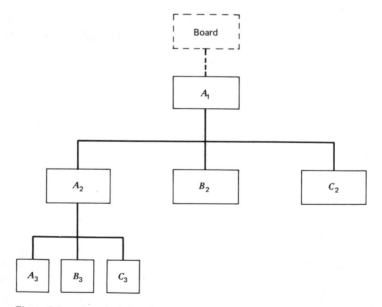

Figure 3.1   A typical three-level organization.

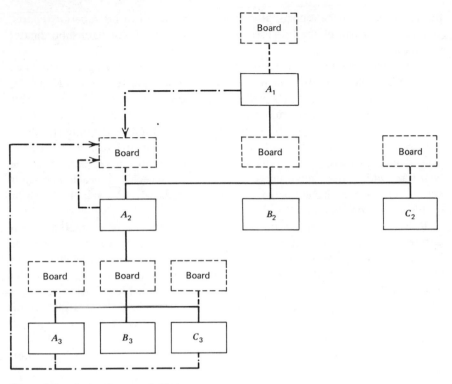

Figure 3.2   A circular organization.

departments, colleges, and overall administration.

Most nongovernmental organizations have boards which, in principle, have ultimate control over the organization. Corporate boards are supposed to look out for the interests of the shareholders but they are also superior to the chief executive.

Let us consider giving each manager a board as is shown in Figure 3.2. Now consider possible membership of the board to which the manager of the middle unit, A_2, could report. It could have the following composition: first, the manager of unit A_2; second, each manager who reports to him—the managers of A_3, B_3, and C_3; and finally, the manager of A_1 to whom the manager of A_2 reports. The manager of A_1 may act as chairman of this board.

This and every board would have three levels of the organization represented on it. The highest and lowest boards require special attention, which I will give them in a moment.

First, look at the organization another way. Each manager is a member of the board to which he reports, also of the board to which his superior reports, and he is chairman of the boards to which each of his immediate subordinates reports.

The boards should not manage but they should have two major functions: to establish policies under which the manager reporting to it should operate, and to evaluate that manager's performance and remove him if doing so seems necessary. Therefore, the immediate subordinates of any manager, acting collectively, can remove him from his position. But the board cannot fire him, it only controls the occupancy of the position, not the occupant. On the other hand, no manager can remove a subordinate without agreement of the board to which that subordinate reports. This means that each manager's performance would be evaluated by those immediately below him as well as by his immediate superior.

It has often been argued that no manager should have more than seven different kinds of unit reporting to him. This is the average number of qualitatively different things that a person can deal with individually and collectively in his mind. If a manager had seven units reporting to him he would participate in nine boards. If each board on which a manager serves were to meet about five hours per month, no more than about a quarter of his time would be so occupied. He would be able to discharge a large part of his responsibility through these boards.

Now consider the lowest-level board. The lowest-level manager or supervisor has no other managers or supervisors reporting to him, only a group of workers. The workers should elect six or seven representatives who would serve on their manager's board. These representatives should meet with their constituency to discuss the issues being considered by the board of which they are part. In this way meaningful participation of those at the lowest level of an organization can be assured. They are given some control over those who have immediate control over them, and they interact with their manager's superior.

Such participation by workers is not intended as a substitute for union negotiations which must take place at a higher level. Therefore, workers' representatives should not include union officials even if they are employed by the company.

Design of the top board requires special attention, which I will give it in the next chapter.

Note that the design I have proposed makes every unit of the system—except the lowest element—participate in management of both the larger system of which it is part and the smaller systems that are part of it. Note also that in the board of its suprasystem each system interacts with every other system that is part of the same suprasystem. Finally, note that in systems of five or more levels, managers at other than the top and bottom of the hierarchy interact with personnal at *five* different levels of the organization because the board above contains two higher levels, and the one below, two lower levels. It is hard to imagine a more effective way of preparing managers for higher positions.

Aside from humanization, the circular organization makes possible such integration of activities at different levels, and such coordination of different activities at the same level, as few organizations can currently enjoy.

CONCLUSION

I have argued that a central problem of our young Systems Age is that of humanizing organizations: increasing the compatibility of organizational and individual objectives. Solution of this problem in whole-oriented organizations requires developing relevant incentives and ways of providing individuals with more meaningful participation in their organizations. Such participation implies giving individuals a role in making those decisions that affect them directly and rewarding them appropriately for improved performance and increased responsibility. There is extensive evidence that such participation produces increased satisfaction and improves organizational performance.

Efforts to democratize organizations have been more extensive in industry than in government. But, as *The New York Times* pointed out, not much has been done even in industry:

> A recent study by the Department of Health, Education and Welfare estimated that only about 3,000 workers in the United States were undergoing. . .basic [humanization] experimentation. . . .
>
> Still, a growing number of companies employing hundreds of thousands of workers, "white collar" as well as "blue," are trying to make the workday a little less dull without at the same time hurting production schedules or profits.

Historians of the future may well look back on this effort as one in which there was "too little, too late."

CHAPTER FOUR

THE ENVIRONMENTALIZATION PROBLEM

*Businessmen have no choice but to respond to be-
coming reformers themselves, making a conscious
effort to adapt the market system to our changing
social, political and technological environment.*

*The question really comes down to this: Will
business leaders seize the initiative to make necessary changes and take on new responsibilities
voluntarily, or will they wait until these are
thrust upon them by law?*

DAVID ROCKEFELLER

In the Machine Age nations and corporations were thought to have little or no
responsibility either to their environments or to other organizations and
individuals within them. Nations and corporations were considered to be
virtually self-contained and autonomous. The natural environment was
believed to be capable of absorbing any amount of use by man and of
recovering fully. It was considered to be an unlimited source of every kind of
resource. Ownership of property was equated to a license to do with it
whatever one wanted.

Developed nations and corporations colonialized and exploited underdeveloped societies and their physical environments. They were considered to
be entitled to whatever they could get away with in the outside world. *Laissez
faire* was the dominant philosophy in both national and corporate affairs.

That some should suffer the consequences was considered to be "natural" because struggle and conflict were assumed to be necessary for survival. Only the fit survived. Fitness was conceived both in terms of ability to adapt to changing natural conditions and ability to compete in society (a euphemism for "fight"). Progress was believed to be the product of the struggle for survival. Its cost had to be paid by the weak.

In short, nations, corporations, and individuals gave little thought to their natural or social environments and those who occupied them.

As the Machine Age began to end so did these attitudes for a number of reasons. Men began to suspect that the supply of natural resources was not unlimited and even began to fear that some might run out in their lifetimes. The quality of the environment, man-made and natural, began to deteriorate visibly, and the rate of deterioration seemed to exceed the recuperative capabilities of either society or Nature. Those in the environment who were exploited and left in a disadvantaged state began to organize themselves into effective protest groups and brought moral and physical pressure to bear on those responsible for their state. The health and welfare of environment and environmental systems were forced into the consciousness of nations and corporations by pressure groups formed around a variety of issues including ecology, racial equality, consumerism, and underdevelopment. Disadvantaged countries and the disadvantaged within both developed and underdeveloped countries began to press for a more equitable distribution of wealth. These and other issues around which such pressure groups formed are discussed in subsequent chapters.

In systems thinking every purposeful system is considered to have an environment and to be part of one or more larger (supra) systems. For example, a city can be taken to be part of a state, a state part of a nation, and a nation part of a family of nations. A company can be taken as part of an industry and industry as part of an economy. Each such system can be considered to have an effect on, and to be affected by, at least one system of which it is part. It also interacts with other systems in its suprasystem. Cities, for example, interact with other cities; states, nations, corporations, and governmental agencies do likewise.

All of a system's environment is part of one or more of its containing systems. Its environment consists of all those things—physical and social, man-made and natural—that are external to it and either affect or are affected by its behavior. Hence a system's environment consists of what that system is open to and what is open to it.

Environmentalization is the process of putting into a system's mind its relationship to the whole of which it is part. It is the converse of humanization in which a system's relationship to its parts are put into its mind.

Humanization efforts are based on the conviction that every system should assume a larger responsibility for the welfare of its parts. In environmentalization there is a complementary conviction that the parts should assume a larger responsibility for the welfare of the whole.

CORPORATE RESPONSIBILITY

Mounting public pressure on corporations to behave in more socially responsible ways has given rise to a major debate in corporate circles. The debate focuses on the question: Should or should not a corporation involve itself in activities and programs that are intended to improve its physical and social environment? This question arises only when such involvement consumes corporate profits; when it produces profit there is no issue. The answers to this question reflect the four basic attitudes toward the present and future; inactivism, reactivism, preactivism, and interactivism.

The Reactive and Inactive Views

Reactivists and inactivists oppose an increase of corporate social responsibility. The former want to return to less regulation and control of corporations by government, and the latter want no more than currently exists. Their positions have been forcefully stated and defended by Professor Milton Friedman, presidential advisor and University of Chicago economist: "There is one and only one social responsibility of business—to use its resources and engage in activities designed to increase its profits so long as it stays within the rules of the game, which is to say, engages in open and free competition without deception or fraud." He maintains that businessmen who spend corporate funds to improve the environment are taxing their shareholders, workers, or customers, and are doing so without their representation. Such businessmen, Professor Friedman maintains, are "unwitting puppets of the intellectual forces that have been undermining the basis of a free society."

We need not concern ourselves with the consistency or validity of Professor Friedman's argument. It is sufficient for our purposes here to show that it leads to corporate behavior that is detrimental to the environment. It follows from his position that a firm should obey rules and regulations imposed on it by government, but should do no more than this for its environment. Its preoccupation should be with maximization of profit. But those who hold this position oppose increased taxation and regulation of corporations because they reduce corporate profits. They also oppose government efforts to improve the corporate environment because these almost always involve increased taxation or regulation.

For example, consider the beverage industry in the United States which has taken a strong position opposing any change in regulation or law that would affect its containers or packages, whatever its effect might be on the solid-waste and litter problems. This industry employs a large lobbying force whose function is to obstruct efforts to regulate beverage containers and packaging, and it does so at every level of government—local, state, and federal. While this industry supports governmental responsibility for the environment in principle, in practice it has opposed every effort by governments at every level to improve the environment in any way that might affect its profits.

Because of such activities by a large number of companies and industrial associations governments are almost completely immobilized in the environmental area. Although several hundred pieces of ecological legislation have been proposed at all levels of government, only a very few have survived the corporate onslaught and been enacted.

To be sure, many of the legislative and regulatory proposals considered by governments are defective and would not work well if enacted, but it is almost impossible for governments to design effective legislation and regulation in the face of corporate opposition to any possible action by them. Without cooperation from industry effective legislation and regulation is unlikely to be drafted; if drafted, to be enacted; and if enacted, to be implemented effectively.

When an environmentally oriented law or regulation is passed, inactive and reactive companies try to make it fail in every way they can. They exploit whatever ambiguity there may be in its statement. They contest its legality and probe its limits in the courts. They make enforcement so difficult that government must create a large regulatory agency to carry it out. Such bureaucracies develop their own inefficiency, inertia, and, often, corruption. In many cases such agencies become more responsive to corporations that they are supposed to regulate than to environmental needs. For example, the Federal Trade Commission has often been accused of being more responsive to companies than to their customers.

Not all companies or industries take inactive or reactive postures with regard to social responsibility. Sears, for example, has cooperated extensively with the government in the development and evaluation of effective safety standards for consumer products, and Hershey has done the same in food testing and control.

The principal argument directed against corporate collaboration with government or unilateral corporate acceptance of greater social responsibility is that it is detrimental to stockholders' interests which focus on profit. But there is evidence of growing stockholder support of corporate involvement in social programs. For example, Alvin Toffler pointed out:

> The invention of new investment vehicles, such as mutual funds, that are consciously motivated or constrained by noneconomic considerations. The Vanderbilt Mutual Fund and the Provident Fund refuse to invest in liquor and tobacco shares. The giant Mates Fund spurns the stock of any company engaged in munitions production, while the tiny Vintage 10/90 Fund invests part of its assets in industries working to alleviate food and population problems in developing nations.

The New York Times reported that the trustees of Yale University, a large investor in many corporations, recently "endorsed the concept that institutional investors, such as university endowment funds, have a responsibility to speak out when the companies whose shares they own are taking actions they deem harmful to society."

Moreover, there is reason to believe that in the future many will become stockholders in corporations not primarily to obtain a return on their investment but to increase corporate responsiveness to environmental problems. For example, Ralph Nader's Raiders purchase stock in the companies they investigate. This legitimates, in their view, their pressure on companies to release data and to become involved in more socially responsive programs.

Preactive Views

The inactive and reactive positions are based on the belief that increased social responsibility necessarily involves sacrifice of corporate profits. Preactivists deny this. They believe that increased social responsibility can lead to increased profits in the long, if not the short, run.

A booklet published in 1971 by the Committee for Economic Development (CED), a group of prominent businessmen and educators, puts forward three preactive positions in the debate over social responsibility of corporations. One of these was formulated by two Yale professors of economics, Henry C. Wallich and John J. McGowan. (Dr. Wallich* was senior economic consultant to the Treasury and a member of President Eisenhower's Council of Economic Advisors.) They wrote that "the proposition that corporate involvement in social policy is contrary to the stockholder's interest in both misleading and irrelevant," because of the diversification of stockholders' investments. They argued that corporate activities become worthwhile to the diversified stockholders that would not be of value to the stockholder in a

*Now a member of the Federal Reserve Board.

single firm. The diversified stockholder has his economic interests advanced when firms undertake programs whose benefits for the corporate sector exceed their costs.

Wallich and McGowan explain: "If there are investment opportunities which would lead to improved environmental conditions, a better labor force, or whatever, and the returns appropriable by the corporate sector as a whole exceeds costs, then they should be seized." Thus they aruge that many social programs engaged in by business can be justified by the benefits that result rather than by consideration of social pressure. Note that this argument is compatible with the assumption that the corporation's principal responsibility is to its stockholders. I shall examine this assumption below.

In the same CED booklet Professor William Baumol of Princeton University argues for consortium arrangements in which groups of corporations, for example, "benefit from a regional theatre in the community." He continues: "If those companies form an association in which each pledges to bear its share of the deficit of the theatre, provided all members do . . . each management will be able to say to its stockholders that the outlay is a simple matter of economics and self-interest."

In the third contribution to this booklet Rensis Likert, former director of the University of Michigan's Institute for Social Research, argues that the reactions of a corporation's various publics are critical: "Corporate sensitivity and responsiveness to these reactions on its immediate and long-term profitability and success is in its own immediate self-interest. Thus, social responsibility has a direct impact on corporate profits."

The positions of Wallich and McGowan, Baumol, and Likert are preactive because they attempt to minimize the effect of social pressures on the corporation. Their positions are based more on a desire to prevent undesirable consequences to the corporation than on a desire to improve its social and physical environment. Maintenance or improvement of the environment is never posed as a legitimate corporate objective in its own right. It is justified only by its contribution, however indirect, to profits.

Because the payoffs from corporate acts of social responsibility are often difficult to measure and are often slow in coming, there is considerable interest in improved ways of measuring social benefits of corporate actions. According to *The Wall Street Journal* business executives want such measures because:

> . . . as they come under increasing pressure to pursue social as well as financial goals, they are anxious to demonstrate in "objective" terms that their enterprises do indeed benefit society. The current absence of agreed-upon standards makes it hard to put forth a convincing case to satisfy critics, they

complain. Moreover, in conventional profit-and-loss terms, the cost of any current social activities actually makes their performance look worse to stockholders.

Some preactive managers have shown considerable ingenuity in avoiding the measurement problem by converting environmental problems or public pressure arising from them into opportunities for measurably increasing profit. In so doing they have found ways of simultaneously serving more effectively both society and their stockholders.

For example, Standard Oil of Indiana has been having increasing difficulty in maintaining the profitability of its service stations in or near predominantly black urban ghettos. It could easily have decided to abandon such stations but it took a more innovative and socially oriented approach to the problem. It contracted with an architectural and planning group of a black neighborhood's self-development organization to prepare a preliminary design of a service station to be located in black urban communities that would not be subject to continuous theft, would be well operated and maintained, and would be profitable to both the company and the neighborhood.

The design group interviewed about 800 residents of the ghetto and analyzed their needs as well as the company's. It then produced a design for a community service station that was to be owned and operated by a community self-development group, but financed and supplied by the company. It was unique both in form and function. In addition to the usual services, it included a shop that would sell parts and accessories for automobiles, motorcycles, and bicycles; a do-it-yourself repair and main-tenance center; training facilities and programs; a club room, and offices to be rented. Its parking area was convertible to an illuminated basketball court. The station was ringed by a well-lit translucent plastic wall broken by entrances and exits. The wall was designed to carry information about neighborhood events. Landscaped resting places were provided for casual meetings and conversation by day or night.

When the design was presented to the company's executives they responded enthusiastically. The design group was commissioned to prepare detailed working drawings. The finished design was evaluated economically by the company and it decided to go ahead. The search for a suitable location for the prototype is now going on.

A simpler example of a company that saw a profitable way of serving the public's interest in the environment is one that developed and produced meters for measuring the polluting content of liquid and gaseous wastes.

As I noted earlier, to the extent that social responsibility can be made profitable, there is no issue. Preactive companies either seek ways of converting social problems into corporate opportunities or they try to show that support of environmental improvement eventually pays off, even if that payoff cannot be measured. They try hard to measure it because they—like reactive and inactive companies—accept profit maximization as the dominant corporate objective.

An Interactive View

Reactivists, inactivists, and preactivists assume—implicitly or explicitly—that the meaning of profit and profit maximization is clear, but this is far from true. To a certain extent, profit is a figment of the accountant's imagination. Significant amounts of it can be created or destroyed by manipulating one's accounting system and financial policies.

Professor C. West Churchman, one of the most prominent philosophers of management science, has shown just how ambiguous and arbitrary these concepts are. His argument is too technical to reproduce here but his summary of it catches its essential flavor:

> As long as we can assume that the entrepreneur wants to maximize the profit measured in dollar units, and we do not ask why he has such a motive, we seem to succeed in developing a scale of value, even though there are serious difficulties in using this scale to define a profit maximum . . . [But] in fact no such scale does exist, or more moderately, there is no known accounting system which supplies the kind of data needed to permit us to use maximization of profits as a basis for evaluating decisions.

One might argue that although the meaning of profit maximization is not clear it should nevertheless be used because it is almost universally accepted as a corporate objective. But, according to Professor H. Igor Ansoff, a prominent authority on business planning at Vanderbilt University: "In actual fact objectives are currently one of the most controversial issues in business ethics. Distinguished writers have sought to remove profit from its position as the central motive in business . . . "

The influential and very respectable *Harvard Business Review* carried R. N. Anthony's indictment of profit as immoral and socially unacceptable. A number of alternatives are being widely discussed. For example, E. Solomon suggested maximization of a company's net worth; W. Baranek, maximization of the market value of the firm; and W. J. Baumol, profit-constrained maximization of growth. Peter F. Drucker, one of the most prominent thinkers on corporate affairs, has argued that survival is the central purpose of the firm. Although he considers adequate profitability necessary for survival, he asserts that " 'profit maximization' is the wrong concept whether it be interpreted to mean short-range or long-range profits."

Concern over social responsibility of the firm has produced what Professor Ansoff has called the "stakeholder theory" of objectives:

> This theory maintains that the objectives of the firm should be derived from balancing the conflicting claims of the various "stakeholders" in the firm: managers, workers, stockholders, suppliers, vendors. The firm has a responsibility to all of these and must configure its objectives so as to give each a measure of satisfaction. Profit which is a return on investment to the stockholder is one of such satisfactions, but does not receive special predominance in the objective structure.

One version of this theory was formulated by then professors R. M. Cyert and J. G. March of Carnegie Institute of Technology. They argued that the objectives of the firm should be extracted from a negotiated consensus of those participating in it. Note that they view the corporation as a part-oriented organization, one whose purpose is to serve the purposes of all its participants and those affected by its behavior. This differs significantly from the view taken by Dr. Friedman who conceives of the corporation as a whole-oriented organization whose sole objective is to make a profit and thereby provide a return to its stockholders.

Most of those who believe that profit maximization should *not* be the dominant corporate objective nevertheless think that it *can* be such an objective. But, I believe, that even if we knew what profit meant and could measure it precisely, it could not serve properly as a corporate objective.

Profit consists of money that is available to a firm to use as it sees fit, including—but not necessarily—payment of dividends to stockholders. The great American wit Ambrose Bierce defined money as "blessing that is of no advantage to us except when we part with it." Its value is purely instrumental, extrinsic; it has no value in itself except to misers, and corporations are not miserly. The value of profit lies in what it can be used for. Profit is to a corporation what oxygen is to an individual; necessary for its survival, not the reason for its existence. Maximization of profit is no more meaningful a statement of a corporate objective than is the maximization of oxygen for an individual. The objective of a corporation should be stated in terms of what profit can be used for.

To understand what profit can be used for we must have a clear conception of what a corporation does. Typically it converts labor, energy, and/or matter into usable goods and services. Doing so involves it in interactions with six types of participants.

1. *Employees* with whom the corporation exchanges money for work. These comprise white-collar and blue-collar workers at all levels including managerial.

2. *Customers* with whom the corporation exchanges goods and/or services for money.

3. *Suppliers* with whom the corporation exchanges money for goods and/or services. Suppliers include governments that provide public facilities and services for which the corporation pays through taxes.

4. *Investors* and *moneylenders* who make money available to the corporation now in exchange for payment later.

5. *Debtors* to whom the corporation makes money available now in exchange for payment later. These include other companies in which the corporation invests, banks in which it stores money, and governments whose bonds it buys.

6. The *public* that it affects by what it does to its environment and that, through government, regulates its behavior.

Note that these exchanges involve both individuals who are part of the corporation and other individuals and organizations that are part of its environment. These participants in corporate affairs are the *stakeholders*.

The stockholders clearly are not the only ones who invest their resources in a corporation. All the participants and those affected by it invest some type of resource (including themselves) in it. Why should the stockholder be singled out and be permitted to dictate corporate objectives? The usual answer is that they run the greatest risk of losing their resources. This is sheer nonsense. The average employee probably has more to lose by his employing corporation going out of business than does the average stockholder.

In one corporation I was able to estimate, using a random sample of employees, the average percentage of their incomes that was derived from the company. The same was done for a sample of stockholders. These percentages were multiplied by the number in each group so as to provide an index of the relative importance of the company to these participants. The number obtained for the employees was much larger than that obtained for the stockholders.

Analysis of the six exchanges in which a corporation can be involved makes it clear that a corporation consumes goods and services provided by others and makes possible consumption by others by providing them both with the money necessary to buy goods and services and with goods and services to buy. When a corporation harms the environment—for example, by contributing to the pollution of a lake—it reduces the value of the property around the lake and of activities on it. The amount of this reduction is the amount consumed by the corporation.

If the value of what a corporation consumes is greater than the value of the consumption that it makes possible, it operates at a loss to society; otherwise it operates to the benefit of society. The amount of consumption a corporation makes possible, less its own consumption, is the *net social consumption* it produces. This quantity is very different from profit. For example, in calculating profit wages have a negative value; in calculating net social consumption wages have a positive value. In the short run a corporation could produce positive net social consumption without making a profit; it could even incur a loss. But if it continued to do so it would not be able to operate because it could not generate the necessary capital. This is why profit is essential. But the principal objective of a corporation should be to maximize the rate of growth of corporately produced net social consumption. Such as objective imposes a parts-orientation and an environmental concern on the corporation that adopts it.

Corporations cannot isolate themselves if our society is to continue to develop. Many corporate managers disagree with this view. According to Alvin Toffler: "They continue to act as though the economic sector were hermetically sealed off from social and psycho-cultural influences."

Public pressure to involve corporations in environmental problems will continue to grow as social problems grow. Such pressure should not be interpreted as evidence of lack of faith in the corporation as a social instrument, but rather as evidence of the belief that corporations can do more to help solve social problems than perhaps even government can.

In most cases, a corporation acting by itself cannot change the environment significantly; the collaboration of other organizations is usually required to do so. Hence part of a corporation's activity should be directed toward organizing other parts of its environment in such a way as to bring about needed changes in the environment. It is unlikely that a corporation will be able to urge others to do what it is unwilling to do itself.

Few corporations take on a social or environmental problem as they would a business problem unless it threatens them in a direct way. They do not usually view social problems as opportunities either to exercise social responsibility or to improve their environment in such a way as to benefit the corporation. They attempt rather to minimize the ability of the environment to threaten them and thereby also minimize their ability to benefit from the solution of social problems.

In the Systems Age, corporations increasingly will have to seek ways of solving their own problems in ways that benefit their environments, and of solving social problems in ways that benefit them as well as society.

For example, Anheuser-Busch, of St. Louis, has supported university-based studies of racial, ecological, and health problems. These studies have been carried out from the point of view of society at large, not from the point of view of the company. The company has supported dissemination of the results of these studies even when, as in the case of the study of solid waste and litter reported in Chapter 10, the results were not compatible with positions taken by the company and the brewing industry. The company subsequently modified its position in light of the findings and is now engaged in supporting activities that can be beneficial both to society and itself. For example, it iniated the national "Pitch-In" antilitter campaign and the National Center for Resource Recovery. It discontinued a container-reclamation program that had good public relation value but that the university showed had no significant effect on solid waste or litter.

Anheuser-Busch uses a university-based research group as representatives of society at large and seeks its advice as to what policies and programs it should adopt on social problems. The policies it adopts and the programs it supports cannot be justified in terms of profit maximization. It does so because it wants a better social and physical environment and feels a responsibility for helping bring it about. And this company has found that it can do so without depriving its stockholders of a more than adequate return on their investment.

Corporate use of advocates—from without, as a university-based research group, or from within—is an effective way of confronting itself with social and environmental problems and the opportunities they present.

Advocates inside, or outside of, the corporation should have two major functions. First, they should examine and evaluate all corporate behavior that affects the environment or that could and fails to do so. They should seek to make corporate actions more effective from the environmental point of view. Second, they should study environmental problems so as to uncover ways in which the company can contribute to their solution, profitably if possible, but even if not profitably. This may involve creation of new businesses or new ways of conducting old ones. It may involve creation of new products or services, or creating new sources of supply. For example, it was a group of ecological advocates that advised the company previously mentioned to manufacture pollution-metering equipment because it would be needed to gain control over the physical environment. This is now a profitable component of the corporation's business.

The advocates within a corporation should be gathered into an organizational unit that reports to the board of directors through an executive for environmental affairs. If this is not done, the job security of the advocates can be constantly threatened by those interested in narrowly defined corporate objectives. The board, of course, will have to appreciate the significance of such efforts as the environmental-affairs group engages in. To be sure that it does, and to meet the requirements of humanization discussed in the preceding chapter, the board should be differently composed than it usually is.

It will be recalled that the corporation was described earlier in terms of six types of interaction involving employees, customers, suppliers, government, investors, and debtors. The usual corporate board includes representatives of only the investors and that subclass of employees called managers. The board of a systems Age corporation should include representatives of each of the stakeholder groups. That is, the board should have members who look out for the interests of each of the six groups of participants as well as of the corporation as a whole. Public representatives should be selected so as to assure corporate concern with at least four environmental problems: racial equality, ecological improvement, sexual equality, and protection of consumer interests. Advocates of these issues should be incorporated into the board.

Concern with the corporation as an entity should be the preoccupation of its managers and their representatives on the board. Their task is to balance the various interests and extract from them policies that enable the corporation to fulfill all of its functions effectively, including maximization of the rate of growth of its contribution to social consumption.

GOVERNMENT AND THE INDIVIDUAL

Social problems are not created and are not solvable by corporations alone. They have only a minor role to play in many of these problems. On the other hand, the government and the individuals it represents are involved in every environmental and social problem.

Consider the ecological problem. Urban trash collection procedures are the largest single contributor to urban litter. It is estimated that about 90 percent of the public agencies responsible for collection and disposal of solid waste use either unsanitary open dumping or air-polluting incinerators. The Atomic Energy Commission is the principal producer of the radiation hazard. The development and use of pesticides now considered to be damaging to ecological balance was stimulated and partially financed by government. Slums develop despite planning commissions and zoning ordnances; water supplies diminish and deteriorate despite water commissions; open spaces disappear despite recreational departments; and so on and on.

The segmentation of government into relatively autonomous agencies of which no one can deal with *all* aspects of an environmental or social problem leads to as much indifference to improvement in these agencies as can be found in any private organization. One expects environmental and social responsibility from government but often does not get it.

Agencies such as the Office of Economic Opportunity and the Environmental Protection Agency were created to deal with particularly pressing problems but they are seldom given either the power or the resources required to affect the problem significantly. They are examples of governmental "tokenism."

Advocacy is required in government as well as in private organizations. For example, each level of government should have one or more advocates of racial equality who examine actions of all governmental agencies at that level for their impact on such equality. An advocate should report to the highest level decision maker in the stratum of government in which he works. No single department or agency has responsibility for racial equality but almost every agency can have an impact on it. For this reason some type of surveillance and coordination is required. There is precedent for such advocacy in the citizen review boards currently used in several cities to monitor police activities.

Government alone cannot solve environmental and social problems. Nor is corporate cooperation sufficient. Cooperation from individuals is also essential. Equal opportunity for all races, for example, is as much a matter of indiviudal attitudes and behavior as it is of governmental and corporate behavior. Individual behavior is frequently not as irrational or antisocial as it appears to be. It is often quite rational when viewed with respect to the implicit and explicit incentives created by the government.

For example, as previously noted, commuters into many urban areas who drive cars over bridges or through tunnels are given commuter discounts on these facilities. Doing so encourages those who contribute most to urban congestion to continue doing so. Less frequent users of these facilities pay a higher price for their use. Rational use of automobiles could be encouraged by a more sensible pricing system. Suppose, for example, that instead of charging a fixed fee per automobile on bridges and in tunnels there was a charge of, say, 25 or 50 cents per empty seat in the vehicle. This would encourage car pooling and use of smaller cars, both of which would reduce congestion and air pollution. Charges for parking could also be made proportional to the size of the vehicle.

Absentee owners of urban housing often find it profitable to allow their rented properties to deteriorate because taxes on property are proportional to its assessed value. A poorly maintained property is worth less than one which is well maintained, hence taxes on it are reduced. As the value of property comes down chances for converting it into a multiple-dwelling unit increases. Thus slums are encouraged by a confluence of governmental policies. If depreciation of property value were taxed as well as its value, or if the cost of maintenance or improvement of private property were tax deductible—as it is in some countries—properties would be better maintained.

One could go on indefinitely pointing out how public pricing of services and facilities could be altered to bring individual and organizational behavior into harmony with social objectives. Doing so does not involve distorting prices, but rather changing them so that they better reflect social costs. Racial segregation, traffic congestion, air pollution, and deteriorating property involve social costs to the public. By making these costs explicit through rational pricing, individual, organizational, and social rationality could be encouraged.

CONCLUSION

Social systems operate in a social and physical environment. Conditions of the environment are both affected by and affect the behavior of the systems it contains. Improvement of the environment and its impact on the systems it contains requires each of these systems to consider how it can improve the environment and itself together.

The increasing rate of technological and social change is reflected in the increasing rate of environmental deterioration. Change need not produce deterioration. It could lead to an improved environment. To make it do so we must reverse the current trend to a more constructive one. This can be done by bringing into public and private organizations advocates of environmental improvement and giving them access to the power and resources required to assure contributions to improvement of the environment. In addition, we require explicit public pricing that reflects the contribution to environmental deterioration by individual and collective behavior.

A person who damages another's property is legally liable for the cost of repairing the damage. Similarly, a person who damages a commonly shared environment should be liable for the cost of restoring it. Unless such a pricing system is introduced, the quality of the environment could deteriorate to a point that precludes its restoration.

PART TWO

———

IN PARTICULAR

CHAPTER FIVE

EDUCATION

*Piecemeal reform and concessions to student
pressure, most educational experts agree, will
not be sufficient. What is needed is a frontal
assault on the existing school structure that will
replace outmoded teaching methods, impersonal
or authoritarian teacher-student relations and
obsolete behavior codes with new forms and ideas
more in tune with the times.*

NEWSWEEK

It is apparent that there is a crisis in education and that it is shared by many
nations. Widespread and continuing student activity—protests, demonstrations,
and uprising—provide evidence that a revolution is taking place. In 1970
Newsweek reported: "Last year some 6,000 'incidents'—ranging from racial
strife through protests to arson attempts—were registered in the nation's
public high schools." Less active but equally disillusioned students are
dropping out of, or absenting themselves from, school in increasing numbers.
And this is happening at a time when most societies place a higher value on
education than they ever have in the past.

Students are not the only ones who are disillusioned with the educational
system; many adults are as well. For example, Charles E. Silberman, in his
widely discussed book, *Crisis in the Classroom*, his report of a study of
American public schools commissioned by the Carnegie Foundation of New
York, wrote:

> It is not possible to spend any prolonged period visiting public school classrooms without being appalled by the mutilation visible everywhere—mutilation of sponteneity, of joy of learning, of pleasure in creating, of sense of self . . . Because adults take schools so much for granted, they fail to appreciate what grim, joyless places most American schools are, how oppressive and petty are the rules by which they are governed, how intellectually sterile and esthetically barren the atmosphere, what an appalling lack of civility obtains on the part of teachers and principals, what contempt they unconsciously display for children as children.

Our public schools might be excused for all this if their students were learning what they are expected to, but they are not. Levels of attainment in such basic skills as reading, writing, and arithmetic are dropping. Teachers in many urban and suburban schools are more occupied with matters of discipline than with subject matter. To many observers the primary function of schools is no longer educational; they have become institutional baby-sitters, day-care centers, low-security sleep-out detention homes, and places for those between infancy and adulthood to grow up without bothering their parents or being bothered by them.

In a letter to *The Washington Post* Nadine G. Sparer, a teacher in the Washington, D. C., school system wrote: "We have a 'right' to teach and educate children as we were trained to do and *not* be surrogate parents, baby-sitters and policemen."

In his recent book on education James Herndon commented on schools as an alternative to jail: "If their parents do not see that they go to school, the parents may be judged unfit and the kids go to jail . . . . No matter how bad school is, it is better than jail. Everyone knows that, and the schools know it especially."

The objectives, methods, and content of education at all levels are being called into question. Education seems far less concerned with preparing the young for the future than with getting them to accept the present and to appreciate the past. Public education seems to keep itself deliberately detached from the pressing problems of the day. When it is confronted by these problems it tries to constrain itself to either "objective discussion" of the issues or such token activities as picking up litter around the school, visiting the city dump on Earth Day, or calling on a school for the "other half."

In his review of James Herndon's book quoted above, Edgar Z. Friedenberg, professor of education at Dalhousie University in Halifax, Nova

Scotia, observed: "Even the most enthusiastic supporters of the "free" or "experimental" school movement . . . are beginning to express severe misgivings about whether young people need schools at all." Schools fail "to help them relate to what is really going on in their community."

Ivan Illich of the Center for International Documentation in Mexico is one of the principal proponents of elimination of schools. He recently wrote: "The pupil is . . . 'schooled' to confuse teaching with learning, grade advancement with education, a diploma with competence, and fluency with the ability to say something new. His imagination is 'schooled' to accept service in place of value . . . " Therefore, Illich concluded, "public education would profit from the deschooling of society."

To be sure, much, if not most, learning takes place before schooling is begun and after it is completed. Without the benefit of formal teaching preschoolers learn a great deal, including a language. On the average, children entering school today are better informed and aware of more things than were their predecessors. This is largely a result of their exposure to television and the increased mobility of their parents that has enabled them to visit more places, see more things, and meet more varied types of people than did children of preceding generations. Learning comes naturally when curiosity is fed by exposure.

But most schools appear to put a lid on children's minds. Curiosity and creativity are suppressed. Learning is equated to memorization, thus converting it into work and differentiating it from play. Only a relatively few are ever able to reunite work, play, and learning in later life.

Most children who perform well in school do so to "beat the system," to please their parents, or because it takes too much effort for them to do otherwise. To many, school is a maze one must go through in order to reach freedom, including freedom to learn. Those who do well in school are more likely to be stimulated to do so at home than in school. The successful products of our educational system are normally those who would have succeeded even without it. On the other hand, those who are not motivated to learn at home are unlikely to be so motivated at school.

Colleges and universities are no more effective than are lower-level schools. Like hospitals, institutions of higher learning are run for the benefit and convenience of the "servers" rather than of the "served." It is a marvelous tribute to many of the young who have learned despite the regimentation, discipline, and uninterrupted presence of the teacher in the public school that they continue to learn in colleges and universities despite the almost complete absence of regimentation, discipline, and the teacher.

The ailments of our educational system have been diagnosed and prescribed for by many. Parts of the system have already been experimented on and changed a great deal. Some changes have yielded modest local improvements, but seldom systemic ones. Most changes have been reactive: directed at correcting specific critical deficiencies. Some preactive liberalizing reforms have been directed at increasing permissiveness in individual schools, but not in the system as a whole.

It is obviously easier to criticize education than to correct it. What is not so obvious is that it cannot be significantly improved by correcting its deficiencies independently of each other. Patching up will not do it. Education neèds an extensive redesign, one that will bring it into the Systems Age.

Few have tried to redesign education in broad interactive terms. To do so requires recognizing that the current system is a Machine Age product of reductionistic, analytical, and mechanistic thinking. We need a system that is the product of expansionistic, synthetic, and teleological thinking. Before attempting such a redesign let us consider how Machine Age thinking has affected the educational system we now have.

MACHINE AGE EDUCATION

Most of our schools are industrialized disseminators of information and instruction using materials and methods that were appropriate when students—like factory workers—were thought of in machinelike terms, particularly as black boxes whose output would hopefully exactly match what was put into them.

The simple fact is that what the education system expects of students can be done better by computers and other "mental machines," and students know this. Computers can remember more and recall, compare, and calculate more quickly and precisely than human beings can. Teachers forget that forgetting what is irrelevant is one of man's most important abilities. The young do not want to be put into competition with machines; they want to learn to do what a machine cannot do and they want to know how to use and control these machines. They cannot learn how to do so in a system that treats them like a product to be worked on and put together on an assembly line, a precisely scheduled process in which they are passed from one discrete operation to another. The processing itself is increasingly performed by machines, as are grading papers, registration, and computer-assisted instruction. Think of the damage to one's concept of *self* that results from being taught by a machine that has no self or by a teacher who has been taught to act like one.

Today's school is modeled after a factory. The incoming student is treated like raw material coming onto a production line that converts him into a finished product. Each step in the process is planned and scheduled, including work breaks and meals. Few concessions are made to the animated state of the material thus processed; it is lined up alphabetically, marched in step, silenced unless spoken to, seated in rows, periodically inspected and examined, and so on. The material worked on varies widely in quality but the treatment is uniform. The system tries to minimize the number of different kinds of product it turns out because the greater the variety of product, the greater is the production cost. The educational process is considered to be successful if the final product can be sold at a high price. The system even puts brand names and model numbers on its products.

Educators have reduced education to a large number of discrete and disconnected parts. They have dissected education into schools, curricula, grades, subjects, courses, lectures, lessons, and excercises. A system of quantification and qualification has been developed to reflect this atomistic concept of education: examination grades, course grades and credits, grade-point averages, diplomas, and degrees. Formal education is never treated as a whole, nor is it appropriately conceptualized as a part of a process much of which takes place out of school.

Unlike the young of earlier generations, today's students come armed with concerns about the world and concepts of relevance, concerns and concepts that are largely ignored in school. They are overinstructed in what they can better do alone: take things and concepts apart; and they are underinstructed in what is very difficult to do alone: put what they have learned together into an understanding of the world and their role in it. They are given answers to questions they do not ask and denied answers to those they do ask. They are taught to answer questions, not to ask them—despite the fact that progress depends at least as much on the questions we ask as it does on the answers given to us.

Educators make little or no effort to relate the bits and pieces of information they dispense. Subjects matters are kept apart. A course in one subject seldom uses or even refers to the content of another. A student's writing ability, for example, is only evaluated in an English course but not, say, in a history course. An English teacher seldom asks a student to write about something he has learned in history or another course, and if he does, the content is not evaluated. Such compartmentalization reinforces the concept that knowledge is made up of many unrelated parts. But it is only by grasping the relationships between these parts that information can be transformed into knowledge, knowledge into understanding, and understanding into wisdom.

For example, children (and most adults) are never made aware of the fact that mathematics is a language and therefore has many characteristics in common with English, and that there are fields of study concerned with the common properties of all languages (logic and semiotic). Nor do they learn that the uniqueness of mathematics derives from the fact that it deals with the *form* of experience abstracted from its *content,* nor what the difference between form and content is. Mathematics is known but not understood by most who teach it to children. One can know something without understanding it, but one cannot understand something without knowing it.

Emphasis on separateness of subjects was characteristic of the Machine Age. Emphasis on relationships and interactions is characteristic of the Systems Age. Machine Age education is disintegrating; that of the Systems Age should be integrating.

The mechanistic input-output orientation of Machine Age education results in treatment of students as though they were machines with the combined properties of tape recorders, cameras, and computers. The student is evaluated with respect to his ability to reproduce what he has been told or shown. Most examinations are tests of the ability to reproduce material previously presented to the one tested. Examinations are designed to serve the system's purposes, not the student's.

Cheating is more a consequence of the characteristics of examinations than it is of the characteristics of students. Otherwise why would teachers also cheat? They do where they too are evaluated by the performance of their students on examinations. For example, *The New York Times* recently reported the following incidents:

> At one school, P.S. 178, two teachers copied sections of the vocabulary section of the test for their grades—including the actual test illustrations—and used the material to prepare their pupils for the examination.
>
> An acting principal at the same school also showed 15 words from the vocabulary section to teachers at a workshop she conducted and told the teachers to use these words "in teaching situations" with their pupils.

Examinations are usually modeled after the ill-fated television program "Information Please." Like this program, examinations invite corruption of the learning and teaching process. Teachers cheat to stay in the system; students, to get out of it. (I have more to say about examinations below.)

More "advanced" Machine Age teaching is based on the Pavlovian concept of the student as an input-output organism. (The much publicized Harvard psychologist, B. F. Skinner, has modernized the language used to describe this concept, but he has left the concept itself unchanged.) Students are taken to be organisms that can be conditioned to respond as desired by rewarding correct responses and punishing incorrect ones. Therefore, they are repeatedly exposed to the same stimulus until the correct response is given automatically. This method of teaching has recently been further "advanced" by mechanizing the instructor's role in it. The result is called "computer-assisted instruction" or "programmed learning." The student and his friendly computer are placed in an isolation chamber in which the computer can dispassionately try to make the student know as much as it does. If Machine Age educators knew how to program the student directly—and some have tried to do so through subliminal suggestion—they would undoubtedly do so.

Computers and other new technologies can play a constructive role in education. Later I will consider how they can be used.

SYSTEM AGE EDUCATION

Understanding the failure of formal education must begin with recognition of the fact that it is less efficient than at least some informal education. Evidence of this is plentiful. Children learn their first language at home more easily than they learn a second language at school. Most adults forget much more of what they were taught in schools than of what they learned out of them. The bulk of what they use at work and play they learned at work and play. This is even true of teachers. They learn more about teaching by doing it than by being taught how to do it. Most university professors teach subjects they were never taught. In more than twenty-five years of university teaching I have never taught a subject I was taught. The subjects I teach did not exist when I was a student. Most professional school graduates cannot practice the profession they were taught in school until they have practiced it out of school in some type of internship. Most of what they subsequently use in their work they learned during their internship, not in class.

Formal education denies the effectiveness of learning processes that take place out of class or school. These processes should be used and augmented in school. Most learning takes place *without teaching*, but schools are founded on teaching, not learning. As Edgar Z. Friedenberg put it: " . . . schools have a prior commitment to teach rather than help people learn . . . . " Teaching, unlike learning, can be industrialized and mechanized; it can be controlled, scheduled, timed, measured, and observed. But teaching is at most an *input* to the learning process, not an output. Nevertheless, our current educational system operates as though an ounce of teaching produces at least an ounce of learning. Nothing could be farther from the truth.

Therefore, *Systems Age education should focus on the learning process, not the teaching process.*

Learning outside of school is not organized into subjects, semesters, courses, or other discrete units. A child's learning of a language, for example, is not separated from its learning of other subjects but is intimately bound up with it. A child learns a great deal without any concept of subjects and disciplines, and without being pushed into learning by examinations and grades. One might argue that this is only true for things the child wants to learn. But school, one might continue, *must* teach a child what he should know whether he wants to or not. This is a Machine Age argument. In the Systems Age school children should be motivated to learn whatever they ought to learn but never forced to learn what they do not want to. To impose learning is to take the fun out of it, and this is much more harmful to the child than is his failure to learn any particular subject.

It is widely recognized that we learn well what we want to learn and learn poorly what we do not. Formal education should try to *induce* students to want to learn more things than they would without it. When students want to learn something or the need for learning it becomes apparent to them, they will learn it.

Therefore, *Systems Age education should not be organized around rigidly scheduled quantized units of classified subject matter, but rather around development of the desire to learn and the ability to satisfy this desire.*

Even where rigid entrance requirements and long lists of prerequisites are imposed on students, they vary in ability, interests, and what they have already learned. Therefore, the same input to each student will not, and does not, produce the same output. Schools based on the industrial model ignore or minimize the differences between students and thus require them to adapt to educational production methods. The methods should be adapted to students. Individuality should be preserved at all costs. Uniformity and conformity are anathema to progress.

Therefore, *Systems Age education should individualize students and preserve their uniqueness by tailoring itself to fit them, not by requiring them to fit it.*

Learning is not restricted to part of one's life. It takes place continuously. In the past, when relatively little was known and it was added to or changed slowly, formal education could be completed in a few years. As knowledge accumulated, more and more formal education was required to absorb it. Because of the increasing rate at which knowledge increased, the problem of keeping up with additions to, and changes of, knowledge also grew. Refresher courses of many types and durations have become commonplace. "Continuing education"—education after departure from school—is now an integral part of our culture.

As the rate of acquisition of knowledge continues to accelerate—and it will—formal education will continue to be extended and thus will occupy more and more of a lifetime and will approach a continuous process. As it does, it will become apparent that the separation of play, formal education, and work is artificial and counterproductive.

Therefore, *Systems Age education should be organized as a continuing, if not a continuous, process.*

What solves an educational problem or even a system of educational problems at any one time and place is not likely to do so at another time and place. Hence we must give up the search for *a* best educational system, one that operates optimally regardless of time and place, not to mention students.

Therefore, *Systems Age education should be carried out by educational systems that can and do learn and adapt.*

An educational system should (1) facilitate a student's learning what he wants and needs to learn, (2) enable him to learn how to learn more efficiently, and (3) motivate him to want to learn, particularly those things he needs in order to satisfy his own desires and to be socially useful. A major objective of learning should be to facilitate the selection and pursuit of objectives. Objectives are valued outcomes. As previously noted, value is of two types: extrinsic and intrinsic. An extrinsic objective is one that is sought as a means to a still farther objective; for example, one may want to learn how to drive a car in order to go from one place to another. An intrinsic objective is one that is sought for its own sake, only for the satisfaction its attainment brings; for example, in learning how to play a musical instrument for one's own entertainment. Objectives may have both intrinsic and extrinsic value. Driving an automobile may be a source of pleasure to the young, and playing an instrument may be a source of income to an adult.

Learning has both intrinsic and extrinsic value. We seek to learn something just because of the satisfaction that doing so brings. We learn somethings for their own sake, and others because of what doing so enables us to obtain. If learning has no intrinsic value to a person—that is, if it brings him no pleasure—it becomes a burden. If one is forced to learn something he does not want to learn, doing so will lack intrinsic value and what is learned is not likely to be learned well. The quality of one's life depends at least as much on what one has learned for its own sake as it does on what is learned for the sake of something else. Hence education should involve a great deal of free choice as to what is learned, how it is learned, and when it is learned.

Learning for dominantly extrinsic reasons should be directed at increasing the ability to use its products in pursuit of those objectives for which it was intended, not to increasing the ability to regurgitate it during examinations. If a student wants to learn the calculus, for example, in order to design structures, he should be evaluated for his ability to design structures using the calculus, not for his knowledge of the calculus in the abstract. He is more likely to become interested in calculus if he learns it in order to do something else he wants to do than if he is forced to learn it for its own sake.

Educators simply do not know what the students of today will need to know tommorrow. Therefore, they should not impose their conception of requirements on students. This is even true for students in professional schools. Educators of professionals do not know what most of their students will be doing after graduation. For example, in a report prepared for the Carnegie Foundation, W. G. Ireson noted:

> The most important fact brought out by ... surveys over a period of thirty years is that more than 60 percent of those persons who earned [engineering] degrees in the United States, either became managers of some kind within ten to fifteen years or left the engineering profession entirely to enter various kinds of business ventures ... "

In an editorial in *Science* Dael Wolfle noted that one-fifth of Americans awarded doctorates move out of the field in which they received their degree within five years after receiving it, and 35 percent do so within fifteen years. Even if graduates stay in the field in which they were educated, they must replace and supplement much of their school-acquired knowledge to remain effective. Therefore, it is essential that graduates be as flexible as possible, that they want to continue their learning, and that they know how to do so.

The previously noted ability of college professors to learn new subjects to teach to others is much more important than their ability to teach. They should be preoccupied with transmitting their ability to learn, not with teaching what they have learned.

Today the principal instrument of education is a teacher lecturing to a class. A student may learn by being lectured to, but there are alternative ways of learning. Their relative effectiveness varies by time, place, subject, and student. Hence each student should have maximum freedom to experiment with and select the way in which he will learn a subject, as well as freedom to select the subjects he will learn. Consider some of the alternatives.

1. *Some subjects are best learned by teaching them to oneself.* This is particularly true for subjects that one is highly motivated to learn. Such learning may involve using others as resources, but in the way the learner, not the teacher, sees fit. The option of learning a subject on one's own—independent study, as it is called—should always be open to every student for any subject at any time.

2. *Some subjects are best learned by teaching them to others.* This is common knowledge among those who have taught. When a teacher teaches material that is new to him he invariably learns it better than do any of his students. Therefore, many bodies of knowledge, particularly those that are well organized and recorded in books, can be learned effectively by teaching them to others.

Small groups of three to five students can be organized into *learning cells* in which they teach each other different subjects or different parts of the same subject. Experiments with such cells have been carried out successfully with students at a variety of educational levels in several different countries.

Faculty members can help such learning cells in several ways. First, they can prepare a specification of the material that they believe should be learned and the principal sources that can be used. Secondy, they can serve as tutors when asked to. Some questions that arise in a student's mind while learning a subject are not answered in the sources available to him, or answers may be difficult to find. Faculty members or more advanced students can help in this regard.

Students at one level who have already learned a subject can teach it to others at a more junior level, or help them learn it on their own. It is already commonplace to use graduate students to instruct undergraduates in college, but it is not common to use more advanced students in this way in lower-level schools. It should be. It enables the senior student to consolidate and augment his previous learning.

I was recently involved in a course given by seventeen graduate students to six faculty members. The course was on planning in less-developed countries. Most of the students were from such countries and all of the faculty members had worked in them. Whatever the faculty members had written on the subject was made available to the students who then tried to educate the faculty further. It was an exciting and fruitful learning experience for both students and faculty.

3. *Some skills are best learned through demonstration and instruction by one who already has the skill.* Examples are sports, surveying, drafting, fine arts, and use of laboratory equipment and computers, driving a car, and playing a musical instrument. In some cases a student may learn such skills more easily from another student than from a faculty member. He should have the freedom to select his instructor.

4. *Awareness of questions that have either not been asked or answered and synthesis of those answers that are available are best attained in seminar discussions guided by one steeped in the relevant area.* Education should be devoted as much to raising questions as to learning answers. The American anthropologist Jules Henry once asked what would follow "if all through school the young were provoked to question the Ten Commandments, the sanctity of revealed religion, the foundations of patriotism, the profit motive, the two party system, monogomy, the laws of incest, and so on . . . " Ronald Laing, the eminent British psychiatrist, replied that there would be more creativity than society could currently handle, but not more than it should be capable of handling. The conversion from the kind of society we have to the kind we should have requires just such creativity.

Education should also be concerned with a continuing synthesis of what has already been learned and with the extraction of a *weltanschauung*, a world view, from it. Such a view makes it possible to convert information and knowledge into understanding.

5.   *Many students are best motivated to learn and best learn how to do so in attempting to solve real problems under real conditions with the guidance of one who is already so motivated and who knows how to learn.* Therefore, students should work on research or service projects with faculty members or others with relevant knowledge and experience. Apprenticeship and internship are two of the most effective ways of learning (1) how to use what one knows, (2) what one does not know, (3) how to learn it, and being motivated to do so.

Such "practice" may well take place off campus. R. C. Quittenton, President of St. Claire College of Applied Arts and Technology in Windsor, Ontario, recommended: "That increased emphasis be put on work-study projects and out-of-the-classroom learning experiences. . . . We may eventually have no classroom lectures or formal labs and shops at all. Furthermore, some students . . . may never even be on campus, because that is not where the action is . . . ."

Student members of such research cells or work-study project teams should be at different stages of their education so that they can best learn from and teach one another.

Traditional lectures should be available to those who want them but students should have a choice of lecturers. Not all teachers can lecture well. A good lecturer on television or film may be preferable to a poor one in person. The technology of communication can be used to facilitate seminar-type discussions between students and faculty members who are at other schools. Exciting lectures, seminars, and even tutorials should be recorded so that other students can see and hear them at their convenience. The recordings (visual and/or auditory) should be kept in a library that is easily accessible to students. In time, any student in any school should have access to any faculty member of any school by means of such recordings. They would even enable us to keep active those who have retired or died.

Flexible Learning System

A major deficiency of current formal education lies in its formality. The process is almost completely inflexible and unresponsive to individual differences among students and therefore requires students to adapt to it. Effective education should be flexible enough to enable the student to select the form and content of his education. He should have the opportunity to design and try his own ways of learning so that he can learn how to learn and adapt his methods of doing so to the nature of the subject at hand.

A number of the learning methods described above are employed in the recently developed "informal schools" pioneered in England. M. A. Farber, in an article for *The New York Times*, described the English development as follows:

> Informal education . . . has given children much broader choices in what to do and when and whether to do it alone or with others . . . .
>
> Classes and schools have been enriched with familiar and unusual materials, both home-made and commercial, put within easy reach of the child and his imagination. Books of all kinds abound, nestled at times between old tires and bottlecaps, printing machines and sand mounds, stoves, tuned bells and guinea pigs, and devices for teaching number relationships.
>
> The rows of desks are gone from many classes and the children are encouraged to explore their room and their school and to engage in conversation . . . .Neither the children nor what they use are tied down.
>
> The teacher has been loosened up too. The syllabus has been shelved and the role shifted from instructor of whole classes to mobile catalyst, questioner and consultant to individuals and groups.
>
> It is the teacher's job to provide a range of purposeful choices for his pupils, to appreciate what any child is ready to learn at a certain point and to help the child gain the most from what he is doing.

This development is not without its critics who, Mr. Farber wrote, "say it is failing to equip children with basic skills and 'facts' and lessening their qualifications for jobs and their ability to pass academically oriented examinations that determine college admission."

These criticisms reveal two important points. First, revolution in part of the educational system is not enough. Unless the methods used in all parts of the system are coordinated and integrated, old criteria will continue to be used by parts of the system to evaluate the output of new educational processes employed in other parts of the system. Academically oriented examinations that determine college admissions are widely used even though they have never been demonstrated to be strongly related to performance in college. Until college admission criteria are changed they will act as a yoke on experimentation in schools at a lower lever.

Entrance requirements are used to assure uniformity of the raw material that colleges receive. Such uniformity is only relevant to educational process that are carried out like mass production. If education were modified in the ways suggested here, there would be no need for entrance requirements. Only exit requirements would be needed and these would consist of demonstrated ability to do well what graduates want to do on leaving school.

Parent's concern with their childrens' slowness in acquiring basic skills in informal schools is based on an acceptance of an educational schedule appropriate only to formal schools. (They overlook the fact that among students in such schools the percentage of functional illiterates is rising alarmingly.) Basic skills are those needed to learn other things that are also needed. They are normally taken to be reading, writing, and arithmetic. It is worth noting that *talking* is omitted despite the fact that it is more basic still. It is omitted because it is assumed to have been learned before entering school. There is a moral here to which I will return.

Most children who have trouble learning how to read well are not strongly motivated to do so. They live with adults who seldom read to themselves let alone their children. It is difficult to convince a child to learn something that he seldom observes those he most admires using. Children who enjoy being read to and who see others enjoy reading to themselves are usually anxious to learn how to read in order to decrease their dependence on others for it. They also want skills they see adults enjoying. To take a child whose home life has produced no desire to read and force him to learn how to do so because an arbitrary schedule dictates it, is to assure his disenchantment with the process. There are many who have learned to read well but who have never learned to enjoy it. On the other hand, it is hard to believe that one who enjoys reading or being read to will not eventually learn to do it well. Motivation should precede instruction. If this delays a child's learning how to read — or similarly, to write or do arithmetic — then the fault lies at home and in scheduled expectations, not at school.

It is not at all unlikely that before long children will enter school with the ability to read and perhaps even to write and do elementary arithmetic. Television and parents can easily combine to make this possible. The popular children's television program, "Sesame Street," has already made strides in this direction. I have the strong feeling that we deliberately restrain many of our preschoolers from learning to read, write, and do arithmetic before entering school because we do not want them to be out of step when they do. Education that can easily take place at home is being constrained by the ignorance expected of children when they enter school. The desire of elementary schools to receive uniformly ignorant raw material is more responsible for delayed learning of basic skills than anything that is done in school, formal or informal.

In the early 1950s my academic colleagues and I decided that knowledge of computer programming should be required of all those students in the graduate program for which we were responsible. Operating in the traditional mode, we initiated a required course on the subject. Over the next few years we received an increasing number of requests from students for the substitution of an examination on the course's content for the course. We responded by making the course optional and requiring the examination. The course had to be canceled shortly thereafter for lack of enrollment. So few failed the examination that we subsequently discontinued it and listed knowledge of computer programming as a prerequisite for admission to the program. This prerequisite was later dropped because it was realized those who entered the program without the required knowledge quickly acquired it and did so without course work.

There are basic skills in specific fields as well as in life in general. When students want to do that which requires a basic skill they learn it and do so efficiently, and usually on their own. The ability to read, write, and do elementary arithmetic ought to be expected of children entering school. (Think of what this would do to our concept of parental responsibility and how much it would contribute to the education of adults.) If children enter without such skills, the fact that others of their age have them is likely to motivate them to want to acquire them. Once they want to do so they may learn more easily from their contemporaries than they do now from teachers. They should, of course, have adult guidance or instruction available when *they* want it.

Computer-Assisted Learning

I have already expressed my reservations about the use computers as *teachers*. However, I do believe that they can be used effectively to facilitate *learning*.

One cannot program a computer to perform a task that one cannot do oneself. The computer will only do what it is told to do, nothing more, nothing less. Therefore, the computer is, in the Machine Age sense, a perfect student; it remembers whatever it is told and only what it is told, and it does whatever and only what it is told to do. This makes it possible for students to learn a subject—for example, arithmetic—by trying to teach it to a computer. To do so requires ability to use a language that a computer understands, but such languages are now very simple and children have less difficulty in learning languages than do adults.

I was once involved in an experiment in which seven-year-olds were taught to program a large computer to do their arithmetic homework. In teaching the computer how to do their homework they learned with great enthusiasm how to do it themselves.

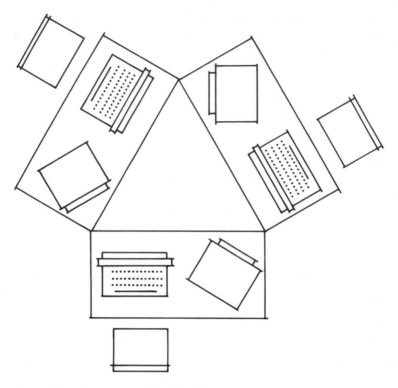

Figure 5.1   A computer-assisted learning setup.

Currently, computerized instruction places the student and his computer in not-very-splendid isolation. Computers should be used to facilitate students working together in social situations, interacting, and learning from, and teaching each other. They can be so used, as the following example shows.

Three consoles with cathode-ray tubes (television screens), typewriters, and light-pen inputs were arranged in a triangle so that each of three students could see the other two and talk with them, but none could see the screens of the others (See Figure 5.1.) The computer addressed the same question to each of the students in writing on their screens. They answered either by use of the light pen or typewriter. The computer than told them how many had given the correct answer, and no more. If all answers were not correct the students had to find out by discussion who had been in error and attempt to correct him. They then put their modified answers into the computer. The computer returned the same type of output. This process continued until all the answers were correct and then moved to another question. Between questions the students were free to consult any material they desired, at or away from the console. The computer did not teach in this situation but it did facilitate students' learning from one another.

In this triangular situation the student provided answers to questions asked by the computer. Education is even better served if these roles are reversed. This becomes possible if computers are used to confront students with relatively realistic situations in which they must determine whether there is a problem and, if there is, how to solve it and test their solution. Let me describe briefly one such use of the computer at the college level, one that has been reported in detail by J. C. Porter et al.

A computerized simulation of a production-distribution process whose characteristics could be completely controlled by the instructor was designed. The instructor could manipulate such characteristics as the number of products involved, the number and capacity of both production and storage facilities, the nature of customer demand, processing times, and costs. In brief, he could play God and control this small simulated industrial world at will. The simulator produced reports of a type common to many industrial firms. These reports were given to students working separately or in teams, as they saw fit. They had to analyze the data to determine if the system had a problem, and if it did, what it was. Once they had formulated and solved whatever problem they saw in whatever way they chose, using any resources to which they had access, they could design and carry out an experimental evaluation of their solution's performance in the simulator. They could then adjust and modify their solution in light of the results obtained. Different students and teams compared their results. The instructor would then reveal his solution based on complete knowledge of the system and compare it with those obtained by the students.

In some cases the students were able to do as well or nearly as well as the instructor by using approaches that differed significantly from his. This enabled the instructor to learn from what the students were doing. Both he and the students became increasingly aware that there are many different ways of solving the same problem, and that the same situation can be converted into many different problems.

These examples show how the computer can be used to humanize and increase the effectiveness of the educational process. Once we get over the desire to mechanize the teacher whose current function, in general, is better eliminated, many effective educational uses of the computer suggest themselves. In none of them should the student and computer be pitted against each other. The computer should be used as an instrument *of* the learner, not as an instrument of others *on* the learner.

Evaluation of Students

Closed-book examinations—the type most frequently used—are poor tests of knowledge or understanding because they are not like real-life situations in which a person's knowledge and understanding are tested or evaluated. They are primarily tests of memory. In real life we are evaluated by how well we get jobs done. We are expected to use all the resources we can bring to bear on the task. In closed-book examinations, on the other hand, the student is deprived of the use of readily available resources. This would be appropriate only if we were training him to survive, as Robinson Crusoe did, on a deserted island.

If examinations must be used to test students they should be modeled on evaluation processes used in the real world. Open-book, take-home, and oral examinations are far superior to closed-book examinations for judging a student's knowledge and understanding, and, of no little importance, they are learning experiences in themselves.

An examination in which the student prepares all or some of the questions as well as the answers reveals much more of his grasp of a subject than does a conventional examination. It enables him to indicate what aspects of a subject he considers to be important and why.

For years I have given my students take-home examinations in which they prepare the questions as well as answers. They are evaluated on both. Their only complaint is that these examinations are too hard. But they are always a learning experience for students and me. When feasible, I let students grade one another's papers. I have systematically compared their grading with my own and have never found a significant difference.

On occasion I have let two students examine each other orally in my presence. Such examinations are usually more revealing of their grasp of a subject than are those that I prepare.

Such examinations as I have suggested are not easy to administer because they consume more time than do those of the conventional type. Most examinations are designed to minimize the work of the teacher. Such examinations minimize the learning that can be derived from them by the student *and* the teacher.

Many examinations claim to test a student's ability to solve problems, but few do so because their authors do not understand the difference between a *problem* and an *exercise*. A problem, as previously noted, is abstracted out of a messy situation. Hence problem formulation is one of the most critical phases of problem solving. But exercises are *preformulated* problems. They do not require formulation nor do they provide the information that was required to formulate them. It is precisely this information which is generally needed to solve a problem creatively.

The ability to solve an exercise is not equivalent to the ability to solve a problem. Exercises are usually formulated so as to have only one correct answer and one way of reaching it. Problems have neither of these properties.

In a conversation with one of my colleagues I was asked how I would go about determining the probability that the next ball drawn from an urn would be black if I knew the proportion and number of black balls that had previously been drawn. He told me that the urn contained only black and white balls. I replied that I would first find out how the urn had been filled. "No," he said, "that is not permissible." "Why?" I asked, "Certainly you have such information." "No, I don't," he replied. "Then how do you know the urn contains only black and white balls?" I asked. "I have it on good authority," he answered. "Then let me talk to that authority," I countered. In disgust he told me to forget about the whole thing because I clearly missed the point. I certainly did.

As essential part of problem solving lies in determining what information is relevant and in collecting it. To deprive a student of the experience of specifying and seeking out such information is to miss most of the point of problem solving. Furthermore, it overlooks the fact that it is harder to ask the right question than it is to find the right answer.

Exercises are purposeless problems. No motivation for solving them is provided other than getting an acceptable grade. Worse still, exercises breed a mechanistic concept of problem solving. For example, my thirteen-year-old daughter was assigned the following "problem" in school. Nine dots forming a square were drawn on a sheet of paper. She was to place a pen or pencil on any point and draw four straight lines—without lifting the pen or pencil—that would go through all the points. The usual solution to this problem is obtained by extending the lines beyond the boundaries of the square formed by the points. (See Figure 5.2)

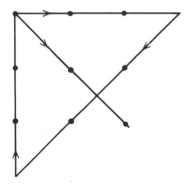

Figure 5.2

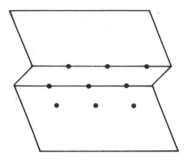

Figure 5.3

My daughter could not find the solution. She asked me if I could. I had seen the exercise before but could not recall its solution. Working on it together we found another way of solving it. We folded the paper as shown in Figure 5.3. Then the top three dots fell on top of the bottom three. Using a felt-tipped pen we drew a line along the folded edge of the paper which simultaneously produced the two lines shown in Figure 5.4. Then after unfolding the paper it was easy to draw three more lines through the remaining points without lifting the pen.

When my daughter presented this solution to her class—giving me credit for it—the teacher told her it was not acceptable because she had folded the paper. My daughter pointed out that the written instructions had not precluded her doing so. "But," the teacher said, "that's what was intended."

This response reflects the teacher's desire to evoke from the student that particular solution that she knew and could pretend to have found on her own. Obviously she should have encouraged the kind of creative response she received. By not doing so she declared that the objective of the exercise was not to find *a* solution, but *the* solution she had in mind. Furthermore, she did

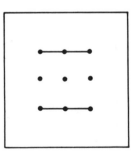

Figure 5.4

not even point out the important methodological principle involved in her solution: that of removing a self-imposed constraint: "you can't go outside the points." What a wonderful opportunity to have discussed the role of constraints in problem solving! As it was, the students learned nothing from the exercise because the teacher had not.

Curricula

Today's education is based on three organizing concepts: subjects, courses, and curricula. The amount of choice among them that a student is allowed increases with his age, but even at the "end" his choices are severely limited. The constraints are justified by the assumption that the teacher knows best what the student needs to know. But, as I argued earlier, this is not, and has not been, the case. What justification was there for the four years of Latin I was required to take in high school? I cannot recall ever having used trigonometry since then either. We do not know what today's students will require tomorrow. It is for this reason that I argued that it is not nearly as important that a student learns any particular subject as it is that he learns how to learn and how to enjoy doing so.

Subjects, disciplines, and even professions are convenient ways of labeling and filing knowledge. But the world is not organized in the same way as our knowledge of it is. There are no physical, chemical, biological, psychological, sociological, or other unidisciplinary problems. The disciplines and subjects are not different parts of the world; they are different ways of looking at the world. Hence any problem can be looked at from the point of view of any discipline. For example, a doctor may see an elderly woman's lack of good health as a consequence of her weak heart; an architect may see it as deriving from her having to walk up three flights of stairs to her inadequate apartment; an economist may see it as due to her lack of income; and a sociologist as a consequence of her family's indifference.

Progress comes as much from creative reorganization of what we already know as from discovery of new things. Einstein's contribution to physics was organizational. All the facts available to him were available to others. In the last two decades science itself has undergone extensive reorganization with the emergence of many new "interdisciplines" such as cybernetics, operations research, communications sciences, and general systems. A filing system can always be reorganized without changing its content, but doing so may increase our access to, and understanding of, that content. Therefore, we should not imbed our current ways of classifying knowledge in students' minds as fixed categories. They should be encouraged to organize their learning in ways that best serve them, not us.

When we isolate a subject we inhibit exploration of its relationship to other subjects. Disciplines are craft unions preoccupied with preserving their academic perogatives. Academic departments do not organize knowledge; they organize teachers and disorganize knowledge. Disciplinary departments and bounded subjects are antithetical to Systems Age education.

A curriculum is a solution to a problem that does not exist. Even if it did exist its solution would change rapidly with respect to time and place. Curricula as now conceived are a denial of the rapid rate of cultural and technological change.

Because what one learns is not nearly as important as learning how to learn, and because questions are at least as important as answers, students should be free to design their own curricula. (To be sure, faculty members should be available to provide help.) It is at least as revealing of a student's quality to evaluate the curriculum he has designed as it is to evaluate what he has gotten out of it. To design a curriculum is to ask a set of questions. What he gets out of it is a set of answers.

Selection of Schools

Much of social progress derives from the struggle for survival. This is as true for organizations as it is for species. Public schools have not had to be concerned with their survival; they are subsidized and have captive customers. They do not have to compete to survive, nor do they have to satisfy their customers to do so. As a result, most school-age children and their parents are in a trapped state. They must take what education is provided to them in a particular school at a particular location.

Any supplier of a service who has assured resources and an assured market has little or no incentive to provide a satisfactory service or to improve it. Public schools are no exception. To survive all they need do is comply with regulations. Experimentation and research on learning and teaching are discouraged; standardization and mechanization of education are encouraged.

Christopher Jenks, a Harvard education scholar, has designed a system to overcome these shortcomings. It is called "the voucher" system and is currently being tried in San Jose, California. What follows is my own variation on Jenks' theme.

The parents of each school-age child would be given an educational voucher worth a specified number of dollars payable by the government to a school that receives it. This voucher would cover tuition and transportation (if required) to any public school, and part or all of tuition in private schools. Parents could apply to any school for admission of their child. They would not have to use one to which their child is assigned because of proximity or political jurisdiction. Children could apply to any primary or secondary school just as young adults do to college today, but cost would not be a factor except for private schools.

Schools that have more applicants than they can accommodate would be required to select from among them at *random*. This would assure as much heterogeneity of the student body as the applications permit. It would also make desegregation of schools possible.

Public schools would have no source of income other than what they receive by cashing in the vouchers they receive. Hence if they do not attract and retain applicants, they would go out of business. Private schools could charge whatever they wanted but parents would have to pay the difference. Private schools that accept vouchers could only redeem them if they selected among applicants at random. This would create competition between public and private schools as well as between public schools.

The voucher system would encourage differences between schools. Needed specialization would take place. For example, if there were a large number of retarded or deaf children requiring education, schools would develop that specialize in their education. (Parents of handicapped children might be given an appropriately larger educational allowance for them.)

By introducing the market mechanism into the educational system its consumers would be encouraged to become familiar with the alternative schools available to their children. Each community would provide a clearing house for information about schools including evaluations by both children and parents.

In this system, schools would learn more effectively from their successes and failures and they would be more adaptive. Individual schools would tend to be more responsive to the needs and desires of the neighborhood of which they are part. Their administrators would be more likely to involve parents and students in planning and policy making. Schools would become more participative as well as more progressive.

Continuing Education

Two trends are developing that will eventually converge and change the educational process considerably. We can, and should, accelerate their convergence.

First, because of the rapid development of new knowledge and the rapid obsolescence of the old, those who have left school are increasingly faced with the need for further education, updating. Most white-collar workers above the clerical level already require occasional reimmersion in the formal educational process. This is particularly true of those in the professions. Witness, for example, the profusion of executive and management development programs.

Norman Macrae, deputy editor of *The Economist*, tried to put some numbers on this trend:

> A man who is successful enough today to reach a fairly busy job at the age of 30, so busy that he cannot take sabbatical periods of study, is likely by the age of 60 to have only about one-eighth of the scientific (including business-scientific) knowledge that he ought to have for proper functioning in his job; and the more learnedly scientific his job sounds, the greater this deficiency will be.
>
> The remedy... has got to be some system for much more continuous lifetime re-education for businessmen and bureaucrats at most levels. This will be one of the big problems of 1972-2012.

The percentage of time spent in learning while at work is bound to increase; hence the distinction between work and learning will become less and less important. Learning will be part of work, and work a part of learning.

Second, increasing numbers of young people are interrupting their formal education for some work experience or exposure to the real world. Many try to combine the two. Furthermore, increasing numbers of graduate students are employed on research and service projects in their universities which deal with real-world problems and provide relevant work experience. Hence just as learning is taking an increasing portion of what used to be years of uninterrupted work, work is entering what used to be years of uninterrupted schooling. Graduation from education to work will be lost in a life pattern in which both go on continuously after an age that is likely to decrease over time.

As these trends develop they will increasingly conflict with incrementally conceived education. The end points of high school and college have always been arbitrary but were convenient in an era in which an educational qualification would last as long as the person who received it. But the life of such qualifications is rapidly shrinking. For example, the medicine practiced at the end of this century will be very different from that of today. Hence a qualification to practice medicine today will not be a relevant qualification then. But most of those who enter medical practice today will still be practicing then. As a result, many professionals and subprofessionals will require repeated requalification (as is already the case for airline pilots and computer programmers). Degrees will become less meaningful and many will become irrelevant. Licenses and certificates requiring periodic renewal are likely to become the rule.

These developments indicate the need for reconceptualizing education as a continuing lifelong process in which the distinctions between formal and informal education and between work, play, and learning become unimportant.

CONCLUSION

There are, of course, many aspects of education that I have not discussed here. I have focused attention on learning that should be the product of the educational process. I have tried to show that we are in the midst of an educational crisis that derives from a conception of education that was suitable for the Machine Age, but not for the Systems Age.

We currently have an industrialized educational system that minimizes the number of choices available to students and that regulates almost every aspect of their behavior. It operates on the assumption that there is only one correct way to do anything, including learning. A teleological system orientation suggests that choice be maximized both in what is learned and how it is learned. It suggests that the emphasis on teaching be reduced and that the purposefulness of students be placed in focus by attempting to motivate them to learn and learn well.

I also suggested that choice of school be made universal so that the market mechanism can stimulate educators to provide better service and to try continually to improve it. Finally, I suggested we begin to design an educational system that provides service over a lifetime, thus maintaining or increasing competence in a world in which the rate of change will continue to accelerate.

CHAPTER SIX

THE GENERATION GAP

*Our youth now love luxury. They have bad manners,
contempt for authority. They show disrespect for
elders and love chatter in place of exercise. Children
are now tyrants, not the servants of their households.
They no longer rise when elders enter the room. They
contradict their parents, chatter before company,
gobble up their food, and tyrannize their teachers.*

SOCRATES

Throughout the development of the Western world there has always been a generation gap. But the gap has grown with succeeding generations. As the rate of change of our technology and culture has increased, and it has done so almost continuously, the difference between the environment in which children were raised and that in which their parents were raised increases.

The gap between the generations born on the two sides of World War II is even larger than one might normally expect because the young (those born after the war) are products of the new Systems Age and the older generation (born before the war) are products of the Machine Age.

I am aware that in what follows I portray youth as "white hats" and those who are older as "black hats" and that the resulting portraits are caricatures; but I have done so deliberately. This chapter is addressed to the older generation of which I am part. Its members are sufficiently aware of their virtues and their juniors' vices. However, they are not as aware of their vices and their juniors' virtues. This chapter is devoted to heightening awareness of these.

To divide the population into the young and old is, of course, a considerable oversimplification. There are many young oldsters, many old youngsters, many in-betweens, and many on both ends. Age is as much a matter of psychology as it is of physiology. Furthermore, the size and nature of the generation gap differs in different subcultures of our society. It is not the same in Harlem as it is in Westchester.

The young form a generation that is not any more homogeneous than is the generation formed by their parents. No generalization about any generation applies to all its members. The young of which I speak are more likely to be the products of middle-class households than of the lower or upper class. Those from the lower class that fit my description are more likely to come from racially segregated communities than from ones characterized as "hard hat" or "white ethnic." This should be kept in mind throughout the discussion that follows. Nevertheless, there are significant differences between contemporary generations, differences that form the gap between them. To understand this gap we must understand what produced it: how the environments before and after World War II differed.

Awareness of this generation gap increased during the 1960s because many of the young in the United States discovered what the young in other countries have known for some time: through organized efforts they can wield considerable political and moral power. They can force responses, however reluctant, from the adult power structure, from the "establishment." Consequently, many young people have taken on the role of a national conscience, calling into question the values that society pursues and, more pointedly, the hypocrisy that attends society's apparent pursuit of its proclaimed objectives. According to Wilma Dykeman:

> ... it is not authority, so much as the hypocrisy of many of our authorities, that our young ones reject. There are enough commandments and too little commitment. It is not our discipline of them that they contradict but our lack of self-discipline. The eyes of youth are clear—and sometimes hard. If we do not like what we see reflected in them, perhaps we'd better look in the mirror.

In a novelette that I recently read the author, Thomas B. Reagan, reflected on his principal character's alienation from his family in a way that strongly reinforces Wilma Dykeman's observations. It is worth quoting at length.

> He often wondered how the great minds who wrote in the New York *Times Sunday Magazine* managed to convince themselves that there never had been a generation gap until 1965. His parents always took him to church and he liked

going. Not merely for the pleasure of hearing about the promised rewards of goodness, but even more for the sake of goodness itself, for the pure kind of satisfaction that goodness brought him. He could look back now and wonder why it had taken him so long to realize that no one *meant* it.

Once, after hearing a particularly moving sermon on loving thy neighbor as thyself, when he was about eight or nine, he brought a little colored boy home to Sunday dinner. His father had hustled the little black fellow, weeping but defiant, out the door and demanded to know what his son meant, dragging every nigger in town into the house. He, naturally, rebutted the exaggeration and reminded his father of the morning's lesson, but his father lectured him on being practical about things and his mother explained that there weren't any darkies in the Holy Land when Jesus was alive, and anyway, they didn't *want* to mix with white people. So he pointed out that one of the Three Wise Men was a nigger, but his parents fell back on their usual last line of defense, which was to tell him—not in so many words, of course—that children should be seen and not heard. . . .

They applauded him when he learned in Sunday school to recite the Ten Commandments of God and gave him story books that proved that honesty was the best policy, but his father made no bones about cheating on his income tax and his mother lied to bill collectors while he stood there listening and argued with streetcar and bus drivers so he could ride for half fare when he was too old.

The young know their parents do not mean much of what they say, but their parents do not know this. This contributes greatly to the gap between them.

There are no social problems that concerned youth consider to be off-limits: war, ecology, civil rights, poverty, sex, drugs, education, and many more. They are not satisfied with just raising issues; they want to do something about them. They take literally the charge that each of them traditionally receives at high-school graduation ceremonies: to remake and improve the world. They earnestly and sincerely believe that unless they do so, there may not be a world at all.

Most adults complain when, having asked the young, "well, what do you propose doing about it?" they receive answers that do not satisfy them. What most adults fail to realize is that the questions bothering the young do not have answers in the sense that adults want them. The young realize this because they are part of the Systems Age and know that "problems" and "solutions" are abstractions; hence they are not so much interested in programs as they are in *processes* through which issues can be progressively resolved or dissolved.

A large part of the older generation is preoccupied with preserving what is good in the current state of affairs, hence tends to minimize what is bad about it. The young are preoccupied with changing what is bad in the current state of affairs and tend to minimize what is good about it. Adults tend to concentrate on avoiding serious errors of commission, doing something wrong; the young tend to concentrate on avoiding errors of omission, not doing something right. The young believe it is more serious to do little or nothing about a critical social problem than to do something wrong about it because in so doing they will learn how to attack it more effectively next time.

The young obviously lack the experience of the old but they believe most of this experience is irrelevant to current crises. The young have a greater concern with the future than with the present; the old conversely. To the old, the young are impractically idealistic; to the young, the old are imprisoned by a false conception of current reality. Adults have a developed sense of the feasible and know how to go about getting what they want but, according to the young, they do not want the right things. The young have a developed sense of the desirable but they do not know how to get it. The young are preoccupied with ends and ideals—with strategy; the old with means and instruments—with tactics.

The young revolt not only because of the hypocrisy and lack of commitment they see in their elders, not only because of the mess they believe their elders have made of the world, but also because of the mess they believe their elders have made of them. They believe that they have been deprived of their *selves* and are busily trying to find them. Such a statement makes little sense to most members of the older generation because they do not know what the *self* is that the youngsters seek. The eminent British psychiatrist, R. D. Laing, who has struck a more responsive chord among young people today than almost any other adult, can tell them.

Laing argues that to rationalize our culture we close our mind to alternatives and close those of our children as well. "Without the most thorough and rapid brain washing their dirty minds would see through our dirty tricks." We accomplish this brain washing by the use of violence under the guise of love:

> Love lets the other be, but with affection and concern. Violence attempts to constrain the other's freedom, to force him to act in the way we desire, but with ultimate lack of concern, with indifference to the other's own existence or destiny.

> We are effectively destroying ourselves by violence masquerading as love.

By restricting what the child can perceive, feel, and think, we destroy its potentialities. "By the time the new human being is fifteen or so, we are left with a being like ourselves, a half-crazed creature more or less adjusted to a mad world. This is normality in our present age."

Our schools, according to Laing, collaborate with parents in this submersion of the self. They do not permit children to discuss or question the basic values on which our culture rests. They close the child's mind and restrict its use. They suppress imagination, creativity, and ingenuity. Children do not give all this up easily. "You have to love them to do that. Love is the path through permissiveness to discipline; and through discipline, only too often, to betrayal of self."

> What school must do is to induce children to want to think the way school wants them to think. "What we see," in the American kindergarten and early schooling process, says [Jules] Henry, "is the pathetic surrender of babies." You will later or sooner, in the schools or in the home.
>
> It is the most difficult thing in the world to recognize this in our own culture.

The young have not been as completely subjugated as Laing's observations would suggest. They are breaking out of the mold into which they have been cast. They are trying to deal simultaneously with the mess we have made of the world and the mess we have made of them. They feel inadequately equipped to correct either. Many are frustrated and take their frustration out in protest and in general hell raising. Ramsey Clark put it well:

> Young people, frustrated, neglected, skeptical and unable to escape the truth that surrounds them, wonder at our purpose. Powerless as are the poor to affect in the slightest way the things that matter most to them, youth can only protest a war that calls on them to kill and die, demonstrate against electronic, chemical and nuclear instruments of mass destruction, endeavor to change the schools that fail to provide fulfillment, seek to stop the bulldozers that destroy the remaining places of recreation and beauty, and try to prevent further pollution of air and water and of foodstuffs by synthetic chemicals.

Some are beyond frustration; they have given up any hope of improvement, hence have withdrawn from society. They are the ones who believe that neither they nor the world has a future.

DIFFERENT BACKGROUNDS OF
DIFFERENT GENERATIONS

Most of the older generation were raised in homes that were in transition from authoritarian households of the Victorian era to the permissive households that dominated after World War II. Dr. Spock, who is often blamed for permissiveness, did not invent it; but he did provide it with a rationale that made it widely acceptable. As a result, society has produced a generation of youth that is less dependent on its parents, more capable of independent thought, hence more critical of its parents than its predecessors were. The young are what their parents brought them up to be: more self-sufficient and individualistic than were their parents. They do not respect their elders because they are older; they respect others only for their commitments and accomplishments.

Most members of the older generation knew and felt the great depression and thus have a sense of what they call "the value of the dollar." Their awareness of the reality of poverty made them place its avoidance among their highest aspirations. They strove to spare their children the financial hardships they had suffered or were afraid of suffering. To a large extent they succeeded. As a result, children of all but those who have remained poor do not place the same value on the dollar as their parents do. It is not that the young place no value on money, but they value it only as a means, not as an end. They tend to take affluence and well-being for granted and do not believe that they necessarily enrich life.

Affluent parents tend to take the poverty of others for granted, but not their own affluence. Their children take their own affluence for granted, but not the poverty of others. Affluent parents tend to blame poverty on the deficiencies of the poor; their children tend to blame it on the deficiencies of the affluent. The older generation is preoccupied with increasing wealth; the younger generation with decreasing poverty and, therefore, with distributing what wealth is already available more equitably.

Most of those who are now adults were raised in home-centered cultures in which life revolved around the family and the immediate community of which it was a part. Most of the young, on the other hand, were raised in a world-centered culture in which they know more about India and China than most adults knew about nearby cities when they were young. Modern transportation and communication have enabled the young to see the world while they are still young. The older generation had to wait until they were old to do so. Places that were abstractions to the older generation in its youth are known by the young people of today, and they are known to be real and to be populated by people, human beings.

The older generation was raised in homes which were the centers of their parents' world; not so for their children. Many of today's parents are more career oriented than home oriented. They do not live their lives nearly as much in and through their children as their parents did. Yesterday's parents aspired more for their children than they did for themselves; many of today's parents aspire more for themselves. Yesterday's parents wanted their children to be better than they were; today's parents want their children to be as good as they are.

The young of today watch their parents and other adults manipulate their moods with alcohol, pharmaceuticals, tobacco, and many other ingested or inhaled products. They are told these are bad or dangerous for children, but they observe the obvious pleasure that adults derive from them. Denied the crutches used by their parents, they have found some of their own. If breaking the law is necessary to get them, this is no worse than what their grandparents did to get access to alcohol during prohibition. Dr. Judianne Densen-Gerber, executive director of Odyssey House in New York City, was reported by *The New York Times* as saying: ". . . by leaving alcohol legal while banning marijuana, the older generation was saying to the younger: 'We can have our habit but you can't have yours.' " She also maintained "that the effects of marijuana had not been proven to be worse than those of alcohol. . . ."

Today's young form the first generation of Americans whose entire lives until very recently have been lived under a compulsary military draft; this while their government repeatedly proclaimed its commitment to peace and engaged almost continuously in war. The young have seen our closest allies condemn our behavior. Throughout most of their lives a credibility gap has separated government from the people, a gap recently extended further by the Watergate incident. A similar gap separates them from parents who support that government without reservations. Dr. Densen-Gerber asserted that one producer of this gap is ". . . the inability of government and political leaders to respond to felt needs, which breeds the atmosphere of dismay and alienation in which addiction flourished."

The young have been raised in an era in which communism and fascism have always been present. They do not feel as threatened by them as their parents do. They have seen that so-called democracies have no monopoly on good, and other forms of government have none on evil. They have been as shocked by our aggressions in Indochina as they have been by Russia's in Hungary. They watch us do business with fascists and communists when it suits our purposes. They watch us prostitute developing countries under the guise of foreign aid. Little wonder that the young do not divide the world into "good guys" and "bad guys" as adults do. They recognize virtue and vice wherever it occurs. They romanticize neither our own virtues nor the vices of others. They do not gratefully and passively accept either the world their parents pass on to them, or the roles their parents want them to play in it. They want to redesign themselves and the world in which they live.

How much redesign of themselves young people have to engage in depends on the kind of family—reactive, inactive, preactive, or interactive—in which they were raised. Reactive parents impose both means and ends on their children; inactive families impose only ends; preactive families, means only; and interactive families, neither.

THE REACTIVE FAMILY

The reactivist's response to what he perceives as the generation gap and the intransigence of youth is an effort to return to the good old days when the young were taught to stay in their proper place, when they were often seen but seldom heard, and when they respected and deferred to their elders. This requires a strong parental hand: authority imposed with generous doses of discipline. Affection and concern are doled out as a reward for compliance with the will of parents; indifference, punishment, or neglect is the payment for lack of compliance.

It is not surprising that children raised in reactive families tend to show affection to parents to the extent that parents comply with their wishes, and that the display of affection is used as a way of getting one's way. Love thus becomes manipulative.

The reactive parent believes in dictating the young's choices of both ends and means until they are old enough to do so for themselves. They are considered to be "old enough" when they make the same choices the parents would without parental guidance.

The reactive family is not only authoritarian and single headed, but also whole oriented; survival of the family is one of its highest values. Divorce is held in disdain no matter how much suffering staying together brings. It is often precluded even after the children have grown up, and they are kept from growing up as long as possible.

Dr. R. L. Laing refers to the reactive family as "nexal." He characterized it as follows:

> The nexal family is. . . the "entity" which has to be preserved in each person and served by each person, which one lives and dies for, and which in turn offers life for loyalty and death for desertion. Any defection from the nexus. . . is deservedly, by nexus ethics, punishable. . .
>
> The condition of permanence of such a nexus, whose sole existence is each person's experience of it, is the successful reinvention of whatever gives such experience its *raison d'etre*. If there is no external danger, then danger and terror have to be invented and maintained. . .

> . . . The "work" of the nexus is the generation of this terror.
> The work is *violence*.

The nexal family has two important consequences. First, if divides the world into the *we* and the *they*. Second, it supports the belief that all other groups must do the same. Within the *we* an ethic of coercion is created. As Laing put it:

> The brotherhood of man is evoked by particular men according to their circumstances. But it seldom extends to all men. In the name of our freedom and our brotherhood we are prepared to blow up the other half of mankind, and to be blown up in turn.
>
> The matter is of life or death importance in the most urgent possible sense, since it is on the basis of such primitive social fantasies of who and what are I and you, he or she, We and They, that the world is linked or separated, that we die, kill, devour, tear or are torn apart, descend to hell or ascend to heaven, in short, that we conduct our lives.

The revolt of youth is largely a revolt against the reactive family and every other kind of nexal group including school, race, religion, sex, and nation. The revolt is a groping for a family of man, for an all-inclusive *us*. But the young seem willing, when frustrated, to settle for less, for a new *we*—the young—and *they*—the old. This is no more rational or less divisive than any other *we—they* dichotomy.

The more reactive society is, the greater is the gap between generations, and the more society is divided into those who want to keep it divided and those who do not.

THE INACTIVE FAMILY

The inactivist believes in limited permissiveness within the family. Children are given freedom in their choice of means, but not in their selection of ends. For example, parents select careers for their children but the children are free to pursue them as they see fit. A high value is placed on family survival, but the family tries to survive not so much through terror and violence (in Laing's sense), as through agreement and consent. Cohesiveness is obtained more by the promise of rewards than by threats of punishment. The family is held together by carrots rather than by sticks.

Inactive parents will tolerate each other—no matter how much suffering living together produces—until the children are grown up and are on their own. Only then will they normally contemplate divorce.

The inactive family also creates and maintains the distinction between *we* and *they*, but it attempts to preserve the *we* not so much as protection against an external *they* as against one's internal self. The family is conceived as a coalition against individual loneliness and isolation. *They* consist of those who can never take one in completely. Inactive parents believe that unconstrained intimacy—protection from self—and unselfish sacrifice of each for the other can only be obtained within the family.

The attitude of the inactive family toward others is indifferent rather than hostile, as it is in the reactive family. Others are tolerated as long as they do not aggress on the family or invade its privacy. Others should be free to do whatever they want as long as they do not reduce the family's ability to do the same.

The inactive family produces less internal conformity than does the reactive family, but nonconformity is constrained so as not to threaten the basic structure and functioning of the family. Long hair, rock music, unconventional clothing, and strange friends are tolerated; but radical politics and religious deviations are not. This type of family tends to produce young people who are more inclined to look for new ways of doing things than for new things to do. They are more likely to question efficiency than values.

THE PREACTIVE FAMILY

Preactive parents are permissive with respect to ends but not means. They give children freedom to decide what they will do, but not how to do it. They tolerate political and religious differences within the family, but they impose constraints on how these may be pursued. Children are taught that "it's not what you do but the way that you do it" that matters. The family dictates manners rather than morals, style rather than substance.

The distinction between *we* and *they* is retained, but with a difference. Its focus is on avoiding social isolation; hence it defines a subculture of which it takes itself to be a part, a *we*-subculture defined by a style of life and a code of behavior. Members of the in-group form a weak but extended family. Members of the out-group are not enemies but they are not friendly. The in-group may be defined by any one or combination of criteria: national origin (ethnicity), religion at birth (rather than of practice), neighborhood, profession, income, and so on.

Preactive parents who cannot get along with each other will contemplate divorce but only if the family's place in its subculture is not threatened by it. Division of childrens' time between divorced parents is common. The family is not sacred to the preactivist. It is primarily an instrument of gratification and convenience. The family is a means, not an end in itself.

Youth who are products of preactive families are likely to think of their families more as a resource than as a haven. This kind of family is more an aggregation than a group. The relationships between individual members dominate the relationship of any individual member with the family as a whole. Preactivists take the family to be a flexible institutional arrangement for raising the young. Its products are likely to consider other social institutions in an equally instrumental way.

THE INTERACTIVE FAMILY

This type of family is only beginning to emerge. It is too new an idea to be well defined or easily recognizable. It is a participative unit that is part oriented. It considers itself to have no function other than serving its members. It is neither an end in itself nor a means in itself. Therefore, when it fails to serve any of its members well they are free either to attempt to redesign, reorganize, or leave it. It is taken to have fluid boundaries, structure, and membership. Membership is voluntary, even to children. It seeks to maximize its adaptiveness to its members as well as to its environment. It is *not* based on a distinction between a *we* and a *they*.

Although contemporary society considers the family to be the primary *social* unit, its membership is determined by *biological* relationships. Geneology is a convenient basis for assigning responsibility for child rearing to adults, but not necessarily a good way. Parents tend to assume that parenthood not only gives them responsibilities with respect to children but also complete control of them. Except for a few legal constraints that prohibit extreme parental behavior, society permits parents to do pretty much what they want to children. They are only under obligation to minister to their offsprings' basic needs but, in the main, they alone judge what these needs are and how they are to be satisfied; and they are often unqualified to do so.

Contemporary adults who find their marriage intolerable are free to dissolve it in most places. Children who find their family intolerable currently have no corresponding freedom. Interactivists believe that children should have the right to appeal to the courts for a change of home, just as their parents do. Society should provide alternatives to children who find their homelife intolerable. Such provisions would remove the moat that now surrounds the family and prevents emigration out of, and immigration into, it. Separation of a child from his parents would not absolve them of financial responsibility for that child.

These conditions would make it necessary for a family to earn a child's attachment to it. The fact that such attachment is now taken for granted is the source of much of the suppression of self in the young to which Laing referred. Giving children some choice with respect to family would do much to weaken the stranglehold that families now have on children. It would provide the family with some feedback on its performance, and it would inhibit inculcation of a *we-they* conception of the world in children.

To be sure, many parents consciously sacrifice a great deal for their children but most unconsciously demand at least equal sacrifices in return. Their sacrifices are voluntary, but their childrens' are not.

Children should learn how to use their family as a resource in their own way. Their parents' conception of how they should be used by children should not be imposed on them. This does not mean that advice and criticism based on affection and concern should not be given freely, but it does mean that compulsion should be confined to only those occasions in which the safety and well-being of the child or others is in jeopardy.

Parents should try to become conscious of the values they never question and the questions they never ask. Once these values and questions are raised to consciousness, parents and children should discuss them, and they should be discussed with others who do not agree with the parents in the presence of their children. For example, most parents impose their religious beliefs on their children. The choice of religion in contrast to atheism or agnosticism, and the choice of a particular religion, should be free based on knowledge of the alternatives. Children should be made aware not only of the fact that many men have reached great heights on the wings of religion, but also that more men have been killed in the name of religion than for any other reason. Religion should be presented to children in the form of a question that he must answer, not as an answer that he must not question.

Parents should especially seek consciousness of any *we-they* aspects of their thinking and behavior. For example, if all their friends are of one religion, one race, one socioeconomic class, and so on, they should attempt to cross the boundaries imposed by these distinctions so that their children are exposed to a variety of people without distinctions being made among them. Every effort should be made to avoid imposing any *we-they* distinctions on children. Such efforts would greatly contribute to the education of parents as well as to that of their children. There is probably no stronger unifying force in a family than shared learning experiences.

Children come into contact with many who are not members of their family. They often pick up constraining ideas from many of those with whom they come in contact. Therefore, parents should continuously review with their children their observations, thoughts, and feelings to be sure they are not accepting answers from others before they understand the questions.

It is almost impossible for adults to avoid hypocrisy, but they can invite others—particularly their children—to point it out to them. If they cannot resolve a contradiction between their proclaimed beliefs and their behavior, they should openly admit to it and not try to rationalize it. Hypocrisy is forgivable, but rationalization of it is not.

The interactive family is an experimental family. It is not equipped with a set of solutions that can be applied without thought to any problem that arises. The family as a whole generates alternative solutions to problems and systematically tests and evaluates them, trying to learn from its own experience as much as possible. Interpersonal relations are brought out into the open where they are discussed, and ways of treating them are sought jointly. Each member of the family is taken to have the right to the affection and concern of the others, but he has no claim on their cooperation. The cooperation of others has to be earned by cooperating with them.

Parents in an interactive family claim no authority by virtue of their age. Whatever power parents exercise over children is vested in them by the children themselves. Such parents do not command respect; they earn it. The interactive family is a generation-gapless family.

CLOSING THE GAP IN SOCIETY

How can effective collaboration between generations be brought about in society?

We must begin by recognizing that the young actually have many of the personal and social values that the older generation pretends to have. Many of the young have a deep desire for peace, equality, a decent environment, absence of poverty, and so on. The older generation—by taking seriously youth's disclosures of its inconsistencies, hypocrisies, and opportunism—can begin to practice what it preaches.

But listening to youth is not enough; the older generation must learn to work with them. Elders must enable the young to do what so many of them were brought up to do: participate. This is not easy, but it is necessary if we are to bring the uncivil war between generations to an end.

Unfortunately, the young are often more interested in winning an argument than in getting something done. Winning alone may not satisfy them; they often require humiliation of their opponent. The young must learn how to talk to adults so that they will be understood and not merely be reacted to. Invective and rhetoric are not effective means of persuasion. The young lack the ability to compromise when compromise is necessary to make progress. They tend to be an "all or nothing" generation.

The generations need each other but neither perceives the nature of its need for the other. Each is condescending toward the other. Hence efforts at discussion of differences between them tend to be token ones and are fated to fail.

I have participated in many formalized joint-generation efforts to deal with a social problem of common interest. Too often these have been fruitless and frustrating to both generations because neither side thought the other understood its position. Each side felt the other assumed it held a position that it did not. Under such conditions discussion tends to degenerate, misconceptions solidify, and hope for cooperation disappears.

How can effective communication between generations be brought about? It is not easy to bring opponents of even the same generation into effective discussion, but there are ways of doing so. Professor Anatol Rapoport of Toronto University, an eminent systems scientist and student of conflict, suggested a procedure that I expand here. To illustrate it I will consider communication between two opponents on the issue of capital punishment. The procedure, of course, is applicable to any issue.

1.   Each participant should listen to the other express his views until he feels he can formulate the other's position in a way that is acceptable to the other. He then attempts to do so. If his effort is unacceptable to the other, the discussion continues until he succeeds. Then the roles are reversed.

If one of the parties wants to maintain a current state—for example, to retain capital punishment where it is used—he should be the first listener. If both seek change, the choice of who comes first should be made by chance. If one wants to abolish capital punishment where it is in use and his opponent wants to maintain it, the former should present his position first and the latter restate it to the former's satisfaction. The reason for this is that the one who wants to maintain a current state is less likely to understand the other's position than the other is to understand his. As the great American wit, Ambrose Bierce, so wisely observed, "there is but one way to do nothing and diverse ways to do something . . . ."

In some cases this first step may be enough to produce agreement. In most cases, however, additional steps will be required.

2.   Once each participant can state the other's position to the other's satisfaction, each should formulate the factual and/or moral conditions under which he believes the other's position would be valid.

For example, in a dispute over capital punishment, the one who is opposed to it should state the conditions under which he believes it would be justified. He might say, "I believe capital punishment would be justified if it prevented more capital crimes than there were executions produced by it." Such statements identify "resolving conditions" and make it possible to convert many differences of opinion to a question of fact; for example, does capital punishment reduce the total number of lives lost through murder?

On occasion one party may take the position that the other's position is not justified under *any* conditions; for example, that capital punishment cannot be justified under any conditions. Then the side that holds the unconditional belief should be called on to propose a method by which two who hold opposite unconditional beliefs can resolve their difference. If he can do so, this becomes the issue to be debated and the opponents would return to the first step. If both parties maintain that such a disagreement cannot be resolved, then the discussion is at an end unless they involve a third party who can propose a method of resolving their difference. This method would then become the subject of debate.

3.   Once the resolving conditions have been agreed to, each party should formulate his concept of how the actual conditions can be determined.

They may agree on these conditions. For example, they may agree to examine four classes of states over the last ten years: (1) states that have used capital punishment over this period, (2) those that have changed from no capital punishment to its use, (3) those that have not used it over this period, and (4) those that once had, but subsequently abolished, capital punishment. They may also agree that if the average percentage increase in capital crimes per year in states that changed from no capital punishment to its use is less than the corresponding average in each of the other three categories, then capital punishment is an effective deterrent.

If the opponents cannot agree on how to determine the match between actual and resolving conditions, they should take this disagreement as the issue between, return to the first step, and proceed through the successive steps until this issue is resolved. Once this issue is resolved, they can return to the point at which they broke off.

4.   Once agreement on how to establish the relevant conditions has been reached, the opponents should attempt to determine what these conditions actually are.

Presumably, this will settle the issue. If such a determination is neither possible nor feasible, they can proceed to the next step.

5.   A table should be prepared in which the different positions being debated form the rows and the justifying conditions of each form the columns.

Such a table for the capital-punishment debate which I have been using illustratively is shown in Figure 6.1.

Positions	Justifying Conditions	
	Capital Punishment Deters Capital Crimes	Capital Punishment Does Not Deter Capital Crimes
For capital punishment	X	Error 1
Against capital punishment	Error 2	X

Figure 6.1   A table of possible errors on the issue of capital punishment.

6.   Now each opponent decides independently which of the two possible errors he believes to be the more serious. If they agree, they should accept the position that has the least serious error associated with it, at least they should do so until the resolving conditions can be determined. If they do not agree, this becomes the issue that they should take back to the first step.

The procedure I have described requires more control of discussion of an issue than opponents can usually provide by themselves. Therefore, a "referee" acceptable to both parties can be very helpful. The procedure is formal but formalism often provides an effective way of resolving disputes, as it does, for example, in courts of law.

The value of such a procedure is by no means restricted to discussions between the young and the old, but such discussions usually require more control to make them constructive than do those between contemporaries. This procedure gives age no privileges.

WHAT CAN HAPPEN WHEN

It is in the universities that we can best see the problems and the possibilities of bringing the two generations together. In the few universities in which students have been given a *significant* participative role they have usually participated responsibly. They have worked hard at participation and have made creative contributions to the institutions of which they are part.

The university research center of which I am part has no formal structure. It has no head; it is managed by a "town meeting" consisting of all participants in the center, faculty and students. There are more than twice as many students involved as there are faculty. The center operates smoothly and efficiently, has a high morale, and absorbs little time in administration. The level of mutual respect is high. The knowledge and skills possessed by the faculty are used extensively and effectively by the center as a whole.

Every decision-making body in a university in which students have equal or greater representation than faculty works well. Those in which they hold a minority position generally do not. Students take lack of equality as an expression of lack of trust. The young who cannot get their way without the approval of their elders are not inclined to listen to them. But when the young can get their way without such approval they almost invariably listen well and consider what they have heard carefully.

I have found it easier to resolve fundamental differences with students than with fellow faculty members, although the route to such resolution is sometimes devious. Here is an example.

One of the graduate faculties of which I was a member contains as voting members four students elected by the student body associated with the program.

Student representatives have made a larger contribution to the development of this program over a number of years than the faculty members have, and the faculty is well aware of this.

Spurred by some of the students in the program who were having difficulty in doing an acceptable master's thesis, the four student representatives decided to try to remove the requirement for such a thesis for those seeking a doctorate. Knowing that I was strongly opposed to such a move, they decided to avoid confronting me with it before the faculty. They waited for a faculty meeting that they knew I was unable to attend. They made their proposal at this meeting and got it accepted.

When I returned to the campus the next day and learned of this, I resigned from that faculty immediately. Within a few hours the representatives were in my office to object flatteringly to my resignation, asking me to withdraw it. When I refused they accused me of being undemocratic, unwilling to abide by the will of the majority. I countered by expressing my rejection of a procedure that denied me the right to discuss an issue important to me with students and faculty before a decision was made. This, I argued, was undemocratic. I acknowledged the right of the students and faculty members to have done what they did, but I insisted on the right to select those faculties on which I wanted to serve. I argued that the right to emigrate is one of the most important provided by a democracy. When membership in a society, large or small, is no longer tolerable to one of its members, he should always be provided with an escape route.

The students withdrew to think this over. They returned the next day and asked if I would be willing to work with them in seeking another solution to the thesis problem that might be acceptable to all parties involved. I was. We found such a solution. The students took the initiative in having it replace the previous decision. But more importantly, they took steps to change faculty procedures so that no member of the faculty could be denied the opportunity to express himself on any policy issue before a decision was made regarding it. (I rejoined that faculty.)

I learned from this experience how important it is to respond to the behavior of the young exactly as one would to the same behavior on the part of older people. The students knew me well enough to recognize that my response was exactly what it would have been had the faculty been responsible for the withdrawal of the thesis requirement. This is what made subsequent negotiation possible.

I have never heard of a case, in or out of the university, in which the young have abused or misused organizational responsibility when it was given to them. They make errors, as adults do, but they learn from such errors more rapidly than adults do. The older generation must learn to give more responsibility to the young and not hang over them when they have it. The more experienced generation should always be available as a resource to the young to be used by them as they see fit.

CONCLUSION

There is an association between age and attitudes toward the future. The oldest members of our population, particularly those who have retired, tend to be reactivists, resentfully riding out what future remains for them. To a large extent they are not reactive by choice but because society has inactivated them.

The oldest members of the working population, particularly those who have reached the peak of power and affluence, tend to be inactivists. They want to stay where they are; they want to stop the clock.

The middle-aged, particularly those still trying to get ahead, tend to be preactivists. They are preoccupied with prediction and preparation for mounting the summit. They are for anything that will ease the climb but against anything that will change the slope to be climbed.

The young, whose future is longer than their past, tend to be interactivists. They are the most capable of accommodating to change and of perceiving the kinds of changes required if social progress is to be made. Because they have a larger stake in that future than do those who are older, they should have a hand in making of it what they want.

As society is now constituted we tend to give age privileges it is not equipped to use to society's advantage, and to deprive youth of those privileges it is equipped to use to society's advantage. For example, consider the custom in universities of requiring young members of the faculty to teach more than older members and of allowing older professors to teach advanced graduate students exclusively. This deprives the young academic of an opportunity for intensive research and social service when he is most productive and creative. The older professor, who is often over the productive and creative hump, is given the time and opportunity to do what he is no longer very good at doing. He, more than the young instructor, needs exposure to, and interaction with, the young in order to keep his ideas turning over. Yet he has least exposure to those who can most challenge his complacency.

The situation in the university reflects a general social attitude toward age. Social institutions operate so as to reduce our contact with the young the older we become. The culmination comes with retirement when most adults are completely severed from any further continuing interaction with youth. It is at this point that they need it the most. As a result we have produced a geriatric subculture that is almost completely occupied in consumption of goods and services, and that plays no constructive role in society. Retirement should not be a period in which the elderly need do nothing for society. Rather it should be a period in which their wisdom and knowledge are fully exploited for their own sakes as well as society's.

The young and the aged should have a responsibility to and for each other. The aged should reenter school to learn as well as teach, to interpret their experience so that it becomes relevant to the young. The young should enter the world of retirement to obtain an understanding of life's *denouement* and an appreciation of man's mortality. They should learn how age affects one's point of view and why it does so. This will enable them to deal more effectively with their elders.

In the eyes of the elderly we can see the reflection of what we are becoming. We can learn that acquiring and arriving does not bring as much satisfaction as striving and sharing.

With the help of the young, the old can approach the end of their lives with a bang, not a whimper. And with the help of the old, the young can approach maturity in the same way.

CHAPTER SEVEN

RACE

[The] economic facts plus a profound change in the feelings of the black community . . . are making for a qualitative difference in the problems of the city. The Kerner Commission warning that we are drifting toward two separate societies, one white and one black, a sort of indigenous apartheid, has not altered the drift.

FRANK H. CASSELL

It took a lot of black protest over the last two decades to produce even a little white response. Urban coalitions and business alliances were formed more in an effort to reduce pressure *from* the blacks than to reduce pressure *on* them. Biracial dialogues were initiated; some white money began to trickle into the black community and a few jobs and blacks to fill them were resurrected. Token remedial programs were installed but not maintained. Weak civil-rights legislation was passed but left largely unenforced. Successes were frequently proclaimed but seldom realized. Attention was diverted from the many efforts that failed by focusing on a few specific gains.

Some progress has been made, but the blacks are still far from enjoying equality of opportunity, let alone of accomplishment. This is reflected in an Associated Press dispatch of July 27, 1971 about a Census Bureau and Labor Department report on the social and economic status of United States Negroes:

> *Income.* Median family income of Negroes was about $6,520
> last year, about 50 per cent higher than in 1960. This was 64
> per cent of white median income. . .

Education. Last year, 56 per cent of all blacks 25 to 29 years old had completed high school compared with 38 per cent in 1960. Between 1965 and 1970, blacks enrolled in colleges almost doubled, up to 7 per cent of total college enrollments.

Employment. Blacks landed more professional and higher paying jobs. Their employment in professional, technical and clerical occupations doubled. At the end of the decade, however, about two-fifths of blacks and other minority group males remained in lower-paying household, labor and farm occupations.

The report said "Even in industries where Negroes are a large part of the labor force, they tend to hold only a small share of the highest paid jobs in large companies."

As black pressure diminishes so does white effort. The white community sighs with relief when the black boil comes down to a simmer.

Progress is responsible for only a small part of the recent reduction of pressure from the black community. A larger part of it is due to the growing realization among blacks that white efforts to solve the problems of the blacks more frequently turn out to be liabilities than assets. In addition, according to black leaders I know, a large number of potentially militant blacks have been neutralized by narcotics.

The pressure is off, but not the problem. A few token programs are continued in the hope that future eruptions can be prevented. Collective protest appears to have been replaced in part by individually committed crimes. Detention centers and jails bulge with blacks who have, or are alleged to have, broken the law, sometimes to feed their addictions and at other times to work off their frustrations. Blacks, increasingly isolated and removed from the whites, even in prison, turn on each other. Witness the Attica prison riots of September 1971. Personal violence is replacing mass violence but has not destroyed the potential for it. Mass violence lies smoldering in urban black ghettos. It can break into flames at any moment.

The black community is part of the environment of the white community. Its deterioration is being felt increasingly in the white community. The portions of the city through which whites feel they can drive, let alone walk, safely are decreasing rapidly. Fear stalks even the streets of suburbia at night.

The white community cannot buy isolation from the black. The two communities are interrelated open systems, parts of the same suprasystem. Effects flow freely between them even if people do not.

THE "PROBLEM"

The race "problem" is not *a* problem; it is a *mess*—a system of interacting problems. In this context "race" means a disadvantaged minority distinguished by its color. In the United States this word usually denotes the blacks, but sometimes refers to Puerto Ricans, Mexican Americans, or the American Indian. Although I focus attention on the black problem in this chapter, the principles are equally applicable to problems involving any minority that is discriminated against.

The black mess consists of two sets of complementary problems: the problems that the blacks have with the whites and the problems that the whites have with the blacks. These types of problem are often confused because one's perception of them is often colored by one's own color. For example, consider the case of one large corporation in which a little less than half of the employees are black, but only a small percentage of its managers are. The company anticipates that more than half of its employees will be black before 1980. It is concerned, therefore, over the prospect of having a corporate plantation consisting of predominantly black workers and predominantly white managers. For this reason it asked the university-based research group of which I am a part to help it in developing educational programs for black employees that would increase their upward mobility.

It was "naturally" assumed by the company that its black employees were less well educated than its white employees. Therefore, we began by examining this assumption. It turned out to be false; on the average the black employees were significantly better educated than were the whites in the same kinds of jobs. Therefore, what appeared to whites to be their problem with the blacks turned out to be the blacks' problem with the whites: the reluctance of white managers to allow black workers to "move up."

Take another example, but this time from the public domain. On June 18, 1971 a black riot erupted in Miami. Was this a black or a white problem? In the Associated Press' account of this uprising it was noted that:

> The focal point of the violent outbreak, the Pic-N-Pay supermarket in the Brownsville section, was entered by state Department of Agriculture agents today and 3,000 pounds of meat condemned and seized. Earlier in the week, 600 pounds of bad meat and produce were confiscated.

Riots do not start without provocation, but lingering racial tension has no first or simple cause; it is deeply rooted in prejudice and discrimination.

The most serious manifestation of our nation's racial mess is the urban black ghetto. It is the most degrading environment in our society. Most of those imprisoned in it seek either to escape by moving up and out, or to escape within it by using narcotics or alcohol.

Most whites and white-dominated communities are inactive relative to the race problem; they settle for an unlegislated apartheid and accept urban black ghettos as long as they do not erupt and pour lava on surrounding white neighborhoods. A few communities are active. How they act depends on their orientation toward the future—whether they are reactive, preactive (predict and prepare), or interactive (make it happen).

THE REACTIVE RETREAT FROM RACE

Most of our cities that are not inactive are reactive. They try to ignore the ghetto as long as they can. When black problems spill over into white neighborhoods, such cities react by increasing repression: putting the blacks "in their place" by strengthening the police, enacting curfews, and withdrawing the right to assemble. Through repression such cities seek to deter any intervention by the blacks in the white community. Blacks are given almost complete freedom to do anything they want in black neighborhoods, but freedom to do nothing they want in white neighborhoods.

Reactive whites support collective repression of blacks, lock themselves in their homes more securely, buy watchdogs, install burglar alarms, arm themselves, and generally withdraw from their environment as much as they can. Those who can, move as far from the blacks as possible. They are adjusted to the prospect of the city's becoming a black reservation surrounded by white suburbs, each separated from the other by six-to-eight-lane concrete moats.

It is clear even to reactivists that such urban "development" will increase the explosiveness of the black population but they are prepared to use larger and more repressive forces to confine eruptions to the black hole of the "doughnut" metropolis. The predominantly black city will suffer from an inability to generate sufficient funds to provide adequate services and facilities to its inhabitants. Witness the current financial difficulties of cities that are, or are becoming, dominantly black. The black inhabitants of dominantly black Newark, New Jersey, draw little satisfaction from the fact that their city is governed by blacks. *The Evening Bulletin* recently reported: "Newark's Negro Mayor Kenneth A. Gibson today told a congressional committee, Newark is 'first in crime, first in venereal disease, first in infant mortality and the first city in America—but not the last—likely to go under because it can't handle decay.' "

Little help comes from reactive corporations that "do their part." According to Frank H. Cassell, Professor of Industrial Relations at Northwestern University:

[Their] strategy has usually consisted of participating in the least risky ventures, minimizing the risk with strings attached to the money contributed in order to control the speed and the direction of the advance, and supporting politically only those dissidents who could be counted upon to merge with the establishment.

Professor Cassell goes on to explain:

Conventional corporate policy is based essentially upon a stable environment with change occurring only at a rate sufficient to be easily absorbed. Because business mistrusts unorthodoxy, it also mistrusts the "bubble up" theory of participative democracy, of community action programs which have been spawned in the cities . . .

Reactive urban white organizations and individuals will give up their cities and place them in solitary confinement if they have to. They are willing to follow the advice of Henry Ford who is reported to have said, "We shall solve the city problems by leaving the city." But the blacks are not part of that "we." Eventually, of course, they will force their way into the suburbs but, to most whites, this prospect appears to be far enough off so that they do not expect to have to face it.

THE PREACTIVE APPROACH TO RACE

The preactive community tries to prevent racial disruption by giving the minorities some cause for hope and by alleviating the most severe of their current problems. It seeks to provide relief from current suffering through public and private welfare. It tries to place blacks in jobs, even ones that provide no satisfaction. It establishes token health, education, and housing programs in the hope that doing so will start self-development. The gift, preactivists, believe, is less important than the willingness to give. Therefore, programs are designed more to demonstrate concern than to provide help. When these programs fail, as they often do, they are rapidly replaced by others that are propagandized in messianic terms. The occasional minor success provides a base for the preactive community's persistent plea for patience while "the complex problems are worked out."

Leaders of the preactive white community spend a great deal of time meeting and talking with black leaders in an effort to work things out. They give encouragement more easily than they do money. Much, if not most, of what money they give is likely to be spent on white experts. This has led to the black quip: "It isn't easy to spend a lot of money to help blacks without giving them any of it." It is now widely acknowledged, for example, that only a small portion of the funds spent in our War on Poverty ever reached the poor.

Affluent preactive organizations—corporations, universities, foundations, and so on—create departments whose function it is to be concerned with minority problems. Corporate departments of community relations are usually put under the direction of an executive who is a nice person, near retirement, and not of much use anywhere else. His department is usually understaffed, underfinanced, and uninvolved in organizational affairs except on ceremonial occasions. But he tries hard to ooze goodwill and hide his frustration over his inability to do anything significant.

The preactive white community believes it can eventually solve the black problem, but that it will take a long time to do so. It believes that significant progress requires taking a number of small steps. In the meantime it propagandizes for brotherhood of man, and attempts to comfort the blacks with demonstrations of paternal concern and maternal commiseration.

THE INTERACTIVE APPROACH

The approach of the interactive community to the racial mess is based on an assumption that history seems to support strongly: *the white community cannot solve the blacks' problems*. Only the blacks can do so. Development of the black community requires development of its ability to solve its own problems. Therefore, blacks must design and manage their own development. They can benefit more from their own mistakes than they can from consuming the successful results of white-directed development.

The interactive community believes, therefore, that *what the blacks have been most deprived of is not the fruit of the white man's labor, but the opportunity to labor for themselves*. Only self-development can bring with it the self-confidence, dignity, and self-respect that makes development possible.

This set of beliefs does not imply that whites in the interactive community must sit by idly while the blacks go it alone. The blacks cannot go it alone in a white-dominated society. They need access to human and material resources controlled by whites. They need whites working *for* them, not *on* them. This requires whites placing themselves and some of their resources at the disposal of the blacks, *to be used as the blacks see fit*.

In the interactive community, whites realize that they can benefit both economically and socially from black economic and social progress. Dr. William C. Finnie, in his doctoral dissertation at the University of Pennsylvania, showed that it would be worth at least $300 per year to the average white family if blacks had an equal share of economic development. He showed this by assuming there was no racial discrimination in the United States and, therefore, that blacks had the same distribution of economic and social characteristics as the whites do. He then calculated what reductions in public and private expenditures—for example, for welfare, police, courts, health services, and insurance—would be possible. He divided the result by the number of white families in the nation.

Interactivists believe that white resources should be made available to blacks as an *investment* in white, as well as black, development. Like all investments, some will fail to pay off, but the black community's ability to provide satisfactory returns on such investments will increase with each failure because of what blacks learn from them.

Control and management of investments, financial and intellectual, should be placed in the black community because so doing maximizes its learning, and that of the giver as well. This belief contradicts the typically reactive corporate position that, according to Professor Cassell:

> . . . is in favor of strong top-down government as against grass roots neighborhood decision making, because the former is perceived as the most "efficient" way to govern. This concept leads the businessman to work through established organizations which are essentially top-down, such as the charity and settlement house boards.

This may bring out the generosity of people, but the giver often overlooks the twin facts that charity makes the receiver dependent upon and even hostile toward the giver, and charity also seems to make the giver hostile to the receiver.

An Interactive Case Study

The concept of black-white relations that I have drawn is not utopian. It has already been realized in a collaboration in which several of my colleagues and I have been involved, one between the university research unit of which I am a part and a neighboring black ghetto. The white research unit is the Management and Behavioral Science Center of the Wharton School of the University of Pennsylvania in Philadelphia, and the black neighborhood is called "Mantua." Until recently Mantua was referred to by blacks in the city as "The Bottom."

Mantua lies one-half mile to the north of the University. It contains about eighty city blocks and has an "official" population of about 15,000 about 98 percent of which is black. By almost any standard it is a critically depressed and disadvantaged area. About 25 percent of its housing units are overcrowded, and more than 50 percent are in substandard condition. Its male unemployment rate was between 15 and 20 percent during the 1960s, more than three times the rate in Philadelphia as a whole. Thirty-seven percent of its families earned less than $3000 per year during this period. More than a third of Mantuans who are over twenty-five years old have had less than eight years of education. About 50 percent of its minors received some type of public assistance, more than six times the city's rate. Sixteen percent of its population from seven to seventeen years old were arrested in 1964, nine times the rate in the city as a whole. Its adult crime rate was more than twice that of the city. Use of narcotics was widespread.

Early in 1968 Forrest Adams, a Mantuan, came to the University for help in preparing a request for neighborhood assistance from a city agency. This help was given to him but he was asked if he would be willing to bring his neighborhood's principal leader to the University to discuss a proposal that the University's Center would like to make to him. This proposal had been carefully worked out in the hope that just such an opportunity would arise. The funds needed for it had already been obtained from the Anheuser-Busch Charitable Trust of St. Louis.

The next day Forrest Adams brought Herman Wrice, president of the recently formed Young Great Society (YGS), to the University for a meeting. YGS was an indigenous group dedicated to the development of Mantua. The Center offered to employ any three people selected from the community by Mr. Wrice. They were to work on the development of their community in any way they saw fit. There were no constraints on how, when, or where they worked. They were not required to be present at the University at any time, but the personnel and facilities of the Center were made available for them to use in any way they saw fit and they were encouraged to use them. The Center would do nothing except by request, but it would attempt to fill every request even if it involved competencies and resources not available to it, by trying to obtain them from other sources in or out of the University.

There was considerable discussion of the question: What is in it for the Center? The answer was: the chance to learn how to be helpful to black ghettos. This was not very convincing coming from members of a university that had previously demonstrated lack of concern with its surrounding neighborhoods, and whose physical expansion was a major thorn in the side of these neighborhoods. But since the proposal involved little risk to Mantua, Mr. Wrice accepted it. He and Forrest Adams selected three Mantuans before the day was over. They signed in on the following day.

The two men and one woman selected from Mantua were hired on a Friday. The following Monday they asked for a meeting with those involved from the Center to review a work plan they had prepared over the intervening weekend.

The Mantuans found the discussion helpful but, more important, they found a willingness on the part of University personnel to pitch in where asked to do so. As a result the Mantuans asked for regular weekly meetings to review plans and accomplishments. In the weeks that followed requests for meetings and participation became increasingly frequent. Before long more than thirty people from the University, faculty members and graduate students, were involved in providing requested assistance. It became necessary for the Center to assign one of its senior staff members, Marvin Rees, and a graduate student to the effort on a full-time basis so that the diverse activities could be coordinated.

In order to stretch the small initial grant to cover the salaries of the three Mantuans for nine months, the faculty members involved did not bill the grant for their services. This turned out to have an unexpected advantage. Subsequently, many other faculty members who were too busy to "sell" their time to the Center gave some of it to this effort.

After about six months of collaboration the Mantua team and the Center jointly prepared a proposal for continued support of their efforts. It was the Mantua team's decision that any additional funds that might be obtained should continue to be administered by the Center. They preferred this for two reasons: it relieved them of responsibility for keeping the books and it assured them continued involvement of the Center. The proposal was submitted to both the Anheuser-Busch Charitable Trust and the Ford Foundation. Grants were obtained from both.

When the Ford Foundation grant was announced one of the members of the Mantua team was asked by a local television interviewer what he thought were the University's motives in the collaboration. He replied: "When the project started I couldn't figure out the University's angle and it worried me because we had been screwed by the University in the past. I'm still not sure what it's up to but I don't think about it any more." Before long the community knew very well what the Center was up to, perhaps better than the Center itself did.

From 1968 to mid-1973, at the time of this writing, a great deal has been accomplished in Mantua by YGS, its subsidiaries, and offshoots—much of it with the help of the Center. Its current and recent activities reveal better than any generalized description can just what has been and Is being accomplished.

Economic Activities

YGS created the Mantua Industrial Development Corporation (MIDC) which brought together, under one roof, eight minority-owned and two white-owned, industrial enterprises. The corporation is owned jointly by these businesses and YGS. The building that houses them was purchased by the corporation with funds obtained from the Small Business Administration. The corporation supplies managerial, marketing, and financial services to its members. It serves as an industrial greenhouse nurturing delicate young enterprises in a controlled environment, helping them grow into healthy independent businesses. In 1971 these firms did about $6 million worth of business and employed just over 300 people. Among their customers are some of America's largest corporations, including IBM, General Electric, Western Electric, RCA, and Leeds and Northrup. Two members of the University's Center serve on the Board of MIDC and have played an active role in making contacts with potential customers of the member-firms' products and services. The story of MIDC has been told by *Business Week*.

The University's Center has also helped a number of small businessmen in Mantua obtain loans from local banks and has provided them with managerial and technical assistance. Much of this help has been given by graduate students of The Wharton School.

YGS helped establish and obtain funding for an employment service that placed about 250 Mantuans in jobs last years. It also serves as a channel for young people into job-training programs.

Building

The principal instruments of physical change in Mantua are the YGS Architectural and Planning Center (APC), the YGS Building Foundation, and Group Builders, Inc., an independent corporation that works closely with YGS subsidiaries. Together they are redeveloping two apartment houses, one with fifty-eight units and the other with twenty-nine. The former will be available with rent supplements.

Thirty-nine townhouses are being built on a parcel of land returned to the community by the University City Science Center—an organization whose major stockholder is the University of Pennsylvania. These units were designed by APC and are being built by Group Builders. The units will be available for rental or lease-purchase from the Philadelphia Housing Authority.

Preliminary plans were recently completed for a shopping-housing center in Mantua. It will have a community center in the middle of shopping facilities and housing above it. The necessary land has been acquired. Financing for construction is now being sought.

Health

YGS operates three medical facilities: a Medical Center that provides general medical and dental services, a Heathmobile that takes service to those who cannot come for it, and a Half-Way House, a heroin-addiction treatment center that provides methadone maintenance. Half-Way House now supports itself out of a modest fee charged for its services. It serves anyone regardless of his or her race, place of residence, or income. More than half of its more than a thousand "clients" come from outside of Mantua, many from upper-income white suburbs.

Education

YGS has helped establish and operate a number of schools and is now planning several others. An Infant Care Center originally provided services for twenty-two children between five and thirty-six months old. They were primarily children of mothers who wanted to return to work or school. With a waiting list of twenty-six, the adjoining house was acquired by the YGS Building Foundation, and APC, which designed the original facility, designed its expansion into the new facility. The enlarged facility accommodates forty-five children.

The Powelton-Mantua Children's School, funded by the School District of Philadelphia, is located on the boundary of Mantua and Powelton, a middle-class neighborhood with a substantial white population. This integrated school is run jointly by parents from both communities. The school uses the English open-school plan. It serves preschoolers and has a kindergarten and early elementary grades.

In 1971 the Benjamin Banneker Center was opened in facilities provided by the University City Science Center. It has since moved into one of Mantua's public-school buildings. It is directed at preventing dropouts and attracting those who have dropped out back into the educational system by providing a "more relevant" education than normal schools do. Relevancy is determined largely by the students themselves. This school served seventy-five 7th grade students in its first year, added the 8th grade in its second year, and plans to add a grade each year until it covers the 12th grade.

YGS personnel work for the School District in three high schools (outside Mantua) and one middle school, trying to provide motivation and incentives to minority students and working to reduce tensions among gangs in the schools. They also assist Philadelphia's Board of Education in selecting and orienting new teachers for these and other schools serving the black community.

A Junior College is currently being planned for Mantua. It will be a formal part of both the University of Pennsylvania and Lincoln University, a predominantly black institution near Philadelphia. The new college will be unique because of its double affiliation. It will have no entrance requirements, but it will have exit requirements: a suitable job or admission to another college. It will provide the first two years of a bachelor's degree program and a terminal vocational degree in several areas.

The Mantua Scattered-Site Middle School, a public school to serve 1600 students from grades 5 through 8, has passed the final design stage and is now awaiting acquisition of necessary funds. A core consisting of a library, gymnasium, auditorium, and community facilities will be located in the heart of Mantua. Classes, laboratories, and other facilities will be strategically placed at three sites so that students will move through multiple gang turfs while they are young enough to do so safely. This, it is hoped, will reduce the significance of turfs to young Mantuans.

In January of 1969 the Community-Wharton Educational Program (CWEP) was initiated at the University of Pennsylvania. Using volunteers—faculty members and students—from The Wharton School, this program offers noncredit courses in business to students who do not have the financial resources required to attend a regular college and have a desire to learn business and seek a career in it. The program is administered by a board consisting of representatives of a number of neighborhood self-development groups. Students are provided with extensive tutorial, counseling, and placement services. About 100 students are served each year. Forty-four of its initial participants have moved into degree programs at Wharton and other schools. A number of the others are now usefully employed in business and industry.

In 1970 YGS and the University's Management and Behavioral Science Center conducted a twenty-two-week Urban Leadership Training Program. The following is a description of the program written by one of its participants, Ronald E. Thompson, for the *Mantua Community Newsletter* of April 1970:

> On February 9 started the greatest event that ever happened in urban history. The event I'm talking about is the starting of the Urban Leadership Training Program. The program started with 21 gang leaders from the Mantua community. The Young Great Society and Mantua Community Planners are affiliated with the program. YGS funds the program. The 21 leaders were picked from different corners which consist of 36th Street, 39th Street, Lancaster Avenue, 41st Street, and 42nd Street.
>
> A few months ago, before the program started, these corners were at war with each other. Many times before the start of U.L.T., social workers tried to gather the corners together, but the problem that would result would be more conflict between the young men. As always, somebody would end up getting hurt.
>
> So far the program is doing very good. The great thing about the program is that the young men have unity among each other. You know yourself that it is good because without unity you do not have anything.
>
> The University of Pennsylvania provides space for the young men. Members of the University faculty and community workers of various fields volunteer to teach the young men different courses. Some of the courses the young men are taking consist of criminology, sociology, black studies, community health services, community planning, housing rehabilitation, radio and TV, and communications. The

> purpose of these courses is to prepare for future black leadership in all fields. . . .
>
> Urban Leadership Training is turning out to be a community organization to fight the problems of the ghetto area of Mantua.
>
> The young men do. . . field work. Recently the U.L.T. brothers did a housing survey of the Mantua area for the Architecture and Planning Center of YGS. The young men also take trips in various parts of the U.S. One trip was taken in the Harlem area of New York where the young men took surveys and analyzed the ghetto neighborhood problems there and compared them with the problems in Mantua. We found out that the way they are living in Harlem is the same identical way we're living.
>
> The program is the first I have known to ever understand gang problems.
>
> I used to be affiliated with one of the gangs before I went into service. I have been home from the service since January. I was in Vietnam. I compare the fighting in Vietnam with the fighting in the streets and find it almost the same. The only thing is that in the streets you are fighting your own brother.
>
> The brothers are not fighting now. This is why the program might be the greatest event in urban history.

Of those who went through the program about half are now working for community development groups. Several have taken jobs in business and industry. A few have returned to their gangs and two have gone to prison for crimes committed before they attended the course.

YGS personnel have given courses and lectures related to the black ghetto at the University of Pennsylvania, Temple University, Villanova University, Morgan State University, and Cheney State College. Master of Science candidates in Education at the University of Pennsylvania earn their first course credits by working in Mantua under supervision of YGS personnel. Westminster and Geneva Colleges jointly send thirty students to Mantua each year for a month's practicum which is followed up by lectures given by YGS personnel at the colleges. YGS also provides jobs to Wilberforce College black-work-study students during their "work" semester.

In 1971 YGS and the Management and Behavioral Science Center jointly conducted two programs for corporate executives to familiarize them with the black ghetto, its problems, and what they can do about them. This program was also written up in *Business Week*.

Recreation and Culture

YGS's first activity after being founded involved an athletic program for young people. Its current athletic program runs throughout the year covering all major, and several minor, sports. It serves both boys and girls. Games are arranged with other communities of different racial composition and socioeconomic characteristics in order to expose young Mantuans to as much of the outside world as is possible. Mantuan teams have competed as far away as Florida. They have captured a number of city championships.

Each summer YGS provides an extensive recreational and work program for young people. In 1972 a camp was set up at Cheney State College just outside of Philadelphia. From Monday to Friday of each week 179 youngsters lived on campus where an equal number of Cheney students served as their "big brothers" and supervised activities not only designed to provide a good time but also to produce a desire to go to college. One of the Cheney students spoke of the program as follows:

> We hope that they can use their own minds and bodies to form the right ways. It's definitely a reciprocal situation whereas the Cheney students are being employed—they're using the skills of their majors, you know. They have a practical experience other than student teaching. They get a sense of responsibility from working with the children and this helps them build their character. The little kids look up to them and that will mold their character. Everybody is giving and receiving at the same time.

A similar camp is operating in 1973.

In Mantua itself 435 youngsters were kept constructively busy on community projects in a Neighborhood Youth Corps program. Projects include repair, maintenance, and cleaning up community facilities.

In cooperation with students at the Philadelphia College of Arts, YGS established a program in 1968 in which classes in drawing, painting, sculpture, and pottery are given in the neighborhood. In addition, the Mantua Academy of Theatrical Black Arts involves fifty young men and women in the dance. This group gives frequent performances throughout the city. Both programs use a cultural center owned and remodeled by YGS.

Early in 1972 the collaboration between YGS and the University was extended when a grant from Anheuser-Busch, Inc. made it possible to create the Busch Center. This new center is run jointly by YGS and University personnel. It is devoted to spreading to other communities the pattern and principles involved in the collaboration that produced it. Similar collaborations have been initiated in several other cities.

There are four essential characteristics of the interactive collaboration described here, characteristics that are being incorporated into projects in other cities. First, the university researchers did not conduct research *on* the community; the community conducted research on the university directed toward finding out how to use it effectively. In so doing they solved the researchers' problem of determining how to be useful to the community. Center personnel would have been rejected by the community if they had tried to do research on it, but even if they had not, they would not have penetrated it as deeply as they eventually did. They developed an expertise on the ghetto by serving it as it saw fit.

Second, only a little of what Center personnel did for the community in the first few years required use of their special technical skills. But they never rejected a request for aid because it fell outside their field. When they did not have the skills required, which was often, they either got the help of others or developed the skills themselves. Center personnel were not above chauffeuring or acquiring empty used oil drums or dirty pond water for a school's fish tank. Initially they spent a great deal of time opening doors and ears in the white community. They helped prepare proposals and solicit support for them. Gradually they earned the right and ability to make suggestions and participate in planning. They even got the chance to use their special research skills as, for example, in preparing an economic-development and land-use plan for Mantua. It took almost four years for the Center to become a full partner in the joint effort.

Distinctions between disciplines and jurisdictional issues that are important to academics and professionals have no importance to those living in a ghetto. They cannot be bothered trying to sort out types of help and they have no patience for those who "pass the buck" on jurisdictional grounds. They want *HELP*, not *help*. They are "turned off" by those who want to help only within the domains of their competencies. Because of its willingness to do anything, the Center discovered that it was competent to do many things of which it had previously been unaware. This led to a significant modification in the way it did its normal work for corporations and agencies of the government.

Administrators and managers of public and private enterprises tend to use researchers as specialists in restricted and highly structured ways. They use them to help with problems which the researchers have propagandized them into believing they have special competence to deal with. The Center stopped telling administrators and managers, or any consumers of its services, how it should be used, but rather began to involve its consumers in systematic efforts to find out how they could best use the Center. Such an approach may well change a profession's conception of its competence and permit it to develop new competencies and thus come to better approximate the practice of systems science. This orientation also gives researchers a chance to become more integrated into the organizations they serve.

The third essential characteristic of the relationship between the Center and Mantua is that no white ideas have ever been imposed on the black community. Nothing has ever been done by the whites involved other than what has been requested of them by the blacks. Once the willingness of Center personnel to work *for* blacks was well established, their suggestions and criticisms were sought. In time the difference in color became irrelevant to the interactions that took place. Deep friendships between blacks and whites were formed. Families of those involved began to interact. Joint activities extended beyond the problems of Mantua. The whites were thus given what is a rare opportunity in our culture: the chance to get to know blacks as people, not as blacks.

Fourth, it became apparent to the Center that what the black community wanted from the white were not gifts or charity, but investments and involvement. Blacks had learned that white donors cannot be counted on for sustained interest because they are subjected to many competing demands for their resources and attention. But an investor does not lose interest once he has made his resources available, and the community found that it often benefited more from the continuing investment of an investor's time than from the funds he provided. Hence, whenever possible, the community sought *partnerships* because these provided the strongest kind of bond between the benefactor and the community, and it gave the community an opportunity to help its benefactor. Obligation is not a nice feeling.

It became increasingly apparent over time that the community and YGS could be as helpful to those who helped it as they could be to the community. Nearly all organizational donors had some kind of black problem of their own. The staff of YGS was often able to help them solve their problems in ways that benefited blacks as well as the donors. This led to the development of a new strategy. YGS and the Center began to look for opportunities to help others without knowing in advance how the community might benefit. Hence one of the functions of the Busch Center is to provide help to any type of organization that has a minority problem.

The design of a service station for black urban ghettos that was described in the preceding chapter was the first project of this type. A number of others followed. For example, early in November 1971 Richard C. Feaster, president of Webb Manufacturing Company in Philadelphia, a producer of canvas products, approached Herman Wrice to discuss his firm's inability to survive in its current location. It was located in a deteriorating neighborhood almost equally populated by blacks, Puerto Ricans, and whites. Webb's employees did not live in the surrounding neighborhood. Their morale and productivity were dropping and their turnover was increasing because of conditions around the plant—vandalism affecting their cars, street crimes affecting their persons, and abuse of the plant itself. Mr. Feaster did not want to move his plant to the suburbs for a number of reasons not the least of which was the cost of doing so. He also had an interest in the problems of the inner city in which his plant was located.

Herman Wrice contacted Dr. Albert Glassman, principal of nearby Edison High School, with whom he had had some previous dealings. This racially mixed school has the highest dropout rate in the city. Using a Federal Grant, Edison was searching for ways of keeping potential dropouts in school. Mr. Wrice suggested moving a group of the "worst" students and a teacher to the Webb plant. Dr. Glassman and one of his teachers, Walter Spector, agreed and the *Edison-Webb Innovators* were born.

Half the students' time was spent in class using space and facilities provided by Webb; the other half was devoted to a community-improvement project. The Busch Center arranged to tie the Innovators into the national "Pitch In" antilitter campaign sponsored by the United States Brewers Association. Oil drums, paints, and other equipment and materials were obtained from a number of local and national firms. The students made 150 "Pitch In" litter barrels and placed them strategically throughout the surrounding neighborhood. This began a continuing fight against litter in the area.

The students voluntarily worked on weekends and holidays in order to turn out the barrels. When these were completed they formed their own company to manufacture "Pitch In" coat patches and litter bags. Several students graduated to full-time employment at Webb.

The improved communications between Webb employees and Edison students alleviated the fears and mistrusts of both. The workers, helped by the students, gave a Christmas party for neighborhood children and through it came to meet neighboring adults. Plant workers are now greeted by, and greet, the plant's neighbors on the streets. They have been invited into their homes and have become involved in their hopes and aspirations. Webb and the neighborhood acquired each other.

Other projects involved bringing a company and two warring factions of black workers together, and reestablishing a company's favorable image in a black community that was seriously damaged by a black labor problem. Several companies are being helped in developing effective ways of conducting market research on black consumers. In each of these cases some black community or groups of blacks benefited, and they benefited in ways that developed their self-respect and self-confidence. Herman Wrice sees to that.

A GENERALIZED INTERACTIVE APPROACH

It is natural to ask whether the relationship between Mantua and the Center at the University of Pennsylvania can be reproduced in other communities using their indigenous resources. This is precisely what the Busch Center was set up to determine. The results to date are encouraging but it has become apparent that intimate black-white relations cannot be developed quickly.

The Penn-Mantua effort is a small one and by itself can have no significant impact on our nation's race problems. But it does suggest how an effective attack can be launched: by initiating a very large number of similar efforts. Consider, for example, a city of 2,000,000 that contains 500,000 underprivileged blacks. Our experience indicates that neighborhoods of up to 25,000 can be treated as development units. This means that 500,000 blacks can be divided into about twenty development units. A city of 2,000,000 like Philadelphia, has more than twenty universities and colleges in its metropolitan area. Furthermore, company headquarters, branch banks, clubs, professional societies, and a wide variety of organizations can play the resource role filled by the Busch Center in the Mantua effort. The wider and more diverse the participation, the better.

Experience with Mantua shows that a resource center needs about $2 per person per year, or $50,000 for a neighborhood of 25,000, to support self-development workers in the neighborhood. Therefore, an expenditure of as little as $1,000,000 per year could help launch citywide black self-development efforts. This is much less than has been wasted, on the average, in cities of this size each year.

Resource groups interested in helping could be placed on a central register. Black neighborhoods could approach, negotiate with, and select those resource groups they want to work with. Together they could apply for funds to support their joint efforts. If a neighborhood lacks a self-development group, the availability of meaningful help is likely to bring one into existence. If more than one group claims to represent a neighborhood, they should be required to reach an accommodation with one another before a project is launched in that neighborhood. How they reach that accommodation should be their business.

A number of these efforts can be expected to fail initially. But even failures will produce learning and new efforts will be built on top of old ones. The blacks must be given the same right to fail that whites have enjoyed for many years. This right is essential if anyone is to learn how to succeed.

Even if we blanket the country with such collaboration as I have described here, it will not be enough. A good deal more will be required to clean up the racial mess. It will require progress with respect to almost every other problem discussed in this book: providing blacks with the ability to provide themselves with better education, housing, recreational facilities, job opportunities, and so on. In short, it will require some modification in just about every public service and private attitude. The problem is how to get such modification under way. A large number of Mantua-like projects might be a way of doing so.

CONCLUSION

Race problems derive from the inability of minority race members to participate equally in the society of which they are a part. Participation does not mean being on the receiving end of majority-conceived development programs. It means giving a community the resources and support it requires to initiate its own development. A minority that has been able to elevate itself will cope with discrimination effectively. Equality of status will follow equality of opportunity and accomplishment.

The interactivist seeks to provide opportunities for self-development. By so doing he seeks to remove the economic and moral burden of segregation and discrimination from the majority, and to reveal the fact that minority group members are human beings capable of helping majority group members improve the quality of their lives.

CHAPTER EIGHT

CRIME

*If you give to a thief, he cannot steal from you
and he is no longer a thief.*

WILLIAM SAROYAN

Crime is winning its battle with law and order. On August 31, 1971 *The New York Times* reported: "The Federal Bureau of Investigation released today statistics showing that both the crime rate and the annual volume of major crime rose substantially in 1970." Because of this, much of the crime reported by police in 1971 was deliberately downgraded to make the situation appear less serious than it is. Reporting on a national survey of law-enforcement officials conducted in 1972, William R. Morrissey, editor of *Justice*, wrote:

> Police officials at all levels claim the desire by state and local police chiefs to please the Nixon administration, in hopes of obtaining greater federal funding, has caused many of them to either encourage or condone the downgrading of crime statistics—falsifying reports of major crimes so they fall into the category of minor offenses—to lower the crime rate in their community.

The inhabitants of American cities do not need to see statistics to be aware of increasing crime and fear of it. The newspapers are full of it. Many city centers and neighborhood streets have been rendered unusable at night; some are not safe during the day. Crimes against property have become so common in some sections of cities that property insurance is no longer available to those who live in these areas. Rampant shoplifting and thefts by employees are closing retail establishments. Fear of mugging and rape has changed the life style of many women. Millions of travelers are inconvenienced by the search-and-seize procedures used at airports; and so on and on.

Arrests increase and prisons bulge, but crime marches on. It has been a long time since it was commonly believed that crime does not pay; it obviously does. As Ramsey Clark, former Attorney General of the United States, observed: "Most crime is never reported to police .... Convictions are obtained in something less than one in twenty cases of even serious crimes against property that are reported to police."

To many born and bred in poverty and deprived by discrimination of legal access to the fruits of our society, crime is almost the only tolerable means of survival. This is certainly the case for many of those suffering from drug addiction. Of these Ramsey Clark wrote: "Thousands of poor people pay as much as twenty-five dollars a day for narcotics—money they can raise only by criminal acts."

Those criminals who are apprehended and convicted are inserted into a correctional system that appears to be coming apart at almost every seam. On March 2, 1970, for example, *Newsweek* reported:

> Carlos Rivera was the fifteenth person within a year to kill himself in New York city jails or police station lockups. . . . None at the time of his death had been convicted of the crime he was in jail for. . . . At any one time 14,000 are locked up in facilities built to handle half that number—two, three and even four men jammed into tiny cells designed for one man.

Those who occupy correctional facilities are seldom corrected. According to Ramsey Clark: "80 per cent of all serious crime is committed by people convicted of crime before. . . . Approximately half of all the persons released from prisons return to prisons, many again and again." The reason is not hard to find. Tom Wicker identified it in an article in *The New York Times*: "Attica— like most prisons—is not a 'correctional facility' at all; the phrase is a gruesome euphemism. No 'correctional officer' there has any real training in correcting or teaching or counseling men; rather, they are armed guards set to herd animals."

A report to the National Commission on the Causes and Prevention of Violence states that prisons provide "vocational training in hate, violence, selfishness, abnormal sex relations and criminal techniques." Similar conditions pertain in other countries. An editorial in the well-known British newspaper, *The Guardian*, asserted:

> The overwhelming evidence is that a large proportion of the people who go into prison at tremendous cost are just as much a security risk to the public when they come out as before

they went in. In many cases prison damages them and makes
them more likely to go on offending.

Will we do anything about crime and punishment in the coming years, and if so,
what? "The crucial test of American character," wrote Ramsey Clark, "will be
our reaction to the vastness of crime and turbulence in which we live." Many
will do nothing because they are not significantly threatened. They can afford to
play the odds and remain inactive because, as Ramsey Clark pointed out, "The
white middle class city dweller . . . is likely to be the victim of violent crime at
the rate of once every 2,000 years, while upper middle income and rich
suburbanites have one chance in 10,000 years."

Nevertheless, an increasing number of people find the effect of increasing
crime on the quality of life to be intolerable. As a consequence "law and order"
has become a major political issue. The proposed remedies can be classified as
reactive, preactive, and interactive. Let us consider each of these in turn.

THE REACTIVIST ON CRIME

The reactive portion of the public responds to increasing crime rates by
increasing its demand for stricter laws more effectively enforced; for more,
better equipped, and less constrained police; for longer and more punitive
imprisonment of those convicted; and for fewer paroles. "Let's face it," said
Senator John Dunne, Chairman of the New York State Committee on Penal
Institutions, "people want more police. . . . They want these [criminal] groups
locked up and then they feel safe—out of sight, out of mind." In short, the
reactivist responds to increasing crime with increasing repression. He argues for
discipline and deterrence because he attributes rising crime rates to increasing
permissiveness in society and in the family.

The reactivist views the criminal as one who is inherently evil, hence
incorrigible. The criminal is taken to be exclusively, or at least primarily,
responsible for his criminal act. After all, the reactivist argues, look at how many
others there are who, though in the same circumstances as the criminal, do not
turn to crime.

The reactivist believes treatment of criminals should be directed primarily at
protecting society from them. This means secure imprisonment, exile, or
execution. Next, those imprisoned should be punished for their transgressions,
and, hopefully, through suffering, driven to penitence and purged of their
criminality. Finally, their treatment should be such as to deter others from crime
by instilling fear of punishment within them.

The reactivist resents the use of public funds for support and treatment of
criminals, but he grudgingly accepts the need to do so. Not only does he want

the system of treatment to be inexpensive, but he also wants it to be unobtrusive—out of sight, out of mind.

When prisoners protest, demonstrate, or riot as they recently did at Attica, the reactivist seeks more repression. He empathizes with the heavily armed guards at Attica whom a reporter for *The New York Times* described as "bearing clubs, rifles, pistols, shot guns and tear-gas launchers." The report went on:

> These guns, moreover, were in the hands of men who left no doubt they wanted to use them. . . . Even the strong belief that an assault on the stronghold in Block D would cause the prisoners to kill their 38 hostages seemed to make little difference to those who had the guns; they wanted to go in.

In brief, the reactivist attempts to deal with crime by dividing people into two classes, the good and the bad. He wants the bad to be apprehended and isolated behind a wall, and he wants this done at minimal cost to the good. He feels that the bad deserve little better than the worst possible treatment. He believes that nothing short of purgatory will produce penitence and that the fear of punishment is the most effective deterrent of crime.

This attitude toward crime has dominated in our country for some time. Not only has it failed to bring crime under control, but it has produced a criminality crisis. Further reactive responses to this crisis will only make it worse.

THE PREACTIVIST ON CRIME

Preactivists and interactivists believe that crime is a joint product of the individual and society. The following passages from Ramsey Clark reflect this belief:

> The anxieties arising from technology cause most of our instability and heighten the desire to manifest contempt for our existing values and to escape to something different. Addicts, alcoholics, and the mentally ill are products of that anxiety and contribute most of the crime in America.
>
> It is the poor, the slum dweller, the disadvantaged who suffer most, and most tragically, the crime of America. It is here that the clear connection between crime and the harvest of poverty—ignorance, disease, slums, discrimination, segregation, despair and injustice—is manifest.
>
> The basic solution for most crime is economic—homes, health, education, employment, beauty. If the law is to be

enforced—and rights fulfilled for the poor—we must end poverty.

Having recognized that the roots of crime go deeply into society, the preactivist despairs of bringing about the fundamental social changes necessary to uproot it and turns instead to reform of the criminal justice system. He argues that reform of this system, not repression of the criminal, is required: "You cannot discipline this turbulent, independent, young mass society as if it were a child. Repression is the one clear course toward irreconcilable division and revolution in America."

The preactivist advocates less punitive and more humane corrective treatment of convicts, and more public and private assistance to those leaving corrective institutions. And he seeks to supplement these reforms with more community agencies and public programs that can divert and redirect potential criminals.

Ramsey Clark has prepared what is probably the most comprehensive preactive critique of, and set of reforms for, the criminal justice system. His main points are based on a breakdown of this system into its basic elements: police, prosecution, courts, and corrections.

His analysis of the current deficiencies within each of these elements reveals several basic needs. More and better personnel and facilities are required to improve the quality of their performance. This, in turn, requires higher salaries to attract more and better qualified personnel, and more investment in better and more facilities. As a result, larger public expenditures are called for. Ramsey Clark laments, "At a time when our major domestic concern is crime and violence, the nation spends more on household pets than on police." Furthermore, he wrote,

> The Federal Bureau of Prisons . . . is responsible for 20,000 federal civilian prisoners, yet its budget for 1968 . . . was $77 million. By contrast, the FBI, one of more than twenty substantial federal investigative and enforcement agencies, has a budget of nearly $200 million. Every year the prison budget is the first of those in the Department of Justice to be cut by Congress. The FBI budget is often increased above its own request.

Clark also calls for emphasis on correction rather than punishment of offenders:

> There is no effort within the criminal justice system that holds a fraction of the potential to reduce crime offered by a vigorous, thoughtful corrections program. Not even efforts directed at the underlying causes of crime, such as health services, education, employment and decent housing, offer the same immediate potential at near the cost.

He points out that despite this: "Ninety-five per cent of all expenditure in the entire corrections effort of the nation is for custody—iron bars, stone walls, guards. Five per cent is for hope—health services, education, developing employment skills."

Prison, according to the preactive reformer, should not seek penitence from its inmates because, as Clark says,

> Remorse comes from within. No prison will create it. But for those who pose America's crime problem penitence has little meaning. By and large, their lives are so empty, they are so full of frustration and despair, they are so sick in mind and body, and their entire life experience providing them grist for thought is so totally lacking in charity that contemplation is more likely to cause anger at society's sins than remorse for their own.

Preactivists, like Clark, believe that a large proportion of offenders are mentally ill and are therefore in need of medical treatment and therapy: "The opportunity for treatment of the mentally ill in prison is virtually nonexistent. Most prisoners suffered from some mental disturbance at the time they committed crime. More have mental health problems on leaving prison than on entering."

Preactive reform efforts are directed toward change of the criminal justice system so that offenders can be rehabilitated effectively. They attempt to make prisons more like hospitals than dungeons, and to give education a central role in correctional programs. Rewards are advocated as incentives to good behavior rather than punishment as a disincentive to bad.

Preactivists seek to protect at least the minimal rights of offenders. For example, Governor Cahill of New Jersey recently proposed matching one civilian with each inmate of his state's correctional institutions so that offenders would be provided with an effective avenue of complaint. Others have proposed such alternatives as use of ombudsmen, "inspector generals," or unannounced periodic civilian inspections of prisons.

A principal objective of preactive reform is to make sentences better reflect the seriousness of the crime and the likelihood of correction of the offender. As Ramsey Clark observed: "Ten-year sentences in lieu of two-year sentences—because we are angry—will not reduce crime. It is not the length of the sentence but the effectiveness of the correctional program that will make the difference."

Furthermore, preactivists want to match the treatment of an offender with the nature of his offense. For example, Clark says of conscientious objectors:

> For society to consume years, or even days, of the lives of these young men in prison idleness and brutality or blight their

personal potential through social stigma is tragically wasteful and desperately wrong. Until laws can be reformed, sensitive correction systems must afford the hundreds of young men serving sentences for violations of the Selective Service Act the chance to make constructive contributions outside the prison environment. We should not make criminals of those who oppose war.

The preactivist advocates programs that will divert the young, particularly those living in slums, from criminality—recreational programs, adult supervision, summer camps, employment, and drug addiction programs. For the preactivist the social worker is a major weapon against criminality and recidivism—the return to crime of those who have been in prison.

In sum, the preactivist appeals to our sense of justice and humanity to pull us through the crisis of crime until we have removed the underlying causes of crime. This, as Ramsey Clark argues, should enable us "to achieve needed reforms, to offer fulfillment, human dignity and reverence for life."

THE INTERACTIVE APPROACH TO CRIME

Preactivists recognize that the roots of crime lie in society, in social conditions such as poverty, discrimination, poor health, lack of education, and substandard and congested housing. But they do not believe that these conditions can be changed quickly enough to affect the crisis in crime. Thus, as preactivists normally do, they accept the environment and seek to reform the criminal justice system within it. The interactivist, on the other hand, does not believe that even the reforms proposed by preactivists are possible without some fundamental changes in society. He does not believe, for example, that the money required to carry out preactive reforms can be extracted out of our society as it currently operates. Therefore, the interactivist does not believe that changes in society and the criminal justice system are separable.

The interactivist assumes a more aggressive posture toward the social environment of crime than the preactivist does. He tries to use the crisis in crime to bring about changes in those aspects of society that breed it. He believes society needs correction even more than the criminal does, and that correcting the criminal without correcting the conditions that breed criminality cannot significantly reduce crime. This orientation leads to an inversion of the problems usually associated with criminal justice. The most fundamental of such transformations is that involving the concept of responsibility for crime.

Recall that the reactivist believes the criminal to be exclusively or primarily responsible for the crime he commits. The preactivist believes that the individual and his environment are jointly responsible for most crimes and, therefore, that criminality is like a disease: the germs must be there in the environment and the individual must be susceptible to them. The interactivist, on the other hand, holds society primarily responsible for crime. He takes the individual's susceptibility to crime to be a product of social influences—an acquired characteristic, not an innate disposition.

Therefore, the interactivist develops a strategy for treating the criminal that is based on the assumption that *his criminal act is the consequence of a crime committed by society against him.* Then, when a person steals to avert starvation, for example, the threat of starvation is taken to be a social crime that requires more attention than the individual theft does. Such crimes can only be significantly reduced by eliminating the possibility of starvation. Race rioting can only be eliminated by removing racial discrimination. This view does *not* imply that the individual criminal requires no treatment but that the treatment he receives is directed to undoing the damage that has been done to him.

The interactivist believes that justice should be more concerned with protecting the individual from society than with protecting society from the criminal. If the criminal is taken to be one whom society has wronged, then the justice system should protect him from further abuse by society. Because the interactivist takes the principal function of the criminal justice system to be the *correction of society,* punishment of either the criminal or society is irrelevant.

Before considering how the criminal might be treated in an interactive criminal justice system some concepts that are central to such a concept should be clarified.

Types of Offender

The performance of a criminal justice system depends primarily on the relationship between the type of offender and the way he is treated. A very large number of ways of classifying offenders—most based on the nature of the crime rather than of the criminal—have been developed. But since the system is supposed to treat the criminal, not the crime, the interactivist bases his classification on three characteristics of the offender.

1. *Those who are dangerous to others or their property* and, therefore, from whom society should be protected. Such a person engages in, or is inclined to, unprovoked aggression on the person of others, or unprovoked destructiveness of property, either for its own sake or for personal gain (where socially acceptable alternatives are available and the need is not desperate).

2. *Those who are dangerous to themselves* and, therefore, should be protected from themselves. A self-destructive person may be either physically or

mentally ill and may endanger himself (and/or others) as a result of his illness. He is his own victim, as in drug abuse.

3.   *Those who are dangerous to no one but who are in danger.* Such an offender is forced into crime by external conditions that he could not overcome. He may be easily pressured, provoked, or influenced into offensive acts by others, or by a personal need deriving from scarcity of a resource essential for survival but not provided by society or others within it; for example, hunger or the need to belong.

Individuals need not be "pure" types; they may incorporate characteristics of several types, and these characteristics may change over time.

Types of Treatment

The treatment of an offender is a resultant of the type of facility used and the way it is managed. Here too "pure" types can be identified. These, taken in relation to the perspectives of society on the offender, may be said to comprise philosophies of correction.

1.   *Deterrent* (controlling). Such treatment is intended to prevent aggression or destruction in or out of a facility, at the time of detention or subsequently. The threat of punishment for doing something and the promise of reward for not doing it are both deterrents, or are intended to be so.

2.   *Clinical* (therapeutic). Such treatment is intended to cure, reduce, or stabilize physical or mental illness, or a character defect recognized as pathological and believed to be actually or potentially responsible for self-destructive or antisocial behavior.

3.   *Supportive* (protecting). Such treatment is intended to remove its recipient from antisocial influences or forces applied to him that he cannot resist except at great cost or risk; to protect him from threats of harm; and to provide him with physical and emotional care of which he has been deprived and which he needs.

Actual treatments frequently blend these pure types in varying proportions. Some clinical procedures, for example, require a good deal of control as well as support, especially at some stages.

Deterrence, therapy, and support do not in themselves necessarily require the placement of anyone in a closed facility. Security, therefore, ought not to be looked at as an aspect of treatment.

Very different types of offender may sometimes need some security. Few are likely to need a high degree of it all the time. Security measures are required in case other methods of control break down. The first task, therefore, is to ensure that these other methods, which should be an inherent part of a facility's organization and management, are well designed and are in fact working as well as possible. Physical security becomes necessary only insofar as social security breaks down. If a facility's staff is able to maintain it as an open facility, there is no need for a perimeter.

Security measures may be required to safeguard either the boundary of a facility or to protect groups or individuals inside from each other or from themselves. The level of security maintained should depend in either case on the frequency expected in the breakdown of social controls. Physical security should be a reserve system, for emergency use only. Where the emergencies become too frequent the ground rules of the social control system have to be changed.

Now let us be more specific.

Treatment of Those Dangerous to Others

Those who are believed by the interactivist to be dangerous to others would normally be thought of by the reactivist as intrinsically evil. The reactivist would "lock them up." The interactivist recognizes that others have to be protected from them but this does not require punitive incarceration. Rather, treatment of those dangerous to others should be designed to provide them with a full and satisfying life while protecting others from them as long as they remain threatening. Depriving such an offender of completely free access to others does not necessarily require denying them access to him.

The offender believed to be dangerous to others would be placed in a community that differs from others in only several respects. Its members would be watched sufficiently to assure their not harming one another, and they would not have the freedom to leave until they were believed to be cured. Others who desire access to them could have it. For example, the criminal's family could come to visit or live with him in this "coeducational" community. He would have the opportunity to work for a living in that community and support himself and others—like his family—in or out of the community. Furthermore, he would pay rent, taxes, and buy the goods and services he needs for normal living. Society at large would cover the costs of security and surveillance, and of therapeutic and correctional programs provided in the community.

The correctional community should have a sound economic base, producing goods and services required both inside and out. Its business and industry could be based on supplying local, state, and federal governments with goods and services they require. Private industries would be encouraged to open branches in such communities. Governments would contract with them to build and operate such facilities. Publicly supported colleges and universities would be required to provide educational programs within the community.

When a convict is no longer dangerous to others he would be free either to leave or remain. "Corrected" in this context means not only that he no longer poses a threat to others but also that he has the skills and resources necessary, and the opportunity, to reenter society in an environment other than the one that produced his criminality.

Those who commit crimes within such a community would be withdrawn to another in which separation, surveillance, and security of inmates would be greater. There would be a hierarchy of such communities, but each would be designed to be as normal as possible. This means that they should also be designed to be essentially self-supporting.

Inmates who show signs of progress would be given furloughs to visit others outside the community. Such leaves would be increased in frequency and duration as the offender improves.

Such communities as are described here might be preferred by many who have not committed crimes to those in which they live. They need not commit crimes to get access to them. Such communities should be open to outsiders. The correctional community should be so designed as to make the inmates reluctant to leave and outsiders anxious to enter. Voluntary movement into these communities would constitute a significant pressure for social change in so-called normal communities.

Personnel who administer and maintain such communities for the state would be required to live within them for at least part of their time. They would, of course, be free to come and go as they wanted.

Those who cannot imagine such a community should reconsider West Berlin which meets many of the conditions I have set down. All ingress and egress are controlled, but within it a normal productive life can be lived. Significant differences do not reduce the similarities.

It is not surprising that reflective and responsible prisoners in the current system desire to change it in directions similar to those described here. For example, *The Evening Bulletin* reported:

> The inmates at Washington State Prison are . . . asking for $1 million to build a prison they designed themselves.
>
> . . . The plan was conceived by the convicts themselves, the architect was a prisoner. . . .
>
> Architect-inmate Don Anthony White . . . said his design is "simple . . . Like it has windows and lots of light so that residents can let the world in. And the windows open to allow fresh air in."
>
> "It is designed to exemplify a normal living situation, so that

> we, as abnormal people from an abnormal situation, can see what normalcy is and relate," White said.
>
> ... Correctional staff and families would live right in the complex.
>
> "Residents would study or leave the facility on a work-release basis and those who worked would pay room and board," White continued. "This would eliminate greatly the dependence of the individual as well as the cost of the project.
>
> "Even at maximum outlay, the state would be paying approximately half what it is currently paying to keep us here. . . . And keeping us here is unproductive."

Interactive correctional communities could be experimental in many ways. New types of low-cost housing could be tried without the restrictions of archaic building codes. In particular, prefabricated units that could be assembled by the inmates, or units that could be manufactured by them could be used for their own housing. Innovations in education, transportation, environmental control, and almost every type of social service and facility could be tested in such communities. Such communities could also be operated as experiments in participative democracy. They could incorporate many of the adaptive-learning procedures advocated in this book. They might well become model communities for others to emulate.

Treatment of Those Dangerous to Themselves

Those convicts who are believed to be dangerous to themselves—for example, alcoholics and addicts—would be placed in a community whose principal function is to provide the medical services they require. In other respects this community would be much like one for those dangerous to others. There would, of course, be modifications in the type of security system used. Wherever possible inmates would be used to help take care of each other as has been done so successfully by Alcoholics Anonymous. When a convict no longer constitutes a threat to himself he would be allowed to return to normal society if he so desires.

The community for those dangerous to themselves would be open to anyone who wants treatment within it. There is evidence that it would be used voluntarily by many. For example, consider the following report which appeared in *Parade:*

> Instead of jail, Minnesota now sentences drunks to three days in one of 52 new "detoxification centers." There, the

alcoholic is given a bath, bed, sleeping pill, and some "morning after" psychological counseling.

The detoxification centers are so successful that 50 per cent of admissions are now voluntary. Moreover, nearly a third of those who come to the centers, sign up for long-term rehabilitation, also offered by the state.

Treatment of Those Dangerous to No One

Even if one assumes that most crimes are due to social conditions it does not follow that every criminal has been damaged by society or is dangerous to himself or others. Some have responded to a unique nonrepetitive set of (1) internal or (2) external conditions. Crimes of passion and need may be of the first type; political crimes may be of the second type.

A person who steals food to avert starvation may not be dangerous to himself or others once the threat of starvation is removed. He needs a job or income more than he needs punishment. Societal revenge should not be the basis for treatment of such an offender; individual welfare should be.

A juvenile who has been forced to commit a crime by others is not helped by detention, but by being removed from the pressures that forced him to crime and by being given proper adult guidance.

Those criminals who are judged not to be dangerous to others or themselves but to have responded to social conditions not under their control, are best treated by removal from those conditions. Punishment in any form is not likely to have any positive effect on them. They should be permitted to function in society in a useful way.

This is particularly true of juveniles and young adults. Instances of their being treated within society by removal of the pressures that produced their crime are increasing. For example, *Parade* reported on an experiment at Yoke Crest near Harrisburg, Pennsylvania:

> . . . in a converted 20-room former mansion that has no cells, locks or bars, 19 convicts are serving sentences for serious crimes ranging from attempted murder to embezzlement.

The residents are free to move in and out of the home, as are their neighbors.

> Eventually the resident looks for a job, then goes to work on the outside, while still living at Yoke Crest. When he has saved enough money, found a place to live and proven himself able to function in the normal world, he "graduates." Even after leaving Yoke Crest, however, he is

asked to come back for a group session every two weeks or
so. . . .

It costs about half as much to keep a man at Yoke Crest as it does to keep
him in prison and his stay is usually shorter.

The use of houses like this one for treatment of juveniles is increasing. *The
New York Times* described several such institutions on the outskirts of
Topeka, Kansas:

> Under the new concept, also being tried in Europe, a
> genuine family atmosphere is created for teen-age and
> preteen-age victims of divorce, abandonment and parental
> hatred by placing half a dozen of them in a "normal"
> environment—a house of ordinary design run in an ordinary
> manner by a couple whose only task is to serve as mother
> and father. . . .
>
> Every effort is made to treat the youngsters as if they were
> the couple's own children—permanent members of one, big
> happy family. They go to neighborhood schools, receive a
> weekly allowance, help with the dishes, cut the grass and go
> out on dates.
>
> Here on a small farm on Topeka's western outskirts, far
> from littered alleys and domestic squabbling, there are two
> of the new homes, one for boys and one for girls. Other
> homes can be found in cities like New York and Los Angeles
> or towns like De Kalb, Ill., and Mount Vernon, Wash.

The conscientious objector is another type of "criminal" who is seldom
dangerous to himself or others. If the draft is considered to be moral then
society needs to discourage such objection. Some parts of society try to do it
by imprisonment; others use constructive social service as an alternative. This
alternative is much less likely to produce a real criminal. The question
concerning the morality of the draft is one I consider below.

Classification of Convicts

It is clear that in the concept of correction presented here classification plays
a major role. Two kinds of classification are involved: classification of
individuals and of treatments.

How an offender is classified depends not only on the classification system
used but also on the amount of information about him that is available to the
classifier. It also depends on the orientation of the classifier, who inevitably

brings his own and his community's biases to bear, and the number and variety of facilities available for handling the offender. Thus classification varies with time and place. Therefore, it should be reviewed periodically or whenever new information about the offender or a new type of facility become available. No disposition of a convict should ever be final.

The best predictor of what an offender's behavior will be after he is released can be his behavior before release *if* the pre- and postrelease environments are similar. Because of this the interactivist seeks to create communities of convicts that are as normal as possible, and to provide them with as much interaction with normal communities as security considerations permit.

Errors in classification are always possible. In the current criminal justice system a convict is seldom given the benefit of any doubt; he is usually given the harshest treatment that is justified by the available information about him. This is a consequence of placing a higher cost on turning someone loose prematurely than on retaining someone longer and more restrictively than is necessary. Concern with security currently dominates concern with rehabilitation. The interactivist seeks to reverse this priority.

Now let us consider interactive views of some other aspects of the criminal justice system.

The Courts

It is clear that legislative bodies have the decision-making function in democratic societies, and that the executive branch of government has responsibility for supplying the legislative branch with the information it needs and for implementing the decisions made. What is not clear is who has the control and problem-identification functions. These functions are not currently systematized nor does any part of government have designated responsibility for them. The interactivist believes these functions should be performed, at least in part, by the courts.

According to the interactivist the courts should not only have the function of enforcing the law but also for evaluating it. This means that the courts should serve as a memory and comparator in an adaptive-learning system of government such as is described in Chapter 2 and the Appendix. It should also have at least partial responsibility for the diagnostic function. In order to perform these functions, the courts would require submission by legislative bodies of explicit statements of the expected effects of laws they have enacted and the bases on which these expectations rest. The courts would then compare actual performance with what was expected and if the differences are found to be significant, they would signal a "deviant."

Diagnosis would then be required. The courts and/or legislative bodies should be provided with researchers who are capable of carrying out the required diagnoses. If the diagnoses are performed by groups serving the legislature, then the courts should review the results. Whoever performs the diagnostic work, the courts should maintain a record of it and the corrective actions taken. They should prepare summary reports of the control process periodically and release them to the public. This would enable public pressure to develop when legislation fails to do what it was intended to do.

Courts, aided by government attorneys, should also serve as symptom and presymptom identifiers. By analyzing the types of cases brought before them, and how the mix changes over time, the courts and government attorneys can identify significant changes in social behavior and conditions. Attention to these changes would indicate whether governmental action is required. Hence the courts should also provide legislative bodies with formulations of problems to which their attention should be given.

As I have already indicated, society should be tried in court along with each alleged criminal. It should be the court's responsibility to determine what social conditions, if any, are responsible for the crime—such as inadequate parental care, poor education, lack of satisfying work, and so on. Information of this type should be accumulated and analyzed. The results should be disseminated to both the public and legislators.

In brief, the courts should provide much needed feedback to legislative and administrative branches of government and to the public on society's actual performance. This would facilitate more effective response to, and anticipation of, social threats and opportunities.

Law

It is much easier to pass a new law than it is to modify or eliminate an old one. The body of law is large, hence exhibits a great deal of inertia.

To the interactivist crimes that are committed provide an implicit critique of society, hence of its laws. Analysis of crimes can make the critique explicit and indicate what changes are needed. Laws that the general public does not respect do more harm than good because they invite widespread violation and thus undermine respect for the law in general. This was the case, for example, when alcoholic beverages were prohibited in the United States, or when, in some cities, activities on Sundays were severely restricted by "blue laws." There are many obsolete laws on the books, laws that are disregarded; for example, laws that prohibit sexual intercourse on Sundays in some places. When a law is generally disregarded, analysis of the reasons for it offers an opportunity for social improvement.

The military draft is a case in point. The morality of a draft law and an undeclared war are brought into question by conscientious objectors and draft dodgers. Many argue that there is no practical alternative to such a law, particularly when a nation is involved in war, declared or not. There obviously is, as Professor Ronald A. Howard of Stanford University has observed:

> A fairly obvious use of the pricing system is in the manning of the armed forces. We should simply pay high enough wages and fringe incentives to volunteers to attract whatever number and variety were required by our military commitments; there would be no draft. Those members of society who had what were to them more desirable life opportunities than serving in the armed forces would be free to follow them. Since there would be no compulsion, every serviceman would have willingly accepted his lot and, consequently, could be expected to perform his duties with greater enthusiasm and efficiency. Of course, the expense of such a military establishment would exceed present cost under the draft system. This cost would be passed on to all of society by increased taxes, thus sharing the burden of military service indirectly among all taxpayers. If the nation were to engage in an unpopular war, it is probable that the pay of the servicemen would have to be increased to attract the necessary number. The increasingly high expenses would serve as a very proper feedback on the true cost of the whole adventure. Conversely, a war that had the support of the populace would find many dedicated citizens who would serve for nominal pay.

Consider another example of how lawbreaking can be used to indicate where the law should be changed and how. I visited Iran a few years ago as a scientific consultant provided by the United Nations. In a conversation with one of Iran's cabinet ministers he put the following problem to me. As best I can remember his words, he said:

We have a national monopoly, a state-owned tobacco industry which is the second largest source of income for the government; the first being the oil industry. We have factories which produce a number of different brands of cigarettes that are sold through government licensed stores for from 15¢ to 35¢ per pack in American money. We also import American cigarettes and sell them for 55¢ and make a good profit from these sales. But this profit has been decreasing because of increasing smuggling. Smugglers bring American cigarettes in from Kuwait on small fishing boats at night. They are brought up to the major cities, like Teheran, where they are sold by unlicensed street vendors for about 50¢ per pack. This illegal business has been growing rapidly, thus reducing government sales and profits.

The reward we offer for information leading to apprehension of smugglers does not lead to many arrests, so we are considering increasing the reward. Clearly, if we make it too high it would be self-defeating. Is it possible to determine the amount of reward that would maximize government's net profit?

In the conversation that followed I probed to determine how profitable the government's importation and sale of American cigarettes was. Once this was established we determined how much profit was being made by the smuggling operation. It turned out that the smugglers were making a larger profit per pack than was the government even though they sold a pack for less. Therefore, I recommended that the government either go into the "smuggling business" itself or legalize and tax it enough to yield the desired level of profit. Unfortunately, I do not know if anything ever came of this suggestion.

The same kind of thinking involved in my suggestion to Iran has led some states and local governments to legalize gambling, or some forms of it, and to derive an income from it by taxation. Governmentally operated lotteries are becoming commonplace. Recall that one of the major sources of revenue for federal and state governments is taxes on alcoholic beverages. Some states, like Pennsylvania, even control its distribution and sale. England handles narcotics in much the same way. Doing so not only enables her to reduce illegal traffic in drugs considerably, but also to identify and treat a large number of addicts.

Laws that are frequently broken should be reexamined and reevaluated periodically. This does not imply that all frequent offenses should be legalized; but it does mean that possibilities for innovative improvement of law and society would be increased.

Police

Preactivists have suggested many possible reforms that would increase the effectiveness of the police. Most of these are directed at raising the rate of apprehension of offenders, not at crime prevention. Crime prevention has never been a central function of the police. The interactivist believes it should be, hence advocates creation of a new preventive police force. The preventive police officer (man or woman) would have no power of law enforcement or arrest. He would not be armed in any way. But he would be conspicuously uniformed so that he could be easily identified.

The preventive policeman's principal function would require his getting to know the neighborhood to which he is assigned and the people in it. To facilitate this process, he would be required to live in that neighborhood. The neighborhood should be small enough so that he can cover all of it on foot or bicycle. He would be there to help people or to help them get help whenever they needed it. He would be expected to know and understand the conditions in his neighborhood that breed crime and thus direct the activities of appropriate public and private agencies to their correction. His activity in the community would be completely positive—oriented to making it a better place in which to live.

When he sees criminality developing he would take corrective action, but if apprehension or forceful intervention is required, he would call on others to perform it.

This preventive policeman should be able to be contacted by anyone in his area at any time, day or night. When someone in his area is arrested he would be responsible for being sure the one apprehended knows his rights and receives whatever assistance he requires; for example, that proper legal aid is available. He would similarly help any ex-convicts who return to his area.

He would work with schools, clubs, and other organizations in the community to help make it as self-policing an area as possible. Put another way, his principal function would be to protect people from society and others who might abuse or misuse them. The preventive officer would testify in court on the crime-producing conditions operating on anyone from his area who is being tried for a crime. He would serve as a witness against the state, not as a witness for it.

The preventive policeman would require all the skills and training of a social worker and more, but his orientation would not be toward the alleviation of suffering so much as toward the removal of its causes.

Victims of Crime

Those victims of crime who can least afford to sustain the losses imposed by it often cannot afford insurance of person and property against crime. Property is not insurable in many low-income neighborhoods because of their high crime rate. The interactivist believes that where insurance against crime is not otherwise available, government should either provide it or subsidize private companies that do so. The amount paid out by government to victims of crime would provide valuable feedback on the effectiveness of anticrime programs. It would also provide a more reasonable basis for determining how much should be spent on efforts to reduce crime. If the cost to the public of such a government-backed insurance program increased too rapidly it would indicate the need to invest more, or to invest more effectively, in efforts to prevent crime.

Even if a criminal is not primarily responsible for his crime, he should be made more aware of the cost of crime to its victims. Therefore, wherever possible, the criminal should repay the government or the appropriate insurance company for its payment to the victim(s) of his crime for the loss or damage incurred. He could do so only if he could earn money, but he could do so in the communities I have described above.

SUMMARY

In this chapter I have described how reactivists, preactivists, and interactivists respond to the crisis of crime. The reactivist believes that the criminal alone is responsible for crime. Therefore, the reactive community treats increased crime with increased repression—more law and law enforcement, if not more order. This means more police, arrests, and convictions; and longer sentences, fewer paroles, and more secure and punitive treatment of those convicted. Treatment of the individual convict is directed at protecting society from him and at punishing him. The intention behind punishment is to produce penitence and to deter others from committing crimes.

The reactive attitude toward crime currently dominates most American communities. In the background, however, there is a growing demand for liberalizing reforms of the criminal justice system.

The liberal reformer normally has a preactive attitude toward crime. He conceptualizes it as a type of illness that possesses the criminal, the source of which is his environment. The environment, however, is usually taken to be too hard to control or to require too much time to bring under control. Therefore, preactive reforms are largely restricted to the elements of the criminal justice system. They are directed at producing more enlightened and humane police, prosecution, and courts. Proposed treatment of convicts is based on the belief that most of them can be corrected or cured through appropriate medical, psychiatric, and educational services, and by a type of detention that does not deprive them of their dignity and self-respect. Preactivists prefer to treat the convict in the normal community, when possible, reserving prison for those who are a serious threat to others.

The interactivist places primary responsibility for crime on society or social conditions. Therefore, each element of the criminal justice system is reconceived so as to lead to social changes that reduce society's crime-producing capabilities. Criminals are classified as dangerous to others, themselves, or no one. The interactivist advocates secure but otherwise normal and supportive communities for those who are believed to be dangerous to others or themselves; communities in which they can lead a full and satisfying life, into which they can bring their families, and to which their friends can come freely. Treatment would be readily available. Such communities would provide considerable opportunities for participative government and experimentation with new social facilities and functions.

The convict who is dangerous to no one would not be incarcerated in any way, but would be relocated in a normal community so that the pressures that produced his crime are not present. He would be given a chance at a normal life in an improved environment.

Commitment of convicts would terminate when, and as soon as, they are no longer dangerous to themselves or others. Sentences would not be of predetermined duration.

Interactive courts would play a central role in society's management system. They would have primary responsibility for society's control function: evaluating consequences of legislation and diagnosing failures. They would also have the function of identifying current and coming problems. Society would be constantly on trial before them.

Laws would be continuously reviewed and occasionally revised in the interactive community. Laws that cannot be enforced or do not have popular support undermine respect for the law in general. Their revision or withdrawal would be undertaken systematically.

The interactivist believes that police should take on an additional function: protecting individuals from their environment. A new arm of the police is advocated, one which has no power of arrest or law enforcement but which is involved in preventing crime, in assisting individuals who are misused or mistreated by others or by society in general. Preventive police would have responsibility for seeing to it that society's obligations to its members are being fulfilled. The objective of this function is to minimize social crimes of which individuals are victims.

Finally, the interactivist believes government should see to it that victims of crimes are compensated for losses or damage due to crime. Criminals should repay the government or its agents for such payment. Such an obligation by the criminal only has meaning if he can earn money while "incarcerated." He could do so in the communities the interactivist advocates for offenders.

If crime is to be reduced, victims of it must understand the criminal at least as well as he understands them. If, as the interactivist believes, most criminal acts are the product of social crimes against the criminal, then, in a sense, all actual and potential victims of crime share responsibility for society's criminality. Criminals will not be corrected until society is.

CHAPTER NINE

_____

HEALTH

*Nothing could be worse in our society today than
to say we need another three to five billion for
medical care, and then simply duplicate or multiply
the arrangements we now have. This would get us
nowhere. It is the fundamental transformation in a
variety of our arrangements that I think is signalled
by these cost changes. The permanent problem is
the need for more productivity. . .brought about
by structural changes in the practice and organization of medicine.*

JOHN F. DUNLAP

I recently heard a very-high-ranking official in the Department of Health,
Education, and Welfare—in an off-the-record talk—point out that although per
capita expenditures for health are greater in the United States than in any
other country, the health services provided are far from the best. About $90
billion are spent annually on health, and costs are inflating at a rate of 12 to
15 percent per year. He pointed out that this not only creates a major
problem for those with low income but, when catastrophic health problems
are involved, for upper-income people as well. Despite a rapid increase in
expenditures on health in the last two decades the life expectancy of those
who reach thirty years has not changed and the incidence of death due to
coronary diseases and cancer is increasing. He also pointed out that even in
our scientifically oriented culture most medical practices are of unproven
efficacy; hence modern medical practice is not as far from that of the
primitive medicine man as physicians would like us to believe. Finally, he

155

noted that there is no national plan or strategy for improving our health services, nor are there any national standards for adequacy of health care.

Many of the deficiencies of our system derive, I believe, from the identification of health with the absence of disease or defect. For example, the *American Heritage Dictionary* defines *health* as "optimal functioning with freedom from disease and abnormality."

The World Health Organization (WHO) has tried to go beyond this simpleminded notion: "Health is a state of complete physical, mental and social well-being and not merely the absence of disease or infirmity." Commenting on this definition, Steven Polgar, director of the Carolina Population Center, observed: "The definition of health given by the WHO includes *social* as well as physical and mental well-being. This reflects a concern with a person as a member of human groups."

The WHO's definition and Polgar's comments on it indicate some of the important dimensions of health but they transfer the burden of its meaning to its synonym *well-being*. However, Polgar implicitly suggests a way out of a regress from one nonoperationally defined concept to another: "If disease is seen as an individual's departure from perfectly well-meshed social and physiological performance, health, by contrast, becomes an *asymptote*—an ideal that can be approached but never attained in actuality." Use of the concept *performance* enables us to become both more specific and more operational in defining health.

Mind and body are two aspects of the system called a person. They are the sources of a person's desires and needs, and the instruments that enable him to fill his needs and satisfy his desires. A need is the absence of something that is necessary for either survival or satisfactory mental or physical performance. A person, for example, may need calcium for survival, but he may not know this, hence have no desire for it. On the other hand, he may desire something that he does not need; for example, ice cream.

Health has two aspects: one is associated with what a person desires and how well his desires match his needs (*aspirational* health), and the other with how well he can satisfy both his needs and his desires (*instrumental* health). To the extent that body and mind can be used effectively in filling a person's needs and reaching his objectives, he is instrumentally healthy. Perfect instrumental health, like perfect efficiency, is an ideal. Instrumental health is a relative concept since there is no absolute standard of efficiency for human behavior. In practice this aspect of health is determined comparatively. A child is judged to be retarded, for example, by comparison with other children of approximately the same age raised under approximately the same conditions. On the other hand, a person is not said to be unhealthy because he cannot fly, but a bird who cannot fly would be. Thus the comparisons involved in establishing instrumental health must be made with respect to a relevant class of organisms operating under similar conditions.

The ranges of physical and mental performance that define normality among members of the reference group may have to be changed from time to time. For example, as diet improves, physical capabilities increase and health standards are raised.

An unhealthy tooth is one that does not function well. It cannot be used to bite or chew food effectively. If it is removed the effectiveness of the mouth for eating may be reduced; hence the instrumental health of the mouth may be impaired. If the missing tooth is replaced by a false one that performs satisfactorily, the health of the mouth is restored. Health does not necessarily require the natural state of an organism. Medical research is yielding an increasing number of effective replacement parts for living organisms.

Instrumental illness may be due to infection, malfunctioning parts, injury, and so on. Disease is normally thought of as being completely caused by germs. To treat it as such is to take a mechanistic approach to health. As René Dubos has shown, the belief that every disease or illness has a specific and unitary cause is a consequence of the nineteenth century's mechanistic view of the world. Such discoveries as were made by such microbe hunters as Pasteur and Koch gave rise to the germ-theory of disease and the associated belief that serums and vaccines specific to each disease-causing microbe could be developed. Even such general-purpose drugs as sulpha and penicillin were not sought until shortly before World War II. Today, illness is increasingly viewed in systemic terms involving the interactions of many factors including the host, the agent, and the physical, biological, and social environment. The malicious microbe is thus increasingly seen as no more than a necessary, not a sufficient, condition of disease: as one of its producers, not as its sole cause. Malfunctioning of organs and even accidents are also increasingly perceived in producer-product and systemic terms. The mind and body are thought of more and more as open subsystems of the organism, with interactions between them and their environment.

There have been a number of efforts to introduce some standard measures or indexes of instrumental health. These were recently reviewed and augmented by S. Fanshel of Farleigh Dickinson University and Dr. J. W. Busch of New York University. They need not concern us here but it is significant that similar efforts have not been made with respect to aspirational health: what a person wants and how his wants match his needs.

A person who is perceived as having "abnormal" desires is usually considered to be ill. For example, a person with an abnormal desire for drugs, sex, or for harming himself or others is so considered. Health clearly involves what a person wants, but not so clear is the fact that what he wants does not have to be normal for him to be healthy. Leonardo da Vinci's desire to fly was certainly not normal at his time but we would not want to think of him as ill because of it. If we restricted health to normal desires then many of our most creative and innovative people would be considered to be ill. Some of them may be but not because they want things most others do not. Normal desires should not be used in defining aspirational health. We neither want to say that those with normal desires are necessarily healthy, nor that those with abnormal desires are necessarily ill. We need a concept other than normality to define aspirational health.

The definition of aspirational health necessarily involves ethical considerations. Its definition depends on our concept of what people *ought* to want. Clearly, they may not want what they should. Fortunately we need not argue about what they ought to want if we agree that in an ideal state *every* individual would be capable of filling his needs and attaining his objectives. For every individual to have such a capability two necessary (but not sufficient) conditions would have to be satisfied:

1.   That no one wants to reduce the ability of others to fill their needs or attain their objectives.

2.   That no one wants to reduce his own ability to fill his needs or attain his objectives.

If the first of these conditions were not satisfied in the ideal, the attainment of their objectives by some would preclude such attainment by others. Therefore, we can say, first, that a person who wants something the attainment of which he knows will necessarily deprive others of their ability to attain what they want or to fill their needs, is ill. For example, anyone who desires to harm others or to force them to do what they do not want to do—except when what they want to do is harm another or themselves—is ill.

Second, a person who wants something the attainment of which he knows necessarily reduces his own ability to attain another objective that is more important to him, is ill. This does *not* mean that a person who has conflicting desires is necessarily ill. One may want both to read and watch a television program at the same time. Attainment of one may preclude the other but attainment of neither necessarily reduces one's *ability* to pursue the other.

This definition of aspirational health implies that a person who wants to harm himself is ill. The desire to commit suicide is an extreme case. The desire for narcotics or alcohol becomes unhealthy when it requires consumption of amounts that impair a person's ability to survive, to fill needs, or to attain more desirable objectives.

In summary, then, *health is the ability of a purposeful system to fill its needs and pursue its objectives with at least a level of efficiency displayed by most other systems of the same type under similar conditions, and the absence of desire to decrease its own or other's ability to fill their needs and attain their objectives.*

Note that this definition of health applies equally to organizations and organisms. It applies to communities and societies as well.

What has been gained by defining health in this way? It enables us to handle such difficult questions as C. West Churchman, noted philosopher of science at the University of California (Berkeley), raised in a personal communication to me:

> Would we want to say that an individual who devotes his life to religious worship, to the neglect of his family and their needs, is healthy or unhealthy? Who is more healthy, the individual who's addicted to a drug or alcohol, or the individual who's addicted to law and order? The first may lead a harmless life from the point of view of other individuals, while the second may be actively engaged in acts of killing and depriving others of their freedom. Which is the more serious disease, infectious hepatitis or pollution of the environment?

People who want to shoot dissenters, burn the homes of unwelcome neighbors, and pollute the environment are clearly ill by the definition of health offered here. The definition not only identifies a type of illness largely ignored in our society, but it also suggests that this type of illness is pervasive.

HEALTH SERVICES

The kind of health services that a society provides or tries to provide to individuals depends on the attitude it has toward planning in general and toward health planning in particular. There are different types of health services associated with reactive, preactive, and interactive planning postures. Health inactivists—for example, the "naturalists" or such "supernaturalists" as Christian Scientists—do not believe in health services.

Reactive health services are directed to fixing things that have gone wrong: curing disease and repairing, removing, or replacing malfunctioning parts; in short, to providing *corrective* medicine. Reactive health planners are generally dissatisfied with any effort to make individual health a social responsibility. They support *laissez faire* practice of medicine. Such an attitude is exemplified by that of the American Medical Association which has almost without exception opposed any change that affects the practice of medicine. This attitude implies a system in which the amount and quality of service available to an individual is proportional to his ability to pay for it. Health is largely treated as a privilege, not as a right. The poor are left to the charitable inclinations of physicians and philanthropists.

Preactive health services place more emphasis on preventing illness and injury than on curing them. They involve such things as the development of immunization, early detection of deficiencies through periodic checkups, and propagation of health habits that make illness and injury less likely. This approach is not as concerned with getting at the causes of illness and injury as it is with eliminating or minimizing their effects. It places a lot of faith in research and development and the use of technology in detecting, treating, and preventing illness and accidents. It supports more extensive and equitable distribution of health services than does the reactive approach, but it attempts to bring about such changes without fundamental changes in the social system. Thus it supports private and governmental health plans that finance services within current institutional arrangements; for example, Blue Cross, Medicare, Medicaid, and the Kaiser-Permanente plan. It advocates free health care to those who cannot afford it but it advocates care at a cost to those who can afford it.

Interactive health services attempt to remove the causes of illness or injury by changing the environment and style of life of those who live within it. Interactive health planners are as concerned with such things as safety standards for manufactured products and work environments, nutritional standards for foods, sanitary engineering, and the quality of housing as they are with the practice of medicine. They take a broad view of the health system, hence see the physician as only a part of it, and not necessarily the most important part of it.

Interactivists take good health to be a right of all regardless of their socioeconomic characteristics. Therefore, they seek to restructure society and health institutions so as to guarantee good health services to all. They attempt to do this by building into society incentives that will yield increasing productivity and quality of health services, and better use of these services. They recognize that the practice of medicine is currently the principal means available for treating illness and injury, and that the hospital is the principal means currently available for distributing these services. But they also believe that these are not the principal means of preserving health. Health depends on every aspect of living, hence on every aspect of society and the environment. René Dubos put this belief in the following way:

> . . . there is rapidly emerging in the modern world a set of
> problems that could properly be called social medicine, not
> to be confused with the very different concept designated as so-
> cialized medicine. The health field is no longer the monopoly of
> the medical profession; it requires the services of all sorts of
> other skills. This collaboration will become increasingly
> urgent as the community demands that steps be taken, not
> only to treat its diseases, but also to protect its health.

The danger in this inescapable trend is that the medical
profession may be progressively edged out of many social
aspects of medicine.

If the medical profession is edged out of this development, it will not because
of what others do but because of what members of that profession fail to do.
Let us consider the physician from the interactive point of view.

DOCTORS

Doctors are, of course, the principal instrument through which recognizable
health services are delivered. Their orientation, as previously noted, is largely
corrective and mechanistic. They try to identify unitary and sufficient causes
of illness and treat them, or to repair, remove, or replace malfunctioning parts
of the organism. The similarity of their approach to the organism and the
mechanic's to the automobile has been noted by many.

Because of the expansion of medical knowledge it has become increasingly
difficult for individual doctors to keep up to date on all aspects of medicine.
Specialization has been a necessary consequence of this development. The
general practitioner is gradually disappearing. As Mark G. Field, professor of
sociology at Boston University, observed: "In 1931 four-fifths of all American
physicians were in general practice; in 1966 three-fourths of physicians were
in specialty practice."

Professor Field and others expect the complete specialization of medical
practice within two decades. Although the medical profession has adapted to
this expansion of knowledge it has not adapted to the patients' needs that are
created by the changes in medical practice. The patient is required to adapt to
these changes. He must either learn to make preliminary diagnoses on himself
so that he can select the appropriate specialist to go to, or he must be
prepared to be shunted from one doctor to another until he finds the right
kind of specialist. Use of paramedical personnel and computers in preliminary
diagnoses is being developed (and will be discussed below) but it is currently
available only where doctors are organized into some type of collective
practice, as in a hospital.

In group medical practice a number of specialists work cooperatively out of
the same facility. If organized properly such practice can reduce
inconvenience, not to mention expense, to the patient. To a large extent,
however, it has been organized to increase convenience to the physician, not
to the patients. Even so, it has not developed at a rate compatible with the
rate of specialization of medical practice. As Dr. Sidney R. Garfield, originator
of the Kaiser-Permanente health-delivery system, observed: "it is only in

comparatively recent years that group practice by doctors has been considered respectable (and as yet only some 12 per cent of all physicians practice in groups). . . ."

House calls have become rare events. Doctors do everything they can to avoid them. This has the greatest effect on those in disadvantaged neighborhoods where doctors seldom practice. Therefore, the disadvantaged in need of medical services often must travel considerable distances, often in public transportation. Even when the disadvantaged can, and are willing to, pay fees for house calls, doctors are reluctant to come into their neighborhoods, particularly at night. One can understand the reluctance of doctors to do so but it is difficult to understand their failure to provide a suitable alternative. One would have hoped for some collective effort by medical practitioners to solve this problem.

The lack of adequate medical services for the disadvantaged, particularly in urban ghettos, should be a national scandal, but it is not. What medical services are available are often provided out of improvised storefront clinics largely operated by unskilled or semiskilled volunteers. Yet most of these areas are near to or contain hospitals that will not carry their services beyond their walls. Nor do they encourage use of their facilities by their neighbors for other than emergency care. "Community medicine" is a popular slogan but it is seldom practiced by the doctors who teach or preach it.

Physicians isolate themselves in their offices and hospitals. They work where people are sick, not where sickness is produced. Doctors should be an integral part of the management and operation of all collected enterprises, public and private, evaluating organizational and institutional decisions and activities from the point of view of their impact on health. This means that executive bodies of corporations, universities, government agencies, communities, and so on should include doctors who are retained to maintain health rather than to remove illness, although cure need not be excluded.

Doctors could work effectively in organizational environments with managers, engineers, educators, laborers, and consumers in manipulating their life styles and environment so as to produce and preserve better health. But few doctors would find such practice very satisfying. Their education and training is almost exclusively oriented toward treatment of ailing or injured individuals. The fact that their education is overly extended and largely supported out of private funds also militates against health-oriented medical practice. Some medical students find themselves in as much as $20,000 debt at the time they can begin practice. It is not surprising that most of them seek to earn money as quickly as possible. If we want community-oriented doctors we will have to educate them at public expense. Doing so would also attract a larger number of young people into the profession whose primary interest would be in community medicine.

The reactive nature of medical practice in the United States is due more to the way doctors are compensated for their services than to any other aspect of medical practice. Most people only go to see a doctor when they believe something is wrong with them. Hence they pay for treatment of deficiencies. As a result doctors benefit from illness and injuries, not from the presence of health. This is not to say that doctors are responsible for illness or desire to promote it but, because they benefit more from illness than from health, their orientation is corrective rather than preventive. The incentives to which doctors are exposed are wrong way around. They should be paid for maintaining health, not curing illness.

Payment for maintenance of a desired state is a more rational basis for compensating those responsible for maintaining it than is payment for correction of deviations from that state. Some health plans—for example, the Kaiser-Permanente plan, the Health Insurance Plan of Greater New York, and Group Health Cooperative of Puget Sound—involve prepayment for some (but not all) aspects of health maintenance. Dr. Garfield, originator of the first of these plans, commented on prepayment as follows: "This reverses the usual economics of medicine: our doctors are better off if our subscribers stay well and our hospitals better off if their beds are empty."

Although per capita expenditures for health in the United States are greater than in any other country in the world, our state of health and life expectancy is far from the best. We pay more for considerably less effective health services than do citizens of a number of other countries; for example, Sweden. Virtually every country that is doing better than we are with respect to health has made fundamental changes in the method of compensating doctors for their services.

Countries with the best health records treat health as a right, not as a privilege. There was a time when citizens of the United States did not think of education as a right. Now it is taken not only to be right but a necessity. Even now a few aspects of health—for example, immunization against smallpox—is compulsory. The principle has been established. It needs to be extended.

The main argument against such extension goes as follows. If we were to make health services a right available to all and if compensation for these services to those who provide them is based on either private or public prepayment for health, then the demand for such service might exceed society's ability to provide it. To prove this point the case of Quebec, Canada, is often cited: a publicly supported Medicare program had five million claims made in the first three months. Only 3.5 million had been expected in the first year! This shows how inadequately the existing system copes with current health needs. Despite the heavy demand the system survived and developed the capability of coping with it. Nevertheless, Dr. Garfield put this problem in a different light:

> ... when we removed the fee, we removed the regulator of
> flow into the system and put nothing in its place. The result
> is an uncontrolled flood of well, worried-well, early sick and
> sick people into our point of entry. ... The impact of this
> demand overloads the system and, since the well and
> worried-well people are a considerable proportion of our
> entry mix, the usurping of available doctors' time by healthy
> people actually interferes with the care of the sick.

Dr. Garfield's view of the problem clearly derives from his assumption that
the principal function of the doctor is to provide care to the ill. He also
believes demand should be regulated to meet supply; a curious concept of
service. It would be well if physicians generalized on the advice quoted by Dr.
R. D. Laing:

> H. S. Sullivan used to say to young psychiatrists when they
> came to work with him, "I want you to remember that in
> the present state of our society, the patient is right, and you
> are wrong." This is an outrageous simplification. I mention it
> to loosen any fixed ideas that are no less dangerous, that the
> psychiatrist is right, and the patient wrong.

Furthermore, it is not apparent that a system that brings more well people in
for treatment does not also bring in more who are sick. Even under Dr.
Garfield's assumption the net benefit has to be calculated.

Increased demand could, of course, be met by increased numbers of
doctors (some specializing in treatment of the well), a solution that many in
the medical profession discourage. Dr. Garfield himself described another
alternative: a testing technique for evaluating the health of patients.

> [This technique] combines a detailed computerized medical
> history with a comprehensive panel of physiological tests
> administered by paramedical personnel. By the time the
> entire process is completed the computerized results generate
> "advice" rules that recommend further tests when needed or,
> depending on the urgency of any significant abnormalities,
> an immediate or routine appointment with a physician. The
> entire record is stored by the computer as a health profile
> for future reference.
>
> ... As a new entry regulator, health testing serves to
> separate the well from the sick and to establish entry
> priorities. In addition it detects symptomless and early
> illness, provides a preliminary survey for the doctors, aids in
> the diagnostic process, provides a basic health profile for

future reference, saves the doctor (and patient) time and
visits, saves hospital days for diagnostic work and makes
possible the maximum utilization of paramedical personnel.

Therefore, a suitable filtering procedure for even correctively oriented
medical practice already exists. It simply has to be made more generally
available. Because of the high cost of developing and making such procedures
available they are not likely to come into common use until either collective
practice is the rule rather than the exception, or until hospitals take on a
diagnostic function for other than their inmates.

HOSPITALS

In principle, hospitals should be institutions whose objectives include servicing
the needs of their patients. However, even a casual examination of their
operations reveals that they are more concerned with serving doctors and
other staff members than they are with patients. They are organized to
facilitate the work of medical personnel, not to make the stay of patients as
pleasant and brief as possible. This is particularly apparent in the physical
arrangement of patients and the scheduling of their activities.

Some designers are trying to reconceptualize the hospital in systemic terms
and with a patient orientation. For example, this has been the main thrust of
a series of studies directed by Sheila Clibbon (an architect) and Dr. Marvin L.
Sachs. In these studies new and innovative ways of grouping activities and
allocating space within hospitals have been developed. Such an approach can
produce significant improvements in the functioning of hospitals from the
patient's point of view. But the great need is for reconceptualizing the
hospital as a component of a community health system.

Communities currently tend to show little interest in what their public
hospitals do. As a result, conditions in them are often as bad as they are in
community operated prisons. For example, the following report in *The New
York Times* of an unannounced "grim midnight tour" by four city officials at
Kings County Hospital is not unusual.

> They . . . reported finding the following conditions in the
> Brooklyn institution:
>
> Security officers complaining of their helplessness to cope
> with a rampant traffic in narcotics and liquor.
>
> Patients unable to sleep in wards with all ceiling lights
> ablaze.
>
> Cockroaches in a kitchen.

A desperate shortage of workable respirators.

Doctors, nurses and technicians forced to climb stairs because elevators were not working.

A man who had just had a kidney transplant "boarding" in a general medical ward because no nurse skilled in dialysis was available.

This lack of concern with community-operated hospitals reflects the community's lack of concern with the disadvantaged who alone have to use these hospitals. This, in turn, reflects the dominant attitude toward health: that it is a privilege that only those who can afford it deserve. Collective indifference to the way these institutions are operated can be changed by desegregating them with respect to income and integrating them into a coordinated health system.

Most efforts to organize the hospitals in a community into an effective system have failed because of the desire of each hospital to retain its autonomy. Organizational objectives dominate those of the patients they serve. As a result health suffers and its cost increases. Under present conditions each hospital tries to provide as wide a range of services as possible. Consequently, the system as a whole has too much of some types of facility and service, and too little of others.

Furthermore, hospitals are not well integrated with other medical facilities and care centers; for example, nursing homes, clinics, orphanages, detention homes, and schools. Comprehensive health planning does not occur at any level in the United States, let alone in the community. Each organization plans for itself independently or not at all.

A complete redesign of even the corrective health system is needed. An interactive medical system would be organized hierarchically as the military's health system is in the field. At the lowest level there would be paramedical and some medical personnel located in every concentration of people to provide first-aid and emergency services. They should also have some minimal health-maintaining functions. Such services would be obtainable in schools, office buildings, factories, and residential neighborhoods. They would be within walking distance of almost everybody in urban areas. On top of this base there would be a pyramid of facilities starting with small local general-purpose group practices and clinics, funneling people through intermediate facilities or sending them directly to large regional special-purpose facilities. Regional facilities would deal with such things as contagious diseases, rare diseases, organ transplants, and mental illness. The number of intermediate levels and the services provided at each would obviously depend on the size and population density of the community involved.

The hospital subsystem should not consist of independent hospitals each assigned to doctors but, as in the military, they should be given a geographically defined population to service. All doctors would have access to any hospital in which their patients are placed.

A regionally or community-administered system of this type would make it feasible to maintain a central health-data base in which all patient records could be kept. Individual institutions could be provided with direct access to such a file through small computer terminals. This would reduce duplication of records and assure the completeness of the file used by medical personnel. Other significant economies of scale would also be possible; for example, the concentration of expensive medical equipment in hospitals to which all patients requiring its use could be brought.

Specification of a geographic area to be served by each health facility would increase local interest in that facility. The boards governing facility operations could then contain public members selected by those living in the service area. This would increase the responsiveness of health institutions to their users' needs and desires.

Health Plans

The Kaiser-Permanente health system is widely regarded as the most advanced in the United States. It appears to provide better service at a lower cost than can be obtained by most individuals from their community's nonsystem. But it only serves those who subscribe to it at an average cost per person of about $150 a year. Most of the subscribers can afford "normal" health services.

This system was not designed to serve the health needs of the poor. Dr. Garfield, originator of the plan, recognizes the need to help the disadvantaged but he warns against intervention by the government to provide it:

> The concept of medical care as a right is an excellent principle that both the public and the medical world have accepted. Yet the words mean very little, since we have no system capable of delivering quality medical care as a right. . . . National health insurance, if it were legislated today, . . . would create turmoil. Even if sick care were superbly organized today, with group-practice in well-integrated facilities, the change from "fee" would stagger the system.

Then how go about establishing medical care as a right. Dr. Garfield suggests:

> Quality medical care as a right cannot be achieved unless we can establish need, separate the well from the sick and do

> that without wasting physicians' time. It follows that to
> make medical care a right, or national health insurance
> possible, it is mandatory that we first make available health
> testing and health-care services throughout the country. It is
> our conviction that these services should be provided or
> arranged by the physicians themselves. . . . .

So there it is. Medical care should be reserved for the ill. The government and
public should be kept out while physicians who are largely responsible for the
inadequate system we now have can continue in their own way at their own
pace to satisfy eventually the prerequisites for free medical services at some
unspecified and distant point in the future. There is no plan by the medical
profession to meet these requirements nor is one being prepared or even
contemplated.

What Dr. Garfield fails to realize is that government intervention is not
required so much to finance the kind, quantity, quality, and organization of
services, as it is to create the appropriate demand for such services. Free
service might result in initial chaos but it would accelerate the development of
the capabilities required to provide adequate service to all. With appropriate
planning even that chaos can be avoided.

Kaiser-Permanente started over thirty years ago. It has a little more than
two million subscribers. *It has grown at a slower rate than has the population
of the country.* Together with the other two large plans of its type about
eight million are served. All three together are growing at a slower rate than is
the population of the United States. What is it that Dr. Garfield wants us to
wait for?

Kaiser-Permanente appears to be a good plan, but if this kind of a plan is
to be converted from a regional sickness system to a national health system,
and if it is to be able to serve all regardless of their ability to pay, there must
be governmental planning and financing, and perhaps even management of the
system. Physicians are reluctant to become civil servants. We must choose
between support of this reluctance and the public's need.

THE NARCOTICS PROBLEM

This problem is one of the most pressing facing the United States today. We
have failed as yet to make any significant progress with it. In the meantime it
appears to be the source of an increasing amount of crime and a major
contributor to the deterioration of the quality of life in urban America.
Because of its effect on young people it may also be eroding our future.

Our society's response to addiction has been reactive: increased repression of those who make drugs available and those who use them. Typical is New York's Governor Nelson Rockefeller's effort in 1973 to impose life sentences on convicted "pushers." Laws prohibiting the production, sale, or use of narcotics have completely failed to hold back the rising tide of drug use and addiction. Incarceration of those who supply and use drugs has had no significant effect on either. In fact, sale of drugs is commonplace within many penal institutions.

We seem to have learned nothing from our unsuccessful attempt to enforce prohibition of alcoholic beverages in this country.

Preactivists support the expansion of treatment and rehabilitation centers for addicts. There is no indication, however, that such centers have had a significant impact on the use of drugs or on those who are addicted. Recidivism seems to be more common than cure. Preactivists also support educational programs directed to discouraging the use of drugs. These appear to be about as effective as the Keep America Beautiful campaign has been.

Interactivists suggest a rather obvious way of treating those already addicted. Writing of heroin in *The New York Times*, Albert J. Carhart, a lieutenant on the Linden, New Jersey, police force since 1947, made the following suggestion:

> Take the profit out of heroin. Give injections of heroin by a qualified physician in a government clinic, free of charge to any addict that walks in and asks for one. Have a federally funded, city-run neighborhood clinic staffed by a qualified physician, a registered nurse and a policy officer. . . . .

There is no reason to restrict this proposal to heroin. It could be applied to all "illegal" drugs. The crime arising out of production, distribution, sale, and consumption of narcotics would be eliminated, and the crimes committed currently to support addiction would be as well. The savings in private property and tax dollars from the elimination of such crime would be very large.

There would be a significant reduction, if not complete elimination, of deaths due to overdoses and hepatitis. Rehabilitation would be facilitated. Lt. Carhart explains:

> In a work program the addict gets to meet his peers of yesteryear, preheroin. He talks about work problems, ball games, television. He knows he can get his shot whenever he needs it at the clinic. Much to his surprise, after a few weeks he even forgets that so many hours have passed and he did not feel the euphoric need for a pick-up. He solved his problems by engaging in problems and decisions that are made daily by all of us.

The principal argument used against proposals of this type is that they would make it too easy to get narcotics and, therefore, would encourage people to try them. This argument is based on the assumption that it is currently expensive or difficult to try drugs. It is not. Drugs are easy to obtain and the small amounts initially required to build up an addiction are not expensive. The large cost comes in supporting an addiction whose demand increases. In the system Lt. Carhart has proposed, one who wants to start on drugs will at least have to confront medical personnel who have a chance to try to discourage him or divert him to a less harmful alternative.

Whatever else is required to make a person want to try drugs, dissatisfaction with things as they are is necessary. To the extent that quality of life is improved and people have increased opportunities to realize their potentials in work, play, and school, the desire for a crutch or escape will decrease. We are unlikely ever to remove the need for "external support" for all, but we can keep this need from turning into personal tragedies and a social crisis.

OLD AGE

There is an obvious need to give the aged a more active and useful role in society. Many have suggested that we try to increase interaction between the young and old for the benefit of both. One can cite Arabic nations, India, and China as ones in which such interactions are commonplace. Most of the examples that one could cite are economically underdeveloped countries. In affluent nations there is a significant reduction of such interactions. Thus the relationship between young-old interactions and the level of national economic development requires understanding.

The interactions between different age groups in less developed countries derives largely out of economic necessity. The family is usually the only source of social security, unemployment and old-age insurance. Hence the elderly are retained with the family because the only alternative is abandonment. The elderly also often care for children while the parents are working. On the other hand, in affluent societies retirement and old age are normally supported by accumulated savings and/or public and institutional funds. Thus affluence makes the separation of generations possible, but not necessarily desirable.

Affluence also changes the nature of homelife in other ways that affect the age problem. In less developed countries families do not change their places of residence often. It is commonplace for generation after generation to occupy the same house. This is rare in developed countries. In the United States the average time between moves of families is less than six years. The mobility of families and of members within families militates against multigeneration households. For these reasons living quarters, communities, and institutions have increasingly been designed to serve the needs and interests of the older generation, but most have been very ill conceived. *They segregate the elderly.* To be sure, older people enjoy each other's company but not to the exclusion of those of different ages. Our error has been in developing large isolated clusters of facilities for the aged rather than small clusters integrated into multiaged communities.

This reflects a more general sickness of our culture. As urban life has developed the city as a whole has become increasingly heterogeneous; it houses an increasing variety of socioeconomic types of people. But the city itself is divided into highly stratified and homogeneous neighborhoods built around a few socioeconomic characteristics. This is most conspicuously reflected in the homogeneity of the populations of elementary schools. Racial segregation is only one aspect of such homogeneity.

People in the cities tend to socialize with like people. The need, therefore, is for redistribution of urban population within the city to form more heterogeneous clusters (neighborhoods and blocks) not only with respect to age, but with respect to almost all socioeconomic characteristics. Each neighborhood should contain the same mix of people as the city as a whole does. This should be set as a goal toward which urban redevelopment is directed. Cities are currently developing in the opposite direction.

Some older people have, and create, a much greater problem than others. Much of the difference between them is due to the differences of their inner resources. Many develop interests, work, and hobbies during their younger years that they carry into old age and enjoy at that time. Many can be productive and occupied, if not more so, after retirement than before it. Thus there is a large educational aspect to the old-age problem. The more education a person receives when he is young the less of a problem he is likely to create when he is old. To be sure, it is not just the amount of education that is relevant, but its range and content are relevant as well. Education of the young should not be designed merely to provide a way of earning a living but also a way of living when earning is no longer necessary or possible.

We provide no education for the aged that enables them to enjoy their retirement more than they otherwise would. There is a pervasive feeling that such education is wasted because the elderly can no longer "contribute" to society. They can contribute a great deal, particularly to the young, if they have access to them. In Chapter 6, in the discussion of the generation gap, I suggested ways this might be done. Furthermore, the elderly have earned the right to enjoy some of the fruits of a society that they helped develop.

CONCLUSION

Throughout this chapter I have referred to the *health system*. It is not a system, certainly not an *organized* system. In fact, one might well argue that it is an antisystem; it is devoted to keeping health services independent of one another. For this reason the organization of health services into a system, almost any kind of system, may hold more hope for future improvement than any kind of improvement of the current anarchy.

Health will never cease to be a problem for man. As long as life lacks perfection and death is inevitable, health will be a concern. The nature of that concern will necessarily change as man changes his environment and what he does within it. Health maintenance systems must be capable of learning and adapting if man is to survive, and they must learn and adapt with increasing speed as the rate of social change accelerates. This can only be made possible with increased organization of the relevant services.

René Dubos has seen the future of man's health more realistically and expressed it more clearly than anyone else I know of:

> Among other things, it is man's dignity to value certain ideals above comfort, and even above life. This human trait makes of medicine a philosophy that goes beyond exact medical sciences, because it must encompass not only man as a living machine but also the collective aspirations of mankind. A perfect policy of public health could be conceived for colonies of social ants or bees whose habits have become stabilized by instincts. Likewise it would be possible to devise for a herd of cows an ideal system of husbandry with the proper combination of stables and pastures. But, unless men become robots, no formula can ever give them permanently the health and happiness symbolized by the contented cow, nor can their societies achieve a structure that will last for milennia. As long as mankind is made up of independent individuals with free will, there cannot be any social status quo. Men will develop new urges, and these will give rise to new problems, which will require ever new solutions. Human life implies adventure, and there is no adventure without struggles and dangers.

CHAPTER TEN

_____

SOLID WASTE
AND LITTER

... the two worlds of man—the biosphere of his
inheritance, the technosphere of his creation—are
out of balance, indeed, potentially, in deep conflict.
And man is in the middle. This is the hinge of his-
tory at which we stand, the door of the future
opening on to a crisis more sudden, more global,
more inescapable and more bewildering than any
ever encountered by the human species and one
which will take decisive shape within the life
span of children who are already born.

BARBARA WARD AND RENÉ DUBOS

Our environment consists of everything outside ourselves that either affects us
or is affected by us. More and more of that environment is man-made but this
does not reduce the importance of the natural part of it. Nature supplies the
materials necessary to sustain life and to create man-made environments. The
natural and artificial aspects of our environment interact strongly. The ability
of either to survive depends on what happens to the other but—as Barbara
Ward, Schweitzer Professor of International Economic Development at
Columbia University, and René Dubos, Rockefeller University's eminent
authority on health, noted in their report to the United Nations Conference
on the Human Environment—these two aspects of our environment are
seriously out of balance and, potentially, in deep conflict.

There is a wide variety of assessments of how serious our current environmental situation is, but there is widespread agreement that it is at a crisis stage. Increasing evidence suggests the existence of a point beyond which further degradation of our natural environment is not reversible. There is little agreement, however, on what should be done to reverse deterioration of the environment, who should do it, and how it should be financed. As a result, the environment has become a major political issue. Pressures from environmentalists are forcing political decisions that are often based on inadequate knowledge and understanding of the natural and social forces involved. Therefore, much less is being accomplished than is being done. Piecemeal solutions to the environmental problem are not likely to succeed because of the large number and complexity of interactions between different aspects of the environment and man's behavior in it. Hence comprehensive, coordinated, and integrated planning, not isolated problem solving, is required if we are to bring about significant environmental improvements.

Failure to take complex interactions into account is not a sin exclusively committed by the common man or his political representatives. It has also been committed with embarrassing frequency by scientists who are expected to know better. They too are inclined to look only at immediate effects and not consider later consequences. This was the case, for example, in scientific evaluations of DDT which demonstrated its effectiveness against the insects that were its target. But its effects on other forms of life were not adequately studied before it received science's *imprimatur*. This failure of science to think systemically of such matters is the subject of Barry Commoner's attack on it in his book, *Science and Survival*.

Concerns with the natural environment are of three interacting types. First, there is concern with its ability to support life by providing the air, land, and water required by it. Second, there is concern with Nature's ability to provide the materials and energy that man desires. Third, there is concern with the ability of our environment to please our senses, not to offend them with ugliness, noise, and stench. My concern in this chapter is primarily with the life-support aspects of the natural environment, but it will become apparent that this concern cannot be kept separate from the others. For example, how we reuse or dispose of products and their by-products has a considerable effect on Nature's supply of resources and its aesthetic properties.

Until recently man took the natural environment for granted. He believed it was capable of adapting to whatever he did within and to it. He assumed it would renew itself rapidly enough to support whatever human life emerged in it. But within the last twenty-five years we have come to realize that we can overload parts of the natural environment to a point beyond which they cannot recuperate their life-supporting capabilities without the active intervention of man. That is, we have come to realize that man must support his environment if he wants it to continue to support him. The "death" of

Lake Erie and London's lethal smog of 1952 are notorious products of man's indifference to Nature. London's smog was subsequently reduced by the systematic intervention of man; Lake Erie has yet to be brought back to life.

To *pollute* air, land, or water is to reduce their life-supporting capabilities. Pollution of any one of these is connected to pollution of each of the others. For example, incineration of solid waste to avoid land pollution may pollute the air, and runoff and seepage from open dumping of solid waste on land may pollute water.

I am going to focus on the solid-waste problem for several reasons. First, my objective is to show how measures to improve the environment should be designed, and the principles involved are the same whatever kind of pollution we consider. Second, by dealing with a specific problem area I can show the need to consider many broad aspects of man's environment—natural and man-made—and his behavior in them. The third reason lies in the magnitude of the problem and its urgency. For example, a report on New York city that appeared in *Metropolis* noted: "The disposal of solid waste is probably the most important problem facing the city. The city generates nearly 25,000 tons of solid waste daily, and the volume is increasing at an annual rate of over 4 percent. At the same time the means of disposal are dwindling."

According to Barbara Ward and René Dubos about fifty pounds of solid waste are generated per capita per day in the United States. Think of it: the weight of the waste each of us produces in a few days exceeds our own weight. No wonder Ward and Dubos observed that "all of modern man's metamorphoses—as industrial worker, as city dweller, as recreation seeker, as farmer—leave behind, like the slime of a moving snail, a thickening trail of solid waste."

I will concentrate on household-generated solid waste because the problems associated with it are easiest for most of us to understand, and I will focus on beverage containers because they have been the principal target of most proposed and actual legislation and voluntary programs. The problems centered around these containers invite simpleminded solutions many of which have been tried and failed because systemic interrelationships have been ignored. The beverage-container problem cannot be abstracted from other environmental problems and solved effectively in isolation.

Soft drink and beer containers—cans or bottles—have attracted a great deal of attention because they are a very conspicuous part of a very conspicuous problem, litter. Unlike paper, which makes up a larger part of litter, bottles and cans do not degrade and disappear over time. They "stay there" almost indefinitely unless removed by man.

Containers that contribute to litter also contribute to solid waste. (Litter is improperly disposed of solid waste.) Solid-waste disposal is a more serious but less conspicuous problem than litter. Hence beverage containers are a principal target of antilitter, as well as solid-waste, legislation and programs.

Attempts to deal with solid waste and litter can be classified into the reactive, preactive, and interactive. Consider each of these in turn.

REACTIVE PROGRAMS AND ANTIPROGRAMS

Activities relevant to the environment are divisible into those that are proposed by the environmentalist and those proposed by the antienvironmentalist—those who intend to minimize the effects of environmentalists' actions on them. The principal objective of the antienvironmentalist is to get the environmentalist "off his back." He opposes any program for environmental improvement that significantly affects his behavior or for which he must bear part of the cost. He supports only those solutions that do not affect him. Antienvironmentalists are not so much opposed to environmental improvement as they are to having to pay for or do anything about it. They are inactivists who act only to remove the need for greater activity.

Because of the behavior of the antienvironmentalist the environmentalist often acts as though his principal objective were to punish the antienvironmentalist rather than to improve the environment. The environment sometimes gets lost in the scuffle.

Antienvironmental industrial associations have a policy of combatting any legislation or program that can affect their current ways of doing business. Such associations carry out extensive and intensive lobbying to maintain the current state of affairs. What research they do is directed at revealing the inadequacies of proposals made by environmentalists.

Both the reactive environmentalist and the antienvironmentalist look for somebody or something to blame for the state they are trying to change. Once they can focus blame on someone or something they advocate restrictive or repressive measures which are intended to prevent the problem-producing behavior and to permit a return to a previously acceptable state.

The reactivist's concept of blame and correction is based on notions of cause and effect that come out of the Machine Age. He fails to understand that in systems no part is ever exclusively to blame for a system's failure. Such failure is always a consequence of the interaction of parts, not the behavior of one part taken alone. Obviously a part of a system may fail but its failure is the effect of other parts on it. If a system fails because of the failure of any one of its parts then the system was incapable of adapting to the failure of that part. Such failure to adapt is a systemic deficiency.

For example, the reactive environmentalist's response to litter may be directed exclusively at the litterer on whom he places full blame for the problem. He supports laws that impose fines and other forms of punishment on the litterer. Antilittering laws and fines have failed to reduce litter significantly for many reasons including the great difficulty and costliness of enforcing them, the lack of receptacles for litter, and failure to adequately service those receptacles that are available. Antilittering laws must be conceived in more systemic terms if they are to be effective.

When a corrective measure fails, the reactivist looks for someone or something to blame for the failure and tries to take further corrective action against him or it. He tends to blame the most obvious participants in the problem. If someone makes an effort to solve the problem and fails, he is likely to be blamed by reactivists for not having tried hard enough or for not having been sincere. For example, several major soft-drink manufacturers voluntarily increased the deposit required on their soft-drink containers in New York City from nothing to 2¢ for one-way containers and from 2¢ to 5¢ for returnable containers. When this measure failed to significantly increase the number of containers returned, reactive public officials and environmentalists either blamed the manufacturers for not having tried hard enough or concluded that the deposits were not high enough. In this as in many other cases of failure no understanding was gained by any of the parties involved. As a result, the next measure proposed has no better chance of succeeding than did the last because the last was not designed as a learning experience. Provisions are seldom made beforehand to assure understanding of success or failure. Therefore, all that such trials contribute are some additional unexplained facts and hard feelings. These are added to an already undigestible accumulation of both.

The reactive environmentalist concerned with solid waste and litter begins by looking for a conspicuous culprit and a way to repress or punish him. The most conspicuous candidate is the beverage manufacturer who packages his products in one-way (nonreturnable and nonreusable) containers made of glass, steel, or aluminum. The reactivist then seeks to return to a previously acceptable state by banning one-way containers; for example, S. 1377, a bill introduced to the United States Senate by Mr. Mathias on March 24, 1971. Consider the effects that such a bill might have if it were to be passed.

A Ban on One-Way Beverage Containers

Beverage containers contribute about 3.5 percent of the weight of domestically produced solid waste. Since the amount of such solid waste is increasing by about 4 percent per year, the total contribution of beverage containers to it is less than the current increase per year. Even for the 10 percent of domestically generated solid waste that currently passes through incinerators, beverage containers make up at most 20 percent of the incinerated residues and, moreover, at this point 85 percent of the costs of collection and disposal have already been incurred. Furthermore, the maximum possible reduction of 3.5 percent cannot be obtained because, in large cities where the solid-waste problem is most acute, returnable bottles used away from the place of purchase average only about five trips and are about 50 percent heavier than one-way bottles and from five to fifteen times heavier than cans, depending on the material of which they are made. Hence the maximum reduction that can be obtained is considerably less than the maximum possible. *If returnable bottles were used exclusively, and sales were unaffected, the weight of the contribution to solid waste of beverage containers could increase.* This follows from the fact that the weight of a returnable container divided by the average number of trips it makes is close to the average weight of the nonreturnable container sold for off-premise use. Unless the rate of return of returnable bottles is increased, a ban on nonreturnable bottles and cans cannot assure a reduction of solid waste.

Those environmentalists who support a ban on all but returnable containers cite return rates of fifteen per container. But they fail to distinguish between return rates of retail establishments such as restaurants and bars, and of individuals who consume the beverage at other than the place of purchase. Most returnable containers are used where purchased and are returned much more frequently by the seller than are those used at home by the individual consumer. The return rate of reusable containers taken off premise is likely to drop below five if nonreturnable containers are banned because many who now are willing to pay more for the convenience of one-way containers would be forced to use reusable containers. They cannot be expected to return them as frequently as do those who voluntarily buy them now.

Many have argued that increased deposits on reusable bottles would increase the rate of their return. As previously noted, this was tried in New York City with no success. Obviously, if deposits were made "high enough" return rates would increase. In fact, if they were made "high enough" no beverages would be sold and there would be no beverage container problem. Previous trials indicate that a deposit high enough to increase return rates significantly would have to be much higher than the cost of the bottle. If such deposits were required, counterfeiting of containers would become attractive and almost impossible to control. Furthermore, if such deposits were required in some areas but not in others, it would encourage smuggling of used containers from low-deposit areas into those requiring higher deposits. To prevent such smuggling, containers that are now uniform across the country would have to be made visibly distinguishable for each jurisdiction that had such a program. Doing so would significantly increase container, handling, and filling costs.

The elimination of one-way containers, with or without higher deposits for returnable containers, is very likely to reduce consumption of soft drinks and beer. Retailers and wholesalers would incur increased handling costs with returnable-bottles-only because they are heavier, larger, and require double handling. To cover these costs the price of beverages would have to be increased. Even more restrictive is the lack of the storage space and handling facilities that would be required in retail stores and distributors' warehouses. Furthermore, there are health hazards associated with storage of dirty containers. It would be very costly to rinse each container when it is returned. For these reasons a ban on one-way containers would be very likely to reduce the number of stores selling beverages and increase their prices. Therefore, beverage sales would be very likely to decrease.

Why be concerned with a reduction in sales of beer and soft drinks? Consider only beer and effects other than the obvious ones on jobs and the economy. In 1969, federal, state, and local revenues from excise, sales, and other taxes and licenses relating to the sale of beer amounted to $2.062 billion. A 3 percent reduction in these revenues would be slightly greater than the estimated cost of effectively and efficiently collecting and disposing of all beer containers. The elimination of one-way containers could easily reduce the sale of beer—not to mention soft drinks—by 3 percent or more. Therefore, a ban on one-way containers could reduce government income by an amount larger than that required to collect and dispose of them properly.

Several points have been made: (1) a ban on one-way containers would not solve the solid-waste problem or reduce it significantly even if it worked perfectly; (2) it is likely to produce an increase in the weight of beverage containers in the solid-waste stream; and (3) by reducing consumption of soft drinks and beer, it could easily result in reduction of revenues to governments in excess of the cost of effectively collecting and disposing of all solid waste generated by these beverages.

Now consider the effect of a ban on one-way containers on the litter problem. Beer containers account for about 15 percent of littered items and soft-drink containers for about 5 percent. Therefore, the greatest decrease in litter that could conceivably be obtained by a ban on one-way containers is 20 percent. But this assumes that no returnable containers are littered. They are, and they would continue to be because, for example, people who illegally consume beer in automobiles want to dispose of containers as rapidly as possible. Taking into account the percentage of returnables now found in litter one can only expect about a 12 percent reduction of litter if one-way containers were banned. This would be significant but would hardly solve the problem. Larger reductions can be obtained more easily. For example, recent experiments conducted by Dr. William C. Finnie at the University of Pennsylvania showed that a decrease in urban and roadside litter of from 25 to 50 percent can be obtained by proper location and servicing of litter receptacles. Furthermore, if one-way containers were banned, all littered containers would be glass. Therefore, the amount of broken glass in litter, particularly urban litter, would be likely to increase significantly.

Deposits on One-Way Containers

A less extreme reactive position than that which supports a ban of one-way containers is one that supports retaining such containers but requires a deposit on them. The deposit is returned to the consumer when he returns the used container to any retail establishment that sells beverages or, as more recently proposed, to a reclamation center.

Although such a program is less inconveniencing to the consumer than is a ban on one-way containers, it is more inconveniencing to retailers and wholesalers who must receive, segregate, and handle more types of containers. Such a program was recently initiated in the state of Oregon. It is too early to determine its effects on consumption levels and patterns, on litter, and on solid waste. One effect that appears to be clear is that the additional cost of handling a container is no less than 2¢. This is more than is required to collect such containers in household trash and to segregate them at a central point.

Voluntary Reclamation Programs

A still less reactive program involves voluntary collection of containers by individuals, returning them to reclamation centers, and usually, but not always, receipt of some payment for so doing. This requires no change in retailing beverages.

Reclamation programs for aluminum containers have attained the highest return rates because of the relatively high salvage value of such cans, about 1−2¢. The most successful such program has produced about a 25 percent return rate, but the average is less than 10 percent. Even if all such programs achieved the highest return rate yet realized solid waste would be reduced by less than 1 percent. Furthermore, there is no evidence to indicate that such programs significantly reduce litter or the rate of littering.

If the salvage value of containers were increased to make their return more likely, scavenging of trash cans would be invited. This could produce more litter than such programs can eliminate. It is estimated that about 50 percent of urban litter is currently produced by trash-collection procedures.

Voluntary reclamation programs give the ordinary citizen a chance to do something for his environment that appears to be constructive. But such programs are very difficult to sustain over extended periods of time. Furthermore, as Iraj Zandi, Professor of Engineering at the University of Pennsylvania, has shown in his analysis of such programs in eleven western states, these programs involved about 1,100,000 extra miles of car travel. "How much these trips have contributed to air pollution, highway maintenance expenses and accidents is a story untold." In addition, Dr. Zandi has shown that these programs produced a return of only about one-twentieth of 1 percent of the aluminum produced in the United States in one year.

In his analysis of glass bottle reclamation programs Dr. Zandi has shown that even with a 30 percent increase in recovery rates over the highest yet attained, less than 1 percent would be recovered and municipal solid waste would be reduced by eight one-hundredths of 1 percent. "In addition, it may be asked in passing why we are so preoccupied with glass. Glass is chemically inert, composed of materials most abundant in nature and is compatible with almost all disposal methods. When sanitary landfill is practiced it is one of the most ideal materials."

Summarizing, none of the reactive programs offer any chance of significantly reducing solid waste and some threaten to increase it. They could yield significant reductions in litter but would fall far short of making it a negligible problem. Nevertheless, some of these programs could be very costly to the public, not to mention being an inconvenience.

PREACTIVE PROGRAMS

Preactivists are not preoccupied with looking for someone or something to blame for environmental problems. In general they seek solutions to these problems that involve adding something to existing systems rather than taking something away, as the reactivist is inclined to do. What preactivists seek to add is usually new technology that facilitates extraction and reuse of materials in solid waste. They concentrate on new technology that can convert collection, separation, and recycling of solid waste into an economically self-supporting activity.

There are few communities in the United States whose solid-waste collection and disposal system cannot be significantly improved by use of already available technology. Most communities, however, are unable to finance such improvement. Therefore, one can either seek new ways of financing available improvements or develop new technology that will pay for itself or make a profit, thus attracting public or private investment. The preactivist prefers the latter alternative. The prospect of an improved and self-supporting or profitable solid-waste system is very attractive not only to environmentalists but also to antienvironmentalists who are the principal targets of much of the repressive and punitive solid-waste and antilitter legislation that has been proposed.

The beverage, container, and related industries and businesses have jointly formed the National Center for Resource Recovery in Washington, D.C., for the purpose of accelerating the development of such technology and disseminating information about it. Such purely technological solutions to the solid-waste and litter problems as this Center seeks would have an obvious advantage to the beverage and related industries: it appears to require little or no change in any of their activities. It would require increased use of recycled materials but this would not involve any great inconvenience to container manufacturers or users.

A purely technological solution is attractive to the preactivist because it appears to require no significant change in anyone's behavior and it might be self-financing. Dr. Richard L. Lesher, president of the National Center for Resource Recovery, is a major supporter of the search for such solutions. *Nation's Cities* reports him as having said:

> "The refuse will be shredded for size reduction, classified into organic and inorganic fractions, with the inorganics being further separated into ferrous, non-ferrous metals, and glass. We will also do some hand-sorting of paper products. These components will then be sold to respective industries for recycling."
>
> Dr. Lesher noted that the organic residue from this process can be land-filled or incinerated, although emerging systems will be able to utilize this fraction as a fuel in power plant boilers, fluidized bed incinerators, and pyrolysis plants for energy recovery. Fiber reclaiming systems, composting, and high protein animal feed are other options for using the organic portion of garbage and trash.

Currently, there is not a large market for materials recovered in such ways as Dr. Lesher describes. The lack of market derives from either the fact that recycled materials are generally more expensive than are virgin materials or the fact that a large investment is required to convert production processes so that they can use recycled materials. These financial factors create a more serious deterrent to a purely technological solution than does the lack of suitable technology. Many reclamation programs that have been in effect over the past few years have had difficulty in selling the materials they have recovered. Unless a market is created for them, new technology will be of little use. Creation of such a market requires a great deal more than technology.

Furthermore, we do not know how long it will be before such technology is available. We do know the solid-waste problem is becoming more serious while we wait, and that better technology than is in general use is already available and not being used because the money required to purchase it is not available. Furthermore, as we shall see, even current technology could be made profitable *now* by appropriate governmental action. But even if such action were taken there is no assurance that the required investment in new systems would be made by local governments or private enterprise. The capital requirements would be large. Finally, we can hardly be as hopeful for a purely technological solution to the litter problem as we can be for that of solid waste.

The interactivist will take all that technology can provide, but he does not believe that this will be sufficient to solve either the solid-waste or litter problems.

INTERACTIVE PROGRAMS

The interactivist does not seek solutions (in the ordinary sense) to the solid-waste and litter problems. He perceives that the relevant conditions vary significantly from community to community and each one changes in different ways and at different rates over time. Hence he seeks to develop environmental-improvement systems that are capable of learning and adapting to the varied conditions under which they will have to operate and to the changing conditions they will bring about. For this reason the interactivist requires the following minimal steps in any proposed program:

1. The conditions to be improved should be specified and measured before the proposed program is implemented.

2. The intended effects (expressed in measurable quantities) and the times by which they are expected (the "due dates") should be specified before implementation of the program.

3. Determination of the effects produced should be made at the due dates and be compared with the intended effects. (Interim measurements of progress should also be made to aid in the system's management.)

4. The due-date measurements should be disseminated to facilitate public discussion and decision of whether to continue, modify, or terminate the program. Discontinuation (not continuation) of the program should be automatic unless there is a positive intervention by the legislative or decision-making body that initiated the program.

Specification of the intended effects of a solid-waste program requires an explicit formulation of program objectives. According to the interactivist these should be:

1.   To minimize the amount of solid waste generated per unit time.

2.   To minimize the cost and maximize the effectiveness of collection, treatment, and disposal of solid waste.

3.   To maximize the percentage of solid waste that can be and is separated and reused in an economically justified way.

4.   To minimize the negative impact of solid-waste disposal on all environmental systems.

These objectives should apply to *all* solid wastes, not only to beverage containers which, as previously noted, account for less than 4 percent of such waste. Programs intended to accomplish these objectives should provide every participant in the solid-waste system with incentives to act in ways that promote attainment of these objectives. Unless the cost of proper collection, treatment, and disposal of materials is made explicit to all parties involved, an effective system of incentives cannot be developed. Public and special interest groups should be made as aware of these costs as they are of the costs of production, distribution, and marketing of goods. *This can only be accomplished by imposing fair and explicit charges for disposal of all manufactured nonconsumable materials whose disposal involves a cost to society.*

In the past the direct costs of disposal of solid waste and the indirect social costs associated with the disposal system have not been taken into account explicitly. These costs should be conspicuously included in the costs of products and services because only by so doing will there be an incentive to suppliers and users of goods and services to modify them so as to reduce the direct and indirect costs of their disposal. This suggests a disposal tax.

The cost of solid-waste disposal can be greatly reduced if materials extracted from it can be recycled and reused economically. Industry should be encouraged to develop production processes with greater capabilities of using recycled materials and doing so at lower costs than it can currently. This can be done in several ways:

1.   The current cost to industry of virgin raw materials and their processing depends greatly on transportation costs, depletion allowances, depreciation rates on processing equipment, and taxes—all of which are controlled by the government. These can and should be adjusted so as to make the use of recycled materials more attractive to industry where the raw material involved is in limited supply or its acquisition or processing produces damage to the environment. For example, freight rates for salvaged materials—now higher than for virgin materials—should be reduced. This would increase their use and might benefit freight transporters. Or, to take another

example, the federal government could permit accelerated depreciation of equipment used to recycle or use recycled materials. Such manipulation of costs to industry should be accomplished in such a way as to reflect better the social costs of environmental damage produced by current practices.

2.   Government, if not private, organizations should require use of recycled materials in the goods they buy. The amount required should not impose an economic burden on the supplier but it should change as the economics of recycling and using recycled materials changes. Such a practice would encourage industry to develop more effective ways of recycling materials and of using them.

The technological properties of a solution to the municipal household-generated solid-waste problem are widely recognized. These involve centralized collection, separation, treatment, and disposal. Such a system provides easily demonstrated economies of scale.

As previously noted, current practices generally fall short of our capabilities. Collection can be improved by use of better trucks. The use of heavy-duty or disposable-plastic trash bags instead of metal trash cans provides substantial reduction in the direct costs of collection and in the costs produced by litter from spillage and injuries to workers; and it provides better protection against pests and vermin.

The techniques of waste processing include incineration, shredding, milling, compaction, sanitary landfill, and a variety of lesser known processes. Improvement of these techniques could be accelerated by enlarging the potential market for them. Furthermore, with increased demand for these technologies, their costs could be greatly reduced.

Many salvageable materials can now be mechanically separated from other solid wastes and thus be made available for recycling. Modern incinerators maximize reduction of solid waste, minimize pollution of the atmosphere, and can be used to generate power or heat. Sanitary landfill of compacted incinerator residues, as opposed to open dumping of trash, minimizes pollution of land and water and can create usable and attractive land where it did not previously exist.

But, as already noted, most communities cannot afford the available technology that can improve their systems. Therefore, the key to improving these systems lies in financing them. But they should be financed in a way that provides the incentives required to improve the behavior of every type of participant in the system, and in a way that makes the system learn and adapt.

Now let us consider how this might be done.

Developing, Financing, and Administering Improvement Programs

The details of the procedure described here are not as important as its general characteristics. These are applicable to programs for improving any aspect of the environment.

The procedure involves ten steps:

> 1. *Minimal national standards for solid-waste disposal and resource recovery should be set by the United States Environmental Protection Agency.*

Because such standards are predominantly technical and ecological, there is no need to take account of local conditions in formulating them.

> 2. *The state or federal government should solicit from every community, development programs that are designed to meet or exceed federal standards. These should be accompanied by capital budgets. The state or federal government should develop such additional programs of its own as are required to support local programs, and a budget for them.*

The state or federal government should maintain a body of public or private consultants who can assist communities in preparing program proposals.

The budgets should cover only capital improvements and program-produced increases in per capita operating costs. Full coverage of operating costs is not desirable because it would remove any incentive to the community for reducing them as, for example, by cooperation with other communities in development of regional facilities.

> 3. *A state or federal commission on solid-waste disposal should evaluate and adjust these proposals.*

This evaluation should provide objective professional screening of all plans for engineering and fiscal soundness. Programs with excessively high capital or operating costs should be rejected. Where these high costs are due to small scale of operations, consolidation of facilities on a regional basis should be required.

Capital improvement programs should not run for more than six years without being reconsidered by the commission. This would allow sufficient time for construction and operation of the new systems so that they can be evaluated before additional capital improvements are approved.

> 4. *The state or federal government should determine the total annual costs for all approved programs over the six-year*

period. It should add about 10 percent for surveys, administration, research, and growth in tax credits for recycling (see step 8). *It should then determine the total overheaded cost* (T) *for each of the three consecutive two-year periods in the six-year period.*

This gives the amount to be raised each year by a solid-waste tax. Receipts from this tax (described below) should not be used for any purpose other than solid-waste programs.

Purchase and use of materials obtained from municipal salvaging operations should be encouraged by a tax credit such as is specified below. Because the amount to be paid out in tax credits cannot be predicted accurately in advance, a buffer must be included for this and other uncertainties.

> 5. *The total tax to be obtained from each product category* (t) *should be set equal to the total amount to be raised that year* (T) *multiplied by the fraction of the total weight of solid waste handled publicly in the state in the last year that was contributed by that category.*

Product categories could be beverage containers, newspapers, magazines, bags, cartons, tires, refrigerators, and so on. The categories should be formed so as to be able to tax products in them at the point from which they are sent to the market.

About 25 percent of solid waste consists of garbage, dirt, grass, and stones. Their weight should not be included in the total weight of solid waste used in the calculations specified in step 5.

Weight is used as the key measure because it is the basis for all current charging schemes in solid-waste disposal, and it is an easily measured product characteristic which is already determined for every product at some point of its life. Weight, of course, is not the only property that affects collectibility and disposability. It is not possible, however, to take all other relevant properties into account because, for example, a product's ease of handling depends on the kind of equipment used, its age, and how well it is used. Moreover, the use of more sophisticated indices of collectibility and disposability would probably cost more than the benefits derived from doing so justify.

> 6. (a) *The tax for units in most product categories should be obtained by multiplying* t *for that category by the ratio of the unit's weight to the total weight of its category in the publicly handled solid waste in the state or nation in the last year.* (b) *The unit tax for rigid containers* (including beer and soft drink containers) *should be obtained by dividing* t

*for this category by the estimated number of containers in
the publicly handled solid waste in the state or nation in the
last year. (c) Units whose materials create special problems
in handling or recycling should have their tax appropriately
increased.*

Tax rates for each product category should be based on a survey of the
composition of publicly handled solid waste in the state or nation in the last
year. The survey should be carried out by a private research organization
which has no stake in the results. Note that use of such a base in computing
the tax rate takes into account all materials diverted by households to
voluntary reclamation programs or to other uses. Thus it provides an incentive
for such programs.

Since the product categories used in the survey would have to be fairly
broad, any reduction in solid waste due to what one company did would
provide equal tax reductions to all producers of items in its product class.
Since the company would have borne the cost of the reduction, its net benefit
would be smaller than that of every other company so affected. This would
encourage companies in the same industry to act collectively rather than
individually, which is what is needed to maximize reduction of the amount of
solid waste generated.

Rigid packaging (metal, glass, rigid plastic, and perhaps containerboard)
requires special treatment. As previously noted, if this category were taxed by
weight it would encourage use of lighter materials such as aluminum. If, for
example, the proposed penny-per-pound tax for all nonconsumables that enter
the solid-waste stream within ten years after production—U.S. Senate Bill S.
3058—were enacted, the tax on a twelve-ounce aluminum can would be
0.044¢; on a steel can with an aluminum top, 0.088¢; on a one-way glass
bottle, 0.44¢; and on a returnable glass bottle, 0.65¢. This would clearly
encourage use of one-way aluminum cans. Such cans produce the worst litter
problem because they degrade least over time. They also require much more
electricity in their production than do the alternatives. Production of
electricity is a major source of air pollution and a critical shortage of capacity
for producing it seems to be developing.

A *unit* tax such as is proposed here would encourage use of larger
containers, hence would reduce the amount of material used in containers.

Some materials or products present special problems in separation, disposal,
or collection. Certain types of plastic container—for example, those made of
polyvinyl chlorides—are a case in point because of their air-polluting
characteristics when incinerated. Aerosol containers explode when heated and
thus can damage incinerators. Containers made of more than one material are
difficult to recycle. Taxes for such products should be adjusted to take
relevant characteristics into account.

7. *Reused containers and resold products should not be taxed again.*

This encourages reuse and longer use of products, and it would provide an additional incentive for use of returnable containers.

8. *Credits against the tax should be given to companies that accept and use materials salvaged by publicly funded reclamation facilities.*

The credit should be equal to the net profit to the community of selling separated material as compared with the alternative of not separating it but disposing of it in a sanitary way. Thus the savings to the community of not disposing of a material would be passed on to those who purchase that material for reuse.

9. *The survey of solid waste and estimates of costs should be recomputed at least every two years.*

This should be done annually if time and cost permit. Doing so is necessary to assure responsiveness of the incentives to constructive and destructive actions of industry and business. It is also essential for keeping public programs within budget and on schedule.

10. *The state or federal commission on solid waste disposal or some other unit of which it is a part should evaluate each community's program and progress annually, and discontinue support of those that do not meet federal standards or are otherwise being mismanaged.*

The type of program described by the preceding ten steps has a number of advantages. It encourages use of larger packages and reduction of secondary packaging. In general, it encourages use of less material, lighter material, and design of products with longer life. It encourages manufacturers to use recycled materials. It encourages communities to develop common facilities with economies of scale and it encourages the efficient operation of all facilities. It affects all contributors to the solid-waste problem and takes the spotlight off any alleged culprit. It distributes costs fairly over all involved. Finally, it requires no change in manufacturing, distribution, or consumer behavior but it charges for such behavior when it creates social costs.

Antilitter and other types of environmental-improvement legislation can be designed to have the same characteristics as this solid-waste program has. Such an antilitter program is described in detail in a report of the Management and Behavioral Science Center of the University of Pennsylvania. It differs from the solid-waste legislation proposed here only in details. For example, the tax is based on the proportion of the *number*, not weight, of items in a category found in litter because the cost of removing litter depends more on the number of items involved than on their weight.

The solid-waste tax described here would initially amount to about 0.25¢ per beverage container and the corresponding litter tax would be about 0.75¢ per container. A combined tax of 1¢ per container would not have a significant impact on beverage sales. Furthermore, this tax would be reduced as it accomplishes what it is intended to.

BEYOND SOLID WASTE

Solid waste creates only a part of the environmental problem, but the principles involved in the approach taken to it here are applicable to most other aspects of the problem. Two basic principles are involved in this approach:

1.   The cost of preventing or correcting damage to the environment, or of damage that cannot be corrected, should be added explicity and conspicuously to the cost of goods, services, and activities that produce such damage.

2.   Positive incentives should be provided to encourage individuals and organizations to seek environmentally constructive actions.

The first principle—imposing charges as a disincentive—is based on the observation that people try to avoid a conspicuous and avoidable cost. Therefore, if the environmental costs are reestimated frequently enough to enable charges to be adjusted so as to reflect responses to them, such changes will act as an incentive to search for environmentally less damaging ways of doing things. In a report of a study, *Environmental Quality and New York City*, prepared by the First National City Bank, *Metropolis* cited the following conclusion: "... the principal task of contamination control [is] to assure that waste disposal costs revert back to the polluter. Through effluent charges or taxes on waste, market forces would be brought to bear which would be highly effective as controls." The funds collected from such charges or taxes should be used exclusively for preventing or correcting damage to the environment.

This charging principle is equally applicable to all types of waste. Discharges of pollutants into water should be charged for as they are on the Rhine. According to Robert O. Saunders, a consultant for Arthur D. Little, Inc.:

> The [Rhine River] tax is administered under a user charge
> system, in which corporations receive levies based on their
> treatment and control of pollution. There is also an estimate

of the benefits accruing to the firm from the use of local resources. Thus, an industry such as chemicals, which draws heavily from the Rhine for its manufacturing process, is taxed more heavily than a similar plant in an industry which uses little water in its production.

A similar tax was put into effect in Vermont on July 1, 1971. All dischargers of wastes into rivers and lakes of Vermont are now required to hold permits and to pay taxes if their wastes degrade state waters below certain standards. Saunders, whose firm advised Vermont in developing and evaluating the new tax, commented: ". . . to be a true incentive, the tax had to be structured to reward those polluters who began to make plans for improvement. Accordingly, a sliding scale was developed so fees decreased as improvements are made. . . "

The charge per unit of pollutant discharged should be uniform across the nation to avoid giving some companies competitive advantages over others because the waters into which they discharge pollutants are not as badly contaminated by others.

Some polluting discharges into some bodies of water and most discharges into the air are difficult, if not impossible, to correct. Therefore, measures other than correction may be required. First, limits to, or prohibition of, some discharges can and should be imposed by law. Where the law is broken either accidentally or deliberately a fine should be levied which is equal to an estimate of the social cost involved. Second, even discharges below or within the legal limits should be charged for proportionally to the amount discharged. This would increase awareness of the limited capability of the environment to absorb man-made discharges into it.

Social costs of pollution are not easy to measure but reasonable estimates can be made. For example, the United States Council for Environmental Quality has estimated the damage due to every form of quantifiable air-produced dirt. The estimate was based on a study of eighty-five cities. According to Ward and Dubos the study showed "a fairly clear relationship between faded paint, anemic shrubberies, bad smells and dirty walls on the one hand and, on the other, the price a purchaser was prepared to pay either to buy or rent a house. The dirtier the air, the cheaper the building." The estimated damage to the natural and man-made environments was $4.9 billion per year.

The tax rebate for use of recycled materials in the solid-waste proposal made above is an example of a positive incentive and thus incorporates the second principle of design cited above. I also suggested tax inducements and accelerated depreciation for pollution-reducing equipment and processes. As Robert O. Saunders observed:

> Using the tax system as a means of focusing the economic activity of a capitalistic system is hardly a new idea. It is a well-tested way of using individuals, resources and capital to achieve desired ends. It is a classic means of "reordering priorities" in a capitalistic society. . .
>
> Our experience with the use of tax incentives over many decades shows that their skillful use can turn difficult social problems into greater opportunities. In the tax incentive concept, we have a means to redirect the system, guide its power, and use its efficiency to solve problems—not at a cost but, if you will, a handsome profit.

Note that the conversion of a problem into an opportunity is a characteristic of the interactive approach to messes. The reactive solution to environmental problems consists largely of taking certain things and behavior out of the environment. Preactive solutions consist of adding new things, usually technology, to the environment. The interactivist is willing to do either but he bases his approach on the creation of positive and negative incentives that will lead to the dissolution of the problem.

CONCLUSION

I have tried to show how a major social problem can be attacked through legislation that makes an adaptive learning system of society and whose principal function is to provide incentives that bring individual and social interests in line with each other. The program is designed so that its effects change as needs change. Furthermore, the proposed legislation is also intended as an instrument of social education, one that will facilitate learning by the public about those aspects of ecology that are involved in solid waste.

Put another way, the law proposed here is intended to provide controls in a social experiment. The controls derive from measurement and evaluation of effects and adjustments of incentives. The law does not constrain, restrict, or prohibit; it tries to *induce* all parties involved into acting in their own, and society's best interests.

CHAPTER ELEVEN

TRANSPORTATION
AND THE CITY

*Without established long-range transportation/
land-use planning goals, we are forced, by default,
into following reactionary transportation planning
policies—the functional problem will not wait.
Resolution of the immediate problems could
take several forms, but unless we know what we
want for the future, we cannot make a responsible choice of methods.*

TABOR R. STONE

One hardly needs to argue that there is a major transportation problem in
most large cities of the United States and other countries as well. *Life*
dramatized this fact:

> ... traffic problems in their [European] cities have become as
> bad or worse than America's. Rome has just about given up
> organized effort to regulate parking and keep traffic moving.
> Even the English aren't polite about traffic anymore. And
> recently a man who had lost an argument over a parking
> space was admitted to a Paris hospital with hatchet wounds
> of the head and shoulders.

Congestion on city streets and expressways has increased both average trip
time and variations around the average. It has also made such trips less

enjoyable and more dangerous. Parking space has become more difficult to find and more costly to acquire when found. To top it off, air pollution produced by automobiles is rapidly becoming a threat to survival in many cities. Automobiles contribute up to 70 percent of the nation's air pollution and are responsible for a 3000 percent increase in the urban noise level since 1939.

Public transportation has deteriorated continuously in the United States for at least two decades. It received only 10 percent of the funds spent on urban transportation in 1967. Between 1940 and 1966 the number of paying passengers decreased by 36.5 percent and the number of public vehicle miles decreased by 23.6 percent. Between 1954 and 1961, 159 transit companies were sold, 54 were abandoned but replaced, and 77 were abandoned without replacement.

By 1958 federally supported urban highways were operating at 90 percent of their practical capacity. Congestion has increased continuously since then. New expressways now reach virtual saturation on the peak hours of their opening days.

The prognosis for urban transportation is not very good. Francisco Sagasti and Russell L. Ackoff, in a study conducted at the University of Pennsylvania, showed that if population continues to grow as expected and use of automobiles is not constrained, then (very conservatively) there would be twice as many automobile miles traveled in 1980 as there were in 1960, and more than three and a half times as many by the year 2000. They also showed that maintenance of the 1960 level of congestion in the year 2000 would require 55,000 additional miles of four-lane urban highways. At the conservatively estimated cost of $10 million per mile, these highways would require an expenditure of $550 billion, or an average of $18.3 billion per year for each year between 1970 and 2000. This is more than ten times the amount spent on urban highways in 1967 ($1.4 billion). Such an increase cannot reasonably be expected.

Furthermore, Sagasti and Ackoff showed that if the $550 billion were spent it would replace one problem with another. In most cities the proportion of land in downtown areas devoted to streets, highways, and parking already exceeds 40 percent of the available land. As far back as 1956 it was 59 percent in Los Angeles, 50 percent in Detroit, and 48 percent in Minneapolis. The amount of taxable land is already considerably reduced. Conversion of more land for use in transportation would accelerate the impending bankruptcy of many major cities.

It would be possible, of course, to build multilevel roads and thus decrease the proportion of land used for transportation. But doing so would increase the already unfeasible dollar requirement by a very large amount.

One might argue that the projected increase in demand is too large for several reasons. First, there has been a considerable spread of population to the suburbs with associated development of shopping, recreational, industrial, and commercial centers outside the central-city areas. This movement is a consequence, in part, of the increased personal mobility provided by the automobile and the urban decay resulting from the exodus of the more affluent from the city proper. Present patterns of change in central cities are likely to remain essentially the same for many years and the trend toward leveling metropolitan population density is likely to continue. The central business districts of most cities are not generally expected to regain their earlier dominance. They are likely to continue their decline due to increasing competition from suburban facilities around which most of the affluent will be gathered.

These changes in metropolitan form may absorb some of the "unconstrained" growth in traffic volume. There may also be a wider dispersion of destinations over the metropolitan area and this could alleviate some traffic congestion. Travel may be distributed more evenly over the whole metropolitan area. But such changes in metropolitan areas cannot be expected to have a major effect on the urban transportation problem because they have been taking place over the past few decades without significantly reducing traffic congestion.

Some argue that new developments in communication technology—such as the picture phone, closed circuit television, and facsimile reproduction—will significantly reduce the demand for urban transportation. But this seems unlikely for several reasons. Lyle Fitch and Associates, prominent transportation consultants, point out one: ". . . there is no reason to believe that it [development of new technology] will make the journey-to-work unnecessary. . . and it is the journey-to-work which is at the center of our urban transportation problem today."

Introduction of the telephone did not decrease the demand for face-to-face interaction and transportation; it increased them. The ability to see distant and strange places on television, even in color, did not reduce the desire for travel; it increased it. The picture phone and other developments in communication are more likely to increase desire to be with others than decrease it. Furthermore, the picture phone is not likely to be as common as the telephone is today before the year 2000. Therefore, there is little reason to believe that "normal" changes in urban form or new developments in communication technology will reduce significantly the transportation problems that urban areas will have to face during the remainder of this century.

MACHINE AGE SOLUTIONS

There is no generally accepted solution to urban transportation problems. This is due, at least in part, to the fact that most, if not all, of the solutions that have been proposed are products of Machine Age thinking and reflect reactive or preactive postures toward the future.

Urban transportation does not present *a* problem but a complex of interacting problems, a mess. These require a system of solutions, hence planning. There has been a great deal of urban transportation planning, but little of it has been implemented, and most of what has been has not produced significant improvements.

The reactive transportation planner conceptualizes the system he plans for as a closed mechanical system in which people behave like atoms moving about in accordance with statistical laws. Because he views the system mechanistically he tends to blame its deficiencies on one or more defective parts. He looks for that aspect of the system that he believes causes the trouble and then tries to replace it, if this can be done easily; if not, he tries to repress it. He most commonly identifies the automobile as the cause of the trouble, hence he tries to replace or repress it.

For example, in Rome planners have banned the use of automobiles in a two-square-mile city-center area. To reinforce this ban, bus and streetcar fares have been eliminated during rush hours. In a report of these measures *The New York Times* observed: "The problem of financing the program still has not been solved by the city parliament. The free-ride experiment at the beginning of the year cost Rome more than half a million dollars in lost fares. This was another, if relatively small, addition to Rome's crushing debt burden..." The effect of this experiment on traffic in the rest of the city is not clear. What is clear is that Rome's transportation problems have not been solved.

Marseilles tried to prohibit parking in its downtown shopping district, to reserve five miles of street lanes for buses and taxis, and provided free bus rides. According to another report in *The New York Times*: "The city... considers the free bus service a dead loss and has no intention of repeating it. Observers concluded that the Marseilles experiment had clearly improved traffic in the no-parking district but had worsened the situation in surrounding areas, where motorists hunted new parking spaces, causing mammoth jams."

The New York City chapters of the New York State Society of Professional Engineers have proposed what is almost the ultimate repressive measure: that *all* motor vehicles be banned for eleven hours every workday between 34th and 59th Streets and between Third and Eighth Avenues, except emergency vehicles and those bearing essential supplies. It might be easier to keep people out of this area and let cars use it freely.

Mexico City has apparently succeeded where other cities, including New York, have failed; it has banned most trucks from city streets during the workday. Doing so has not produced free-flowing traffic but it has reduced congestion. At peak hours, however, the difference is not detectable by the naked eye.

Attempts to stagger the workday have been made unsuccessfully in a number of cities including Philadelphia and New York.

Both New York and London have considered charging for use of city streets by motor vehicles in order to discourage such use and to raise funds for improving public transportation. The costs of installing and operating the proposed systems, however, have been too high to justify them.

Note that all measures proposed by reactive planners try to eliminate or remove something from the system—to go back to a previous and less complex state. (Some have even suggested a return to bicycles.) They do not try to meet or eliminate demand, but to reduce or change it by repression.

In contrast, preactive planners try to add something to the transportation system to meet demand more effectively. They propose additional facilities to absorb predicted increases in traffic and travel. The additions often involve new technologies that are not infrequently treated as panaceas.

I have already argued that sufficient additional highways and streets cannot be provided to satisfy unconstrained demand, at least while other aspects of the system remain unchanged. Neither the money nor the space required to do so is available. Nevertheless, some cities continue to plan as though they were. For this reason a number of preactivists look for ways of expanding mass transit and of making it more acceptable to trip-takers. In a speech delivered in Boston on September 21, 1970 John Volpe, then Secretary of Transportation, said, "Public transportation, as I see it, is the great untapped resource for making the city conform to human needs. . . . Public transportation will be safe, clean, comfortable, stylish, and efficient."

Secretary Volpe overlooked important differences between public and private transportation. The differences involve privacy, convenience, comfort, time, and cost. Consider each of these in turn.

Privacy.

Many have observed that the automobile has a deep psychological significance to most of its users. For example, J. B. Jackson, editor of the journal, *Landscape*, wrote:

> . . . the automobile allows one to travel almost at will
> anywhere in the public domain while remaining in a

completely private world unequivocally defined by physical boundaries. The maintenance, defense or even definition of this intensely personal space no longer needs to be achieved by psychological adaptation or cultural understanding or ritual. It is marked off structurally—with clarity and solidity.

... the transportation problems of our urban regions are not going to be solved until we admit to an understanding of the very special spatial features of the automobile, for it is likely that the appeal of the automobile is not just a silly habit easily gotten rid of, but a means of fulfilling deeply rooted concepts of human territoriality.

Convenience.

This refers to the amount of physical effort expended in taking a trip. It is most affected by the amount of walking and waiting required, the number of vehicle changes, and the number of stairs that must be climbed. The automobile clearly has an advantage for most trips because it comes closest to providing door-to-door transport except in the relatively small number of cases in which parking near one's origin or destination is difficult. Most users of public transportation, however, must either walk considerable distances, use more than one vehicle, or wait in discomfort for one or more vehicles.

Comfort.

T. R. Stone, an architectural consultant to the Office of the U.S. Air Force Surgeon General, put the advantages of the automobile with respect to comfort very simply:

The automobile offers many amenities for personal comfort, limited only by one's ability to pay for them. These generally include adjustable seats, individual temperature controls, radio, etc. One can seal himself off from contact with the world outside the vehicle, and be entertained to boot. Significantly, each automobile rider has a seat: none is forced to stand up.

Time.

Although travel time on public modes other than buses and streetcars is sometimes less between points near transit stops than it is in an automobile, most trips on mass transit neither start nor stop near origins or destinations.

Door-to-door time for most automobile trips taken in most cities is less than it is for mass-transit trips.

Cost.

Actual cost-per-passenger-mile is generally lower on mass transit than in automobiles with no passengers, with driver only. But with several passengers the cost of the automobile per passenger is considerably reduced. The low cost of mass transit is partly due to the fact that most of it uses fully depreciated equipment, hence only maintenance and operating costs are taken into account. Even so, most public systems are heavily subsidized. The automobile is less costly than currently subsidized mass transit if one considers only the incremental costs of a trip, and most automobile owners do so.

A number of changes to mass transit have been proposed to make it more attractive. Consider some of the more important of these.

Buses now carry about 70 percent of all urban public transportation passengers. Most cities in the United States completely depend on them for public transportation. Improvements suggested for them range from operational improvements—such as assigning lanes or streets to them exclusively, gearing traffic controls to favor buses rather than automobiles, and using computers to assist in scheduling them—to changes in bus design; for example, reintroduction of doubledeck buses, extralong articulated buses (bus trains), and the establishment of dual mode bus systems capable of operating on both streets and rails.

However, unless these improved systems become the only means of urban transportation, they cannot be expected to have a large effect on traffic congestion. They are not likely to divert a large number of urban travelers from other modes because they will continue to be deficient with respect to—at least—privacy, convenience, and comfort.

Suggested improvements for mass rail transit follow the same patterns as those made for buses. Operational improvements include the use of automatic control systems, simplification of fare-collection procedures, and modifications in vehicle components such as automatic couplers, brakes, and suspensions. Suggestions include improvements in vehicles and guideways. The two most developed examples of such improvements are Pittsburgh's Transit Expressway and San Francisco's Bay Area Rapid Transit System (BARTS).

The transit expressway consists of driverless, rubber-tired vehicles that operate over a concrete guideway at a maximum speed of fifty miles per hour. It uses lightweight cars that seat twenty-eight persons and provide standing room for twenty-six. It is capable of economically serving peak demands of 5000 to 16000 passengers per hour, one way. This system has been implemented as a demonstration project in South Park (Pittsburgh). Its 9000-feet-long track is likely to be extended once some design problems are overcome.

The BART system is basically a commuter rail system that incorporates several new technologies including automatic fare collection and controls. It is the only large-scale improvement of mass transit that is currently under way in the United States. It is intended to be a component of a large urban transportation system for the Bay Area. B. R. Stokes, General Manager of the Oakland BART District, described the system as follows:

> The system aims at a truly balanced transport pattern for the Bay Area: freeway to accommodate the normal flow of auto traffic and rapid rail transit to handle the bulk of the peak-hour commuter traffic. It will be a completely grade-separated system based on about 13 miles of downtown area subway construction, 31 miles of aerial structure, 4 miles of underwater tube, 24 miles of surface track and more than 3 miles of tunnel through the East Bay hills into the commuter pockets of Contra Costa County.

We have to wait for completion of this system to determine its effect on congestion. Some improvement is inevitable, but how much remains a question.

Some pin their hopes on less conventional mass-transit concepts, the most highly developed of which is the Dial-a-Bus or Demand-Activated Bus System proposed by the Stanford Research Institute. This is a hybrid system, somewhere between an ordinary bus and a taxi. It would pick up passengers at their doors or at a nearby bus stop shortly after they have telephoned for service. A computer would "know" the location of the vehicles in the system, how many passengers were on each, and where they were going. It would then select the right vehicle and dispatch it to the caller in accordance with some optimal routing program (yet to be developed). The Department of Housing and Urban Development pointed out that ". . . the Dial-a-Bus might do what no other transit system does: handle door-to-door travel demand at the time of demand. This means that the system would attract more off-peak business than does conventional transit."

Among the approximately twelve localities using such systems are Mansfield and Columbus, Ohio; Columbia, Maryland; Rochester, New York; and Ann Arbor, Michigan. After a year of operation in the last of these cities the system carries only 250 passengers per day and fares collected cover only about one-third of its cost. It is unlikely that this system will ever be able to offer trips of time and cost to the user that are competitive with the automobile or, if it could, that it would significantly reduce peak-hour congestion. The main benefits that might be obtained from it would derive from its provision of mass transit to low-density residential areas, particularly during off-peak hours.

There have been a number of preactive proposals relating to automobiles as well as to other modes of transportation. These include automatic control of traffic which is intended to permit an increase in speed and a reduction in the space between cars without jeopardizing safety. L. E. Flory of the Stanford Research Institute described one proposed development as follows:

> ... first, a stage of improved communication. . . to enable [the driver] to make decisions better and faster; second, a stage where some of the decisions are made for him and he is given warning if he is approaching a dangerous condition; and, third, a stage where the system actually takes control over the car either on a continuous basis or as a limit-type operation which could physically take control if the driver failed to respond properly to the warning system.

This stage-by-stage approach is intended to solve the difficult problem of mixing vehicles with and without automatic controls.

Several designs for integrated vehicle-media systems have been proposed. One is for a Personal Rapid Transit (PRT) system. Such a system was described by the Department of Housing and Urban Development as consisting of automatic individualized vehicles traveling over exclusive guideways which extend over the metropolitan area. Another proposal involves a dual-mode vehicle that combines the characteristics of flexible individualized transport with those of a fast economic mass-transit system. This vehicle would travel for part of its journey over normal streets mixing with other vehicles, and part of it over fixed guideways, possibly under automatic control. Such systems are still at least decades away from economic feasibility.

Some cities—for example, Toronto and San Jose—have already installed computer controls over the cycle time of traffic lights in an attempt to maximize traffic flow under changing conditions. Such controls appear to improve the flow of traffic but they do not produce large improvements. They retard the growth of congestion but they fall far short of eliminating it.

Technological solutions to the transportation "problem" proposed by preactivists either do not promise to do more than patch up the existing system or they involve massive expenditures that do not appear to be feasible. There is no doubt that the problem could be solved technologically if unlimited resources were available but there is no technological solution on the horizon that promises to be economically feasible.

SYSTEMS AGE SOLUTIONS

There is a tendency for transportation planners to adopt an inflexible attitude either for or against the automobile. Some take it to be the devil incarnate and others attribute to it all that is good in contemporary society. Those with a favorable attitude toward it accept it as it is and try to plan for and around it; those with an unfavorable attitude try to repress or replace it by public transport. The interactivist is inclined neither to blame nor to bless the automobile. He tries to retain its advantages while removing its disadvantages, even if this involves changing it in fundamental ways. But he does not believe that automobiles, however they might be modified, can completely remove the need for public transit. At least children, the aged, and the infirm will require it. Therefore, he seeks to design a system in which public and private transport are more effectively combined.

The interactivist does not believe that transportation problems can be solved by manipulating the transportation system alone. Therefore, he considers ways of changing the city itself so as to improve transportation, and he insists on considering the possible effects of any changes intended to improve transportation on other aspects of urban life. The interactivist argues that the kind of coordinated and integrated planning required to significantly improve urban transportation requires (1) some governmental reorganization to enable different functionally defined agencies to interact more effectively and (2) modification of the public-private interface involved in the planning process.

Most proposed solutions to automotive congestion involve changing the highways or the way the automobile is controlled, but not the automobile itself. The interactivist considers how the automobile can be changed so as to help solve the problem it has helped create.

The automobile accounts for about 85 percent of all urban passenger travel and its predominance is likely to continue. Many transportation analysts agree with Donald S. Berry and his collaborators:

> ... of all modes of transportation, the private automobile is best suited for most urban passenger trips because of its inherent flexibility in meeting the needs for involvement of people between widely scattered points of origin and destination. Projected suburban growth in population, industry and business will result in increasing reliance on the automobile for urban area travel.

There are no signs indicating that this increasing reliance on the automobile will diminish in the near future because of traffic congestion. Quite to the contrary, there is some evidence that urban dwellers relocate their jobs or residences rather than switch from the automobile to other modes of transportation. When places of employment relocate so as to increase automotive access to them, they usually move to the edges or outskirts of the city. This creates increased access problems to those who must use public transit or who cannot move from the city proper to suburban locations—particularly minority-group members whose access to suburban housing is restricted.

The Department of Housing and Urban Transportation noted: "The experience of recent years contradicts the belief that traffic congestion will set itself a limit to car ownership. If there is to be any chance of coexisting with the automobile in the urban environment, *a different sort of automobile is needed* with improvements in the supporting systems."

The present design of the automobile, predominantly a five-to-six-passenger family car, is intended to satisfy a wide variety of needs. Automobiles are used for inter- and intracity travel, travel to and from work, for recreation, shopping, and so on. It is not clear that individual or societal needs are best served by one type of general purpose vehicle.

The number of two-car families in the United States increased from 7 percent in 1950 to 25 percent in 1966 and it continues to increase. This and other facts considered below suggest development of an automobile better suited for use within the city at peak hours. Families that own or use more than one car would obtain distinct advantages by using special-purpose automobiles better suited to their different needs. Adequate provisions could and would have to be made for those who can afford only one or no car.

A way of improving transportation significantly is suggested by one characteristic of automotive usage in urban areas: average occupancy rates are about one and a half passengers per car. It is apparent that substantial reductions in automotive congestion could be achieved if the average occupancy of automobiles, particularly for work trips, were increased. Car pooling, however, reduces the advantages of door-to-door travel by automobile. A less inconveniencing alternative would involve the use of a small urban automobile, an *urmobile*.

Automobile users have been moving toward smaller cars. In 1957, 32 percent of the automobiles sold in the United States were four-door sedans and 19 percent were smaller two-door hardtops. In 1967, however, almost twice as many two-door cars were sold as four-doors. Furthermore, the sale of small imports, compacts, and subcompacts has been increasing rapidly, particularly in the very recent past because of the gasoline shortage.

It is generally acknowledged by traffic experts, however, that at higher speeds in free-flowing traffic the effect of reduced vehicle length on congestion is very small. For example, most of the road surface is "unused" when cars travel on it at forty miles per hour or higher. There is more space between vehicles than under them. In a study conducted at the University of Pennsylvania by McClenehan and Simkowitz, it was shown that the effect of reducing car length by half on expressways would be an increase of flow of no more than 10 to 15 percent. However, greater increases would be obtained on heavily used city streets: as much as 70 percent increases would be obtained when congestion reaches the not uncommon level of fifteen vehicles per light. If only a fraction of long cars is replaced by shorter ones, flow would be increased by approximately that fraction of 70 percent.

Curiously, little attention has been given to the effects of reducing the *width* of automobiles as is easily accomplished in a two-passenger automobile in which the passenger sits *behind*, not beside, the driver. Such a vehicle need be no more than three and half feet wide and about six feet long, if it is restricted to a maximum speed of about forty miles per hour. Vehicles traveling at approximately this speed on an expressway maximize its throughput. If traffic were made up exclusively of such vehicles an increase of more than 100 percent on expressways would be obtained. Half of the shoulder could be used for an additional lane. On city streets with three lanes, one for parking, increases of as much as 400 percent could be obtained. This would be enough to take care of the increases forecasted as far out as the year 2000.

Furthermore, parking-space requirements would be greatly reduced. Even further reductions could be obtained by using sliding side doors or front or rear doors so that little space would be required between parked cars. Such cars could easily park at right angles to the curb; they would be shorter than most current cars are wide. They could be made to hook on to each other in trainlike fashion to facilitate towing or taking the family along on a trip. (Towable unmotorized cars could be used for this purpose.) "Towability" would reduce delays caused by breakdowns on expressways. The reduced maximum speed and acceleration of these cars would increase their safety. They would also significantly reduce street maintenance and construction costs.

A large variety of small automobiles—although none like the one envisaged here—are under development. Some of them were described and shown recently in *Mechanics Illustrated* and *Life*. According to *Life*: "Britain, France, Germany, and Italy have all produced sub-minis that make the VW beetle look like an airport limousine. All cost about $1000 in their country of manufacture." In some cases the new designs incorporate pollution-reducing features. It is much easier to meet pollution standards in small cars than in large ones. Furthermore, such vehicles would require considerably less energy per passenger mile than do current automobiles.

The advantage of using subminis for intracity traffic are dependent on the restrictions imposed on the use of larger vehicles. During a transitional period vehicles of different sizes could mix together or they could be segregated by lanes or streets. Eventually, use of city streets and expressways may have to be limited to use of subminis during peak hours or, say, between 7:00 a.m. and 7:00 p.m. on weekdays.

Urmobiles could be made available for short-term rentals and as self-driven taxis. The pickup and dropoff points could be widely dispersed over the city. Commuters could drive their large cars to a parking-pickup point on the urban fringe where a smaller car could be obtained for use in the city. Rented urmobiles could be coin, token, or credit-card operated. Such rental systems are being tried experimentally in Amsterdam and Montpellier. Amsterdam is trying a two-passenger electric car but Montpellier is using an ordinary French car.

It is clear that a change to small urban automobiles—whatever their particular characteristics might be—could be accomplished in less than a decade with relatively few transitional problems. Furthermore, such a change would reduce public and private expenditures for transportation by a significant amount. There would be no loss of privacy, convenience, comfort, or time.

The transition to subminicars could be facilitated and accelerated by charging rationally for use of automobiles and automotive media. Bridge, tunnel, and expressway charges are currently levied on an automobile regardless of its size or occupancy. If tolls were based on *the number of empty seats*, use of smaller cars and higher occupancy of all cars would be encouraged. Furthermore, the unit charge could be varied as a function of demand: it could be higher during peak hours than at other times. (Mass transit charges could be made similarly variable. Some commuting trains already do so.) Parking charges and license fees should also be made proportional to the size of the car.

Whatever is done to the automobile, some public transit will be required. The more attractive public transportation can be made the fewer problems there will be with private transportation. As Secretary Volpe suggested, funds obtained from gasoline taxes should be used to help finance improvements in public transit. Public and private transportation are interactive parts of the same system.

URBAN REDESIGN

Up to this point I have only considered changes of the transportation system itself without considering changes in the urban system that contains it. Transportation always involves origins and destinations. These can be changed by modifying land-use patterns of a metropolitan area. For example, it would be possible to design a city in which average trip length would be significantly reduced and in which travel would be more evenly distributed over it. This could be done in such a way as to serve better a wide variety of other needs.

Cities have developed a pattern of land use in which most sections have specialized functions; they have a narrow range of land uses. There are industrial sections, commercial sections, shopping sections, residential sections, recreational sections, and so on. Residential sections (neighborhoods) tend to serve groups that are homogeneous with respect to socioeconomic characteristics, particularly with respect to income. As a result, different sections of the city have different amenities, facilities, and access to those facilities. Most cities are very heterogeneous as a whole, but their parts tend to be very homogeneous with respect to use and occupancy.

An alternative type of city would be one whose sections are heterogeneous: stratified samples of the city as a whole. That is, each section would approximate a relatively self-contained community with most facilities and services available within it, a wide range of land uses, and a heterogeneous population. The city would consist of a set of interrelated villages, each serving and housing a variety of types of people. If each section provided housing, places of work, shopping, recreation, and so on, the number and distance of vehicular trips would be reduced. Almost everyone could find a suitable place to live near work.

Because of economies of scale some services and facilities would have to serve a number of sections; for example, theaters, museums, and colleges. They could be located so as to serve a group of sections more effectively. The metropolitan area would thus consist of a hierarchy of units: neighborhoods, districts, divisions, and so on. Each of these could be designed to be as heterogeneous and self-contained as possible. Such a community would lend itself to social and economic integration.

The conversion of an existing metropolitan area into one of the type I have described requires planning and control of a type that is not currently practiced. What planning there is in most metropolitan areas is disintegrated and uncoordinated, sporadic and nonparticipative. Each political jurisdiction in a metropolitan area tends to plan for itself independently of what its neighbors plan or are doing. It is also planned for by state and federal agencies usually without coordination with local efforts. Furthermore, different functions are planned for independently of each other within the same community.

Effective community planning, like any planning, must be participative, continuous, coordinated, integrated, and experimental. The structure and planning practices of local, state, and federal governments obstruct the development of such planning. These are not likely to change without massive pressure being applied to them.

In a democracy, public planning cannot be reorganized effectively from above. No one or body has the authority necessary to do so. It must be reorganized from below. Such reorganization can emerge out of the development of neighborhood self-planning efforts. These efforts could then be coordinated and integrated at successively higher levels. Effective neighborhood planning will require a great deal and wide range of technical knowledge but this could be provided by local universities and colleges as well as by public planning agencies.

Self-planning groups have begun to spring up in neighborhoods, particularly in those that are disadvantaged. Some have been operating with considerable effectiveness. They have grown into unofficial governments acting on, and in behalf of, the neighborhood. Some have succeeded in extracting resources from different levels of government by applying political pressure on them. But thus far even successful neighborhood planning efforts have been largely independent of one another. In some cases they compete for access to the same resources.

Urban colleges and universities could help coordinate and integrate neighborhood planning efforts so as to produce neighborhood, district, division, and ultimately area plans. Most institutions of higher learning are not anxious to enter into such activities but they can be pressured into them more easily than government agencies can. They are more susceptible to public pressure than are governments. Many of their faculty members and students would welcome the opportunity to involve their institutions and themselves in community self-development efforts. Such involvement would have a significantly beneficial effect on the educational process.

An effective plan for urban transportation cannot be developed merely by aggregating neighborhood transportation plans. But a city or metropolitan-area plan cannot be implemented without support of most neighborhoods and modifications in at least some. If neighborhood planning is instituted with the help of colleges and universities, with representatives from neighborhoods working together with representatives of relevant government and private agencies and organizations, an implementable area transportation plan might well be developed. If properly organized, such efforts could extract financial support from federal, state, and local governments.

CONCLUSION

Certain conclusions about current efforts to relieve traffic congestion seem clear. Repressive measures taken against the automobile by constraining use of streets for either moving or parking can only have a significant impact on automobile usage and congestion if acceptable alternative modes of transportation are available. They seldom are. In general, public transport in the United States has deteriorated more rapidly than automotive travel; hence more and more trip-taking has shifted to the automobile. The attempt to reduce travel time and congestion by building new highways and streets cannot provide a long-term solution because the funds necessary to maintain the current level of congestion are not likely to be available; and if they were, their use would result in excessive coverage of the city's surface with roadways and parking facilities. The attempt to solve the space problem by going to a multilevel system increases the already unfeasible cost of preventing further congestion on one level.

The two most feasible approaches to the reduction of travel time and improvement of the quality of travel in cities lie in changing the nature of the automobile and in the redistribution of land use in the city.

First, because automobiles currently being used in American cities carry an average of less than two people, and because the maximum density of use of roadways is obtained by vehicles moving at about thirty-five miles per hour, I have suggested development of a small urmobile that would carry two people at a maximum speed of about forty miles per hour, and that would be capable of being attached to each other in tandem. Such a vehicle could be less than three and a half feet wide and six feet long. Two such vehicles could travel side by side in a current lane and as much as 70 percent more cars could fit into a column on city streets. Such vehicles could be publicly and privately owned. Those publicly owned could be coin or credit-card activated. They could be used as drive-yourself taxis that are deposited at designated parking places throughout the city.

City streets would be limited to the use of urmobiles, say, from 7:00 a.m. to 7:00 p.m. on weekdays. "Normal automobiles" could be used at other times and would continue to be used for intercity travel.

Computations show that use of such vehicles could absorb expected increases in automotive travel up to at least the year 2000 without any increase in congestion. The transition from the current vehicle to the proposed subminicar could be accomplished in no more than the expected life of a new conventional automobile.

The second promising approach to relief of congestion and reduction of trip time lies in relocating facilities in a city so that it gradually approaches a collection of villages that are as self-contained as possible. Each village would provide as many facilities as possible within walking distance of home and each village would approximate a proportional stratified sample of the population and facilities in the city as a whole. This would make each "village" as heterogeneous as possible, provide residents of each with virtually equal access to needed facilities and amenities, and would be small enough to allow direct participation of residents in village government.

By proper use of zoning regulations and normal replacement and growth of facilities, the conversion of a currently homogeneously structured city to the proposed aggregation of heterogeneous villages could be accomplished by no later than the end of the century.

By combining the redesign of the urban automobile with the redesign of the city it should be possible to improve significantly the quality of life in the city and to approach equality of opportunity for all city dwellers independently of their background and socioeconomic characteristics. In this way efforts to solve the transportation problem can be converted into a program for general and extensive redesign of the city and life within it.

CHAPTER TWELVE

——————————

UNDERDEVELOPED COUNTRIES

Examining the present population of the globe, we find a tiny group who still live, hunting and food-foraging, as men did millenia ago. Others, the vast majority of mankind, depend... on ... agriculture. They live, in many respects, as their ancestors did centuries ago. These two groups taken together compose some 70 percent of all living beings . . . .

ALVIN TOFFLER

Barbara Ward, Professor of International Economic Development at Columbia University, described our world as "lopsided." She explained: "A small number of states, equalling some 20 percent of the world's population, controls 80 percent of the world's wealth."

In general, developed nations do not consider this imbalance to be threatening because less-developed nations do not constitute a direct military threat to them. The account in *The Mouse that Roared* of a small nation that conquered the United States was comic for this reason. The incredibility of such a conquest is reflected in the story of a cabinet minister of a small less-developed nation who proposed to his prime minister that they declare war on the United States. He defended his suggestion to the astonished prime minister by pointing out that the United States always financed the development of any nation it defeated in war; for example, Germany and Japan after World War II. "But," the prime minister asked, "suppose we win?"

Although less-developed nations do not constitute a direct threat to larger developed nations they do threaten them indirectly. Struggles within or between disadvantaged nations have a way of drawing developed nations into them. Witness Korea, Vietnam, Hungary, Cuba, and particularly the Arab-Israeli conflict. Furthermore, the struggle among developed nations for political influence, markets, sources of raw materials, and military bases in less-developed nations is a continuing threat to world security.

An increasing number of those living in less-developed countries are becoming aware of, and dissatisfied with, the disparity between their standards of living and those of developed nations. C. P. Snow noted that the "disparity between the rich and the poor has been noticed. It has been noticed, most acutely and not unnaturally, by the poor." Improved communication and the increased presence of affluent tourists in deprived nations impress this disparity on the disadvantaged. As a result, discontent is increasing, but despite this, disparity is also. Snow observed: "Just because they [the poor] have noticed it, it won't last long. Once the trick of getting rich is known, as it is now, the world can't survive half rich and half poor."

Few poor nations have yet attained a rate of development equal to, let alone exceeding, that of the more advanced nations. If the less-developed are to catch up it is necessary for them to develop *faster* than advanced nations. The difficulty that a nation faces in trying to catch up is apparent when we consider how difficult it is for the poor *within* a developed nation to do so.

Inhabitants of developed nations are also becoming more aware of the plight of those living in less-developed nations. Again, improvements in communication and transportation have increasingly brought the suffering of the disadvantaged into the view of the affluent. The famished Indians, victims of an earthquake in Turkey or a flood in Pakistan, and those attacked by a plague in the East are no longer abstractions. They and their pain and deprivation are vividly shown on our television screens.

Although awareness of the development gap is widespread, concern with it is not. It certainly is not persistent among developed nations. Within them, however, we can see the application to less-developed nations of each of the four now-familiar types of attitude toward the future.

THE INACTIVE APPROACH TO DEVELOPMENT

There are few in developed nations who *say* we should do nothing about the underdevelopment of other nations, but there are many who do nothing about them. Inactivists do nothing to make the resources that would facilitate the development of others available to them. They prefer a reduction in taxes to an increase in either foreign aid or even internal development programs. Their attitude dominates our national policy at this time. Francis O. Wilcox, Dean of The Johns Hopkins School of Advanced International Studies, cited the evidence:

> ... when the Marshall Plan was launched in 1948, the United States contributed nearly $4 billion annually toward the reconstruction of war-torn Europe. Very little of this was in the form of loans; most of it went as outright grants to the recipient countries. ... The result was the most miraculous recovery of Europe and new strength and hope for the Western World.
>
> In the two decades since 1948 our gross national product has more than doubled in real terms. Despite this enormous growth and despite the great need of the new countries, our foreign-aid program has been sharply curtailed. It still amounts to about the same $4 billion but the dollar is worth only two-thirds as much as it was twenty years ago . . . .
>
> Actually our record is even less inspiring than appears on the surface. Virtually all our assistance is now what is euphemistically called tied-aid—that is, it is devoted to the purchase of American products. Equally important is the often forgotten fact that much of it is now extended in the form of loans that must be paid back by the recipient nations.

Why have we retrenched? Barbara Ward answered by pointing out ". . . the feeling that spending a great deal of money does not give the answer and only leads to waste. This general proposition is buttressed by a whole set of special instances of supposed or reported failure. Together they create a context of thinking which is discouraged, sceptical, or downright hostile."

In reviewing their own nation's development, inactivists overlook its failures and see only its successes, real or imagined. In reviewing the underdevelopment of others, they tend to see only their real or imagined failures, not their successes.

There is persistent suspicion, if not belief, among affluent inactivists that disadvantaged people, taken separately or collectively, are innately inferior. Such a belief reinforces another belief of the inactivist: those who deserve get, and those who don't, don't. Recall that inactivists believe this is, or closely approximates, the best of possible worlds. Some even argue that inequality is God's will. Others maintain that those in less-developed countries are at least as happy as we are and, therefore, should be left alone. Facts that contradict this belief are ignored.

Inactivists also ignore the fact that development and underdevelopment are interdependent phenomena; the development of every advanced nation derives at least in part from the exploitation of less-advanced nations. For example, until recently American companies produced crude oil in less-developed nations and shipped it to the United States for less than they could produce it for in this country. The idea that the difference in cost ought to have gone to the country from which the oil was taken crossed few "developed" minds. After all, it was argued by most of those minds it did cross, it was *our* capital and ingenuity which made *their* oil fields possible. Without it *they* would have nothing. This is a rationalization of the imbalance of benefits. Such an imbalance is exploitation, however benevolent it may be.

Most of us who have goods or services to sell would not think of selling them at a high profit to a needy friend. We are embarrassed to profit from a friend's need. There is no such embarrassment when the needy are foreign, "colored," and not known to us personally. This may be easy to understand but it is difficult to justify unless we believe, as the inactivist does, that inequality is "natural" and that everything eventually works out for the best.

Many developed nations are not willing to spend much on assistance to known friends, but they are willing to spend as much as they can to protect themselves against an unknown enemy. They justify doing so in the name of national security and because of its stimulation of the national economy. The irrationality of such spending led Barbara Ward to ask:

> Is imagination liberated only when destruction is at issue? Are we to be aroused by our fears and hates and never by our loves? If out of all the carnage were to come some sense of man's unlimited resources for the works of peace, then we could still reap some gain from our harvest of unreason. And one condition of such a hope is to realize that money for tractors stimulates an economy fully as much as money for tanks. . . .

But any argument for a more equitable distribution of wealth, including Barbara Ward's, is unconvincing to inactivists who believe that those who have, deserve; and those who don't, don't.

Historically, the development of most of the currently advanced countries was made possible by what Gerald Piel called "coercive deprivation." This involved economic exploitation of a large portion of their own populations or that of other countries. The nineteenth-century historian Alexander Herzen commented on this process as follows: "In order to develop, it is necessary that things should be much better for some and much worse for others; then those who are better off can develop at the expense of others." The "some" could be nations as well as individuals, as was the case in much of past colonialism.

The relevance of Herzen's observation to the development of the United States was noted by Piel:

> . . .it was 35 million steerage immigrants. . . who furnished the working capital for the industrial revolution that got under way at the middle of the nineteenth century. The American Negro's present determined drive to capture and assert his civil rights, after a century of punative emancipation, serves to remind Americans how the savings for the development of their country were corralled.

A more equitable distribution of wealth between and within nations, inactivists argue, would destroy any incentive toward self-development. On the other hand, an inequitable distribution does not generate enough investment capital to accelerate development in less-developed nations. Affluent inactivists do not have to face this dilemma, but disadvantaged nations do.

THE REACTIVE APPROACH TO DEVELOPMENT

The objective of a reactivist's actions, it will be recalled, is to return to a preferred previous state in which no action was required. This characteristic can be found in his attitude toward less-developed countries. In the reactivist's view the best poor country is one that is neither seen nor heard, hence requires no attention. When a poor nation acts up and requires attention, the reactivist tries to react in a way that best serves his own purposes. The recalcitrant nation's interests are not necessarily ignored but they are subordinated to his. For example, the apparent generosity of the United States in the Marshall Plan and in the financial support given to Japan at the end of World War II was primarily motivated by its own national interests. A strong Europe and Japan were believed to be essential to the containment of communism. Had this not been the case, the United States would not have been as generous as it was. This does not deny the presence of goodwill, but it denies that it was sufficient for, or even the prime mover of, its aid program.

Reactivists occasionally respond to the needs of others out of generosity and concern, but usually only in the event of an emergency. They support disaster relief but they do not usually respond, for example, to a continuing state of malnutrition or high mortality in a poor country. They do respond to a famine, plague, or pestilence. Once the emergency is over, aid is discontinued. The reactivist's response to the needs of the disadvantaged is based on the philosophy of the Red Cross rather than that of CARE.

Reactivists support continuing foreign aid only when it is necessary to serve their own interests; for example, to retain military bases or access to needed raw materials. Such self-interest is reflected in the observation of Dennis Gabor, recent Nobel laureate in physics:

> At the present time there exists a drive to speed up the development of the underdeveloped countries. It is not as strong as one might wish, nor is it inspired by purely humanitarian motives. It is mainly a drive of the United States on the one hand, of the U.S.S.R. on the other, and more recently also of China, to get allies and bases all over the world.

In Greece, Spain, Brazil, and many other countries the United States supports governments based on principles of which it disapproves because they are even more antithetical to those of communism. Recall that reactivists are moved more by their hates than by their loves.

The reactivist's principal argument against foreign aid is its failure to buy the loyalty and support of its recipients. For example, in his 1972 campaign for the Democratic Party's nomination for the presidency of the United States, George C. Wallace, governor of Alabama, used this argument to defend his desire to reduce foreign aid. He never questioned the reasonableness of his expectation that the receiver expresses his appreciation by supporting whatever position the donor takes on international issues, even if it is against the receiver's national interest to do so. For Wallace, the main purpose of foreign aid was to "buy foreign votes." He attributed its failure to do so to the ingratitude of the receivers. If one were to apply this principle to one's private giving, gifts would never be made to anyone who, for example, did not support one's politics or religion.

Disagreement does not signify a breach of friendship. It is an essential characteristic of friendship that it can survive disagreement because each party to it believes the other has his best interests at heart however much they disagree. Friendship is not an interaction of two parties each of which has only his own interests at heart. To confuse agreement with concern is a misconception of the first order. To confuse giving that is motivated by self-interest with generosity is even worse. Reactive aid is based on both these misconceptions.

In brief, the reactivist does not see the ability to give aid as a *benefit to be derived from affluence*, but as a cost of maintaining it and, therefore, as something to be minimized.

THE PREACTIVE APPROACH TO DEVELOPMENT

The preactivist desires a more equitable distribution of wealth among nations. He sympathizes and emphathizes with the disadvantaged and is motivated by goodwill and a sense of fairness, and, to a certain extent, by a sense of guilt. He supports aid to less-developed nations because he feels that doing so is right. Giving is more blessed than receiving. Charity is its own justification. This is not to say that preactivists are beyond enlightened self-interest; they also believe we would be better off if everyone else were.

It will be recalled that the preactivist generally looks for solutions to problems through manipulation of resources or use of technology. Therefore, he tends to support financial and technical aid programs and to believe these are sufficient to raise the standards of living in less-developed countries. The preactivist tends to identify development and the Industrial Revolution; he does not see how one can take place without the other. Recall that he believes the future to be largely out of our control, but that its effects on us are controllable. This view is reflected in the observation of C. P. Snow: "Since the gap between the rich and the poor can be removed it will be. If we are shortsighted, inept, incapable of good will or enlightened self-interest, then it may be removed to the accompaniment of war and starvation: but removed it will be. The questions are how, and by whom." This prophetic statement was written before the current effort of the Persian Gulf nations to use the price of their oil as an instrument of equalization.

Preactivists argue that the financial resources required to develop less-developed nations could be made available. For example, C. F. Powell, Fellow of Britain's Royal Society, wrote:

> At present [1964] the total amount given for aid and development amounts to $6 B per annum. A number of estimates have been made of the material resources required for the radical transformation of the present situation. They vary considerably, but most of them fall in the range from $10-15 B per annum for a period of about twenty years. These estimates, while representing great expenditures are well within the resources of the advanced countries. They could be provided, for example, by even a modest measure of disarmament.

Approximately $200 billion per year are currently spent by developed nations for "defense."

Financial resources, argued U Thant, Secretary-General of the United Nations, are not the problem: "The truth, the central stupendous truth, about developed countries today is that they have—in anything but the shortest run—the kind and scale of resources they decide to have. . . . It is no longer resources that limit decisions. It is the decision that makes the resources."

Then why is enough financial aid not provided? According to Dean Francis Wilcox, because of lack of leadership and inspiration: ". . . .what is needed is a dramatic proposal for a massive foreign-aid program that would fire the imagination, encourage the cooperation, and challenge the productive capabilities of the countries involved. . . ."

Proposals made to date have obviously failed to inspire. There appear to be three reasons. First, most, if not all, developed countries believe that they cannot reduce their *non*defense spending by the amount required to help others significantly without seriously affecting their own quality of life. Second, they believe, correctly or not, that they cannot reduce their defense spending by the amount required without seriously endangering their national security. Hence no one country will reduce its defense spending unilaterally. Third, those in power in developed nations do not believe they can retain their power if they increase foreign aid by increasing taxation.

Therefore, preactivists maintain that disarmament and foreign aid are not separable issues; they must be dealt with together. What is needed, they claim, is a dramatic proposal as to how international disarmament negotiations can be carried out. There is reason to believe, they argue, that it is not likely to be carried out without the development of an effective international government. But this is not likely in the near future.

In the meantime, the preactivist proposes at least modest increases in foreign aid. Barbara Ward has made a number of suggestions as to how this can be done: first, reduce tariffs and other forms of protection applied to products of less-developed countries by developed countries; second, guarantee prices on the products of less-developed countries; third, provide greater credit to these countries; and, fourth, establish common markets. Some of these suggestions require international collaboration but of a type for which there are precedents.

Preactivists believe that with the increases in aid such measures, and the knowledge that scientists and technologists in developed nations have, would make possible significant acceleration of development of less-developed nations. The solutions to many development problems are known, they assert. Therefore, underdeveloped nations ought to turn their development over to the intellectual elite of the developed countries. Preactivists expand this argument as follows.

Additional capital for investment can obviously be generated by increasing the return on those investments that have already been made or are being made. This requires increasing efficiency and reducing waste: increasing productivity of natural resources, machines and plants, and men.

One from an advanced country who visits underdeveloped countries cannot help but be struck by their failure to use available technologies effectively. In some cases this is due to lack of adequately trained personnel or to lack of necessary equipment. But in many cases technologies that could be used are not. Sweepers still bend over short-handled brooms despite the disclosure in *The Ugly American,* and others sweep ceramic tile floors in air terminals with stiff-bristled brooms rather than mop them. It hardly seems necessary to make work where there is so much work to be done. It is obviously necessary for a country that seeks to develop more rapidly than advanced countries to exploit available technology at least as well as advanced countries do.

Preactivists realize that technology alone cannot produce development. It must be accompanied by increased productivity of individual workers whether they operate machines or not. Worker productivity tends to lag behind mechanization in underdeveloped countries. Preactivists believe this is due in part to the fact that very little use is made of "soft" technology: industrial engineering, human engineering, and the behavioral sciences. These can be used to redesign tasks for greater productivity or to motivate workers to seek it on their own.

The opportunity for underdeveloped countries to replace low-productivity workers by high-productivity machines is very limited. W. A. Lewis has put this well:

> In the developed countries, one of the chief purposes of applying science to production is to find ways of substituting capital for labor—of doing by machine what was previously done by hand. Such technology is very appropriate to countries where labor is scarce and expensive relative to capital, but it is irrelevant to most parts of Asia, where the problem is rather to devise new technologies which make manpower more efficient without more capital.

Elementary work studies in India have increased productivity by as much as 250 percent. According to preactivists, too few such studies are being carried out in India and other less-developed nations.

Low productivity was epitomized to me by a middle-aged male in a lobby of a large public building in Iran whose function it was to ask those coming to the elevators whether they wanted to go up or down. He then pushed the appropriate button for them.

To make employment is one thing; to make it productive is another. The preactivist believes research is needed to find useful things for people to do and efficient ways of doing them.

Labor-management relations tend to be bad in underdeveloped countries. Caste often separates manager from worker and prevents his motivating them to greater productivity. Therefore, the preactivist argues, we must export management—as well as scientific and technological—skills to these countries.

In brief, preactivists believe that development of less-developed countries is primarily a matter of using what developed countries already know and of receiving from them such resources as they can provide without serious modification of their current internal allocation of resources.

THE INTERACTIVE APPROACH TO DEVELOPMENT

It appears easy to imagine an idealized world in which underdeveloped nations would not exist. In light of the discussion of the preactive view of development one would probably start by imagining a centralized world government to which existing nations are related much as the states of the United States are related to it. Such a world federation of nations would eliminate the need for military forces and this, in turn, would make a great deal of money available to the central government for investment in those parts of the world requiring development. Furthermore, essential personnel could be moved about easily and thus located where they are most needed. And universal compulsory education would eliminate the ignorance that breeds underdevelopment.

To the interactivist the notion that world government would be enough to assure elimination of inequitable distribution of wealth among its parts appears to be naive. How come parts of developed nations are underdeveloped? How can one explain Appalachia, Puerto Rico, black ghettos, Indian reservations, and migratory communities of Mexican-Americans? In view of what is happening in the United States how can one believe that universal compulsory education is enough to eliminate ignorance in segments of a world federation?

As I noted earlier (Chapter 7) the problem of the urban black ghetto is similar in many respects to that of an underdeveloped nation. Such a ghetto has the "advantage" of already being a part of a developed nation. Despite this its development is far from assured. Therefore, why should development of a nation converted into a state in a world federation be any easier? If anything, it would be harder because nations have been less interdependent than have advantaged and disadvantaged groups within nations.

The problem of development is not just one of getting access to, or possession of, the resources *we* think *they* need. It is one of enabling them to use what resources they have and can acquire in a way *they* believe will most accelerate their development as *they* conceive it. This is exactly the same problem that Mantua, the black ghetto in Philadelphia, had. Therefore, an interactive concept of aid to less-developed countries can be extracted out of the Penn-Mantua experience. It is based on three observations.

1.   It is characteristic of developed nations to believe that they understand development and that this understanding can easily be transferred to less-developed nations. In the interactivist's view, this misconception must be removed. *Developed nations do not know how to solve the mess we call underdevelopment.* There is not a single instance of a developing country being responsible for the elevation of an underdeveloped country to the condition of development. No colonial power ever produced a colony as developed as it was. Whatever the reasons, this is a simple fact that we ought to begin to accept and adapt to. We should stop acting as though *we* could solve *their* problems if only *we* were given the chance. We have had the chance over and over again and have failed each time.

2.   We assume that even if we do not have solutions to their problems, given the chance, we could find them. After all, we developed ourselves, did we not? This assumption is based on the belief that development is something that can be given by one who has it to one who has not. Nothing could be farther from the truth.

Development is not just a matter of applying *our* technology to *their* problems. Technology is not a guaranteed harbinger of development. R. J. Forbes, an eminent Dutch historian of science and technology, points out that technology is not culturally neutral. "It is a product of Western ideas and value judgments which without many of the impulses guiding it would be meaningless or even destructive." The imposition of our technology on an ancient culture could be disastrous to that culture. It can lead to "collapse of the class and caste structure on which such a civilization depends." It can also make a small minority of rich people richer and the large majority of the poor poorer.

> The orderly development of technology in any country has many aspects of natural growth. The simple transfer of modern highly perfected forms of technology is no more possible than it is desirable. . . . Increasingly our technology must be seen as systems rather than machines, as it requires education rather than mere training—with all this implies in the way of conflicting values.

Most underdeveloped countries are wise enough not to want to recapitulate all the phases and consequences of development through which the more advanced countries have gone. For example, they would like to avoid very rapid and excessive urbanization, pollution, traffic congestion where it is not already present, and other disorders of development. In addition, as Forbes points out, they would like to preserve some of their indigenous cultural values.

Because we know enough about our own culture to develop it with our technology, it does not follow that we know enough about other cultures to do the same for them. For example, we tend to reason about the overpopulation problem of underdeveloped countries as follows.

If the rate of growth of population of an underdeveloped country could be reduced, then unemployment and underemployment could eventually be reduced and additional investment capital could be generated. Therefore, we should make contraceptives available in these countries (and, some would suggest, abortion) and teach the natives how to use them. We have done so—for example, in India—without success and, more importantly, without learning why we did not succeed.

Powerful economic and cultural forces are involved in population control. Consideration of only one is sufficient to make the point that we often do not know enough about other cultures to apply our technology to them effectively.

In most underdeveloped countries there is no form of social security: insurance against unemployment, illness, and old age. In these countries the family is usually the only form of protection against such contingencies. Hence children are an economic necessity; they depend on parents when parents can provide for them (however minimally) but they are a source of support for parents when parents can no longer provide for themselves. Furthermore, because expected life has increased in most underdeveloped countries more rapidly than have expected earnings, the need for large families has increased.

In most underdeveloped countries parents can turn only to their sons for support because daughters are usually unemployable. T. R. Balakrishnan, an Indian demographer, and Glen D. Camp, a professor at the University of Pennsylvania until his death, determined how many sons the average Indian family required to assure themselves of such support. They found that the average size of an Indian family was almost exactly twice this number. On the average Nature provides one daughter along with every son.

Those who attempt to impose Western birth-control methods on the Indians and others are, in effect, asking them to commit a delayed suicide.

Development, contrary to popular belief in developed nations, has little to do with *wealth*. I came to realize this on the island of Leyte in the Philippines during World War II. After hostilities on that island were over, a group of soldiers with nothing else to do began to convert their camp into a community that provided a high quality of life. They used nothing but native materials with which they were initially unfamiliar, and their imagination and ingenuity. Recall Robinson Crusoe. The natives in the area were dumbfounded at what they saw done with bamboo and nipa. Out of this experience I came to realize that development is not nearly so much a matter of what one has, but of what one does with what one has. Development is the desire and ability to use what is available to continuously improve the quality of life. This ability cannot be given to others even by those who have it. It must be developed in and for oneself.

Development is not a state in which one has access to the products of a developed society. If groups of underdeveloped primitives are housed in plush American facilities and if nothing else is done for them, their environment is likely to deteriorate rapidly to an underdeveloped state. Put a group of developed individuals in the most primitive surroundings and in a short time they will find ways of improving their living conditions and making life more enjoyable.

Therefore, development must begin with the desire to improve one's lot. The Renaissance gave this desire to the Western world. But many underdeveloped countries have not had a Renaissance. Some are still in an age in which death is valued more than life.

Desire cannot be imposed on one by another. To try to do so is cruel as well as futile. Development cannot take place until its time has come: when it is wanted. Therefore, it should always be left as a matter of *free* choice; that is, it should be available to those who want it when they want it.

Next development requires the ability to learn how to improve one's lot. This is the ability to develop and use *knowledge*. We believe such knowledge to be universal, true for all people at all times in all places. Therefore, we are impatient with those who hesitate to accept what of it we offer them. We forget how our Western culture resisted the heliocentric theory of our solar system when Copernicus, Galileo, and others offered it. We forget how alive the debate on evolution still is in some quarters of our society. Even if science is universal it certainly is not culturally neutral. Beliefs must give way before there is room for knowledge. We have little if any skill in making the necessary room in the minds of others.

Finally, development requires the ability to recognize when old solutions no longer work and new ones have to be found; that is, the ability to adapt to internal and external changes. Inhabitants of developed nations have shown a remarkable ability to change their environments to suit their needs and desires, but much less ability to change themselves to suit their environment's needs. Yet what we ask those in underdeveloped countries to do is adapt themselves to the developed world. This request does not bear conviction, coming as it does from people who have shown little inclination to adapt to the underdeveloped world.

3. If we give up the assumptions that we have solutions to the underdevelopment mess and that, if we do not have them, we can find them, then it is still possible that we can educate enough members of less-developed countries to enable them to solve their nations' problems on their own. We have, of course, been trying to do so for years without conspicuous success.

Many of the students from less-developed countries who go abroad for education do not return to their countries, not so much because they are attracted by a higher standard of living (although this has its effect), but because they recognize that the skills they acquire are more salable in a developed country than in a less-developed one. Of those that return home many find that their skills are not in demand and are subject to misuse. Of these some emigrate and others settle into academia where they transmit their irrelevant skills to others in their country.

Universities in less-developed countries seek to emulate those in developed countries almost without exception. There is very little attempt to adapt higher education to national needs. This is due in part to the fact that the textbooks used are generally those written in developed countries, and in part to the fact that faculty status derives from publishing in prestige journals of developed countries. As a result, higher education in less-developed countries is often more relevant to life in the developed world than it is in the country in which it is provided.

We can no more teach others to develop themselves than we can show them. One cannot learn how to play a piano by watching others do so or listening to them talk about doing so. One can only learn by practice. If one practices then watching others and listening to them can help. Learning how to develop, like learning how to play the piano, requires trying, failing over and over again, and eventually succeeding. The role of the "teacher" should be that of giving others an opportunity to learn by practice, encouraging them to do so, supporting them during their failures, recognizing success when it is obtained, and serving throughout as a resource that the learner should learn how to use effectively and that should be available to him to use as he sees fit.

If we do not have and cannot find the solutions to the development problems of others, and, if additionally, we cannot teach others how to solve them, what can we do to help? Developed nations can offer to do for the less-developed exactly what the Penn Group did for Mantua: *they can induce less-developed countries to find out how they can use developed nations in their self-development efforts.* They can do so as follows.

> 1. *Help support a development-planning and planning-implementation group in the less-developed nation.*

Many less-developed countries already have such groups. But many of them are too small to do the job. Hence support for their enlargement would be welcome in most places. Support should be guaranteed for a long enough period to develop plans, implement them, and evaluate results. In most cases five years would be minimal, ten years preferable.

What the indigenous group works on and how should be left entirely in its own hands and those of its national leaders, not in those of the assisting nation.

> 2. *Establish a "resource group" in the developed country to assist the indigenous group in any way the indigenous group sees fit.*

The resource group should contain or have access to practitioners of a wide variety of sciences, technologies, and practical arts, and to many who control public and private resources. This group cannot possibly contain all the skills, or have direct access to all the resources, it may need. Therefore, it should contain "resourceful people" who will not hesitate to approach others who can provide the help they cannot provide themselves.

Both the resource group and the indigenous group should have access to their nations' chief executives, to his staff and cabinet, and to their nations' legislative bodies. Clearly, this access should not be abused; it should be used sparingly but effectively.

The wider the variety of resources on which the resource group can call the better. For this reason universities or general-purpose research establishments might well serve as their homes. This would free them of government control without denying them access to government.

The resource group should not initiate any action on its own but should respond to every request for help that it receives. It should try to do whatever it is asked to do even if failure seems inevitable. It must establish the fact that it is an instrument of the receiver, not the donor. Once it has done so, the receiver may give it the right to act on its own.

The resource group should be supported financially by the donor nation. This support should be sufficient to cover all its expenses and travel of members of both the indigenous and resource groups between the two nations.

How extensive a coverage of less-developed countries could such interactions provide? To answer, some statistics are required. Using 1965 figures, Barbara Ward classified the nations of the world as follows:

    33 Very poor — less than $100 per capita GNP
    38 Poor — $100 to $249 per capita GNP
    29 Middle income — $250 to $749 per capita GNP
    31 Rich — more than $749 per capita GNP

As can be seen, the very poor and the rich could be paired off one-to-one with only two rich countries being required to care for two very poor ones. Or each rich country could take on approximately three others, one from each category above it in the table. This would hardly be a backbreaking load.

To launch these interactions an *International Development Decade* should be declared. It would help dramatize the effort. International scientific, technological, and managerial societies, and universities throughout the world should be called on to collaborate. The decade could be sort of an extended International Geophysical Year.

An international headquarters could be established to serve as an information and conference center. A proposal for the creation of an international development university to serve as such a center has been submitted to the government of France as part of a long-range plan for Paris. As of this writing it has received the support of the French government.

Such a worldwide effort as I have described might well have a significant effect on the United Nations. It could give rise to more cooperation and collaboration among its participating nations. It might lead to a moratorium on defense spending during the Development Decade, and possibly beyond. It might even lead to activation of an idea that has been lying dormant for many years, that of *world citizenship.* An international youth movement could well provide the spark necessary to make this idea catch fire. World government might then be approached by the actions of the governed, not by actions of governments.

CONCLUSION

Effective national development requires the kind of individual and collective commitment that is usually only brought about by (1) a severe external threat from man (as in war) or from Nature (as in the threat of a flood); (2) reconstruction after a man-made or natural catastrophe (as in reconstruction of Japan after World War II or in repairing the ravages of an earthquake); or (3) a revolution. Leaders of less-developed countries must learn how to bring about such a commitment without the help of a threatened or actual catastrophe, or violent revolution.

There is a need for leaders who can create a shared vision of a desirable future and effectively direct pursuit of it. As Donald Schon has observed: "At the root of most innovations significant enough to precipitate a change of state, there are individuals who display irrational commitment, extra-ordinary energy, a combativeness which enables them to battle established interests over long periods of time, and a remarkable skill at guerrilla warfare."

Leadership itself may be either reactive, inactive, preactive, or interactive. Of these the interactive is the most difficult because it seeks to overthrow an old order and establish a new one. It requires widespread acceptance of a new *weltanschauung,* a new view of the world and oneself. Reactive, inactive, and preactive leaders have no need for a new conceptual framework; they work within the established one. They are preoccupied with reinterpreting old concepts and theories in light of new facts, or reinterpreting new facts in light of old concepts and theories.

The interactive leader must find a new and exciting concept of "development," one that does not incorporate as inevitable the evils produced by the development of the more advanced nations. Such a concept will clearly have to be broader and more systemic than previous concepts of development have been. It will have to be one that enables less-developed countries to take a shorter and less painful route to development than developed countries have taken.

I have tried in this book to contribute to the development of such a concept by providing a view of the world and a way of thinking about it that offers a new and richer concept of development, one that applies equally to less- and more-developed countries. Both types still have a very long way to go—all the way to their ideals.

EPILOGUE

We have come a long way together. I hope you found the trip self-justifying. Even if you did you are likely to be asking what destination has been reached. I could reply that there is no destination in the search for an ideal other than the ideal itself, and it can never be reached. But we have reached a stopping point, however temporary. I owe you a conclusion that serves as a starting point for the next phase of your journey. I have tried to provide one that gets down to essentials in form as well as content.

What does this book offer? Speculation and sketches? Between sketches and design, design and implementation, and implementation and improvement, impossibility looms large. Is this true?

If one mess is removed others remain and a new one may replace the old. If all are removed may not the mess that includes them as parts—the all-inclusive mess—remain and be made worse? Is this not what you told us?

Furthermore, most people are re-, in-, or pre-, not inter-, active. What can the latter do to move the masses into a future produced by their will rather than the lack of it, a lack they call *fate*? Into a future in which every man can do what he wills and by so doing enable every other to do the same.

Humanity is a system of attitudes. Can one part change the whole?

The whole can only be changed by its parts or by the whole of which it is part. We cannot change ourselves; we can only change our parts and the whole of which we are part. Only through them can we change ourselves.

Even now the environment imposes changes on man. Every imposition is an opportunity for intervention—for changing the future. There is no lack of opportunity. With what weapon can we attack it?

There is nothing as powerful as an idea whose time has come. The idea is *interaction*. Look back. See why.

The Middle Age was an age of inaction. Life was not important enough to do anything about. Death was. No surprise in an age in which man did not know enough to do anything significant about life. He knew this. He did not know whether or not he could affect death.

The Machine Age was an age of preaction. Man penetrated life with technology, looking for problems to solve, fitting what he found to his solutions: converting windmills to giants to justify use of the weapons in hand, and converting giants to windmills to justify not using his weapons against enemies he feared.

Man learned how to produce, not consume. He consumed other men and himself. He used himself as a weapon against other men. Death became a way of life. War became a maternity ward in which heroes were born and died.

The future happened; it was not made. Destiny was designed by default.

Majority races, sexes, and generations—euphemistically called "minorities"—are rising and demanding a future they can live with *now*. We mistake our part for the whole; not they. They induce the labor that gives birth to the Systems Age.

The Systems Age is an idea and the idea is *interaction*. Of whom with whom?

Observe. The Machine Age gave us machines to replace our bodies, and the Systems Age gives us machines to replace our minds, as instruments of work. Will man have to compete with machines for the right to work? Or is there another whose work he can do? Whose?

GOD's. God's work is to create the future. Man must take it away from Him. How? The only way he can: by submitting himself to his victims for redesign and use as *they* see fit. Together they can realize ideals.

We do not know that we cannot recreate the world. We have not tried. We should, if for no other reason but the satisfaction that trying can bring.

But there is another reason:

TRYING IS AN IDEA WHOSE TIME HAS ALSO COME.

APPENDIX

THE COMPONENTS OF
A MANAGEMENT SYSTEM

In Chapter 2 it was asserted that a management system should perform four functions: (1) identify problems, (2) make decisions, (3) control the decisions made, and (4) provide the information required to perform each of the first three functions. In this Appendix each of these functions is described in a little more detail than was provided in the chapter.

The management system which results from the interaction of the four functions is shown in Figure A.1.

INFORMATION SYSTEMS

An adaptive-learning control system must have information about the problems that do and may face the system it controls. It requires such information to solve, prepare for, and prevent threats, and to exploit or create opportunities. The subsystem that provides such information is called a *management information system*.

Such information systems must deal both with solicited data and information most of which is internally generated on a routine basis, and with unsolicited information most of which is nonroutine and externally generated. Unsolicited information may come in letters, magazines, books, newspapers, telephone calls, face-to-face conversations, and so on. There is usually more unsolicited than solicited data and information to be handled. But automated information technology can be used more effectively and extensively in dealing with preplanned internally generated data and information than with that which is unplanned and externally generated. However, much of the growing body of knowledge and understanding of observation, communica-

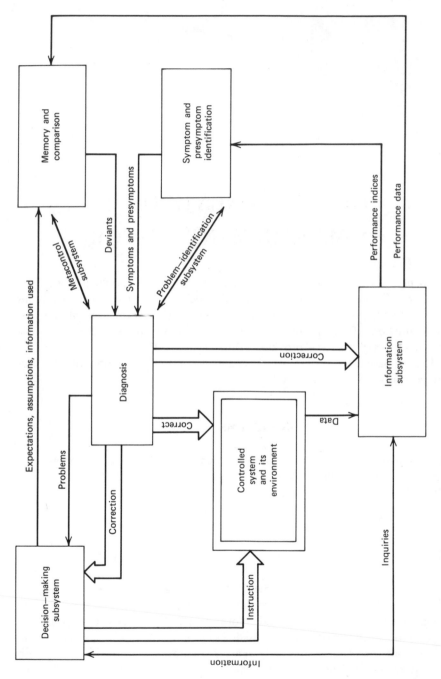

Figure A.1   Schematic diagram of adaptive-learning control system.

tion, and data processing can be used to increase the effectiveness with which man as well as machines can perform as parts of information systems.

Managers are handicapped more by the overabundance of irrelevant information than by the shortage of relevant information. Most managers already have more information available to them than they can effectively handle. Therefore, information systems should be designed not only to generate, transmit, process, store, and retrieve data—much of which can be automated—but also to filter and condense unsolicited information. Filtration and condensation of information cannot be effectively automated at present but significant developments are under way.

Information is required by each of the other three subsystems of the control system but the information system itself must receive information from them which enables it to perform its functions effectively.

Automated information technology has undergone rapid and dramatic development in the last decade but it has only begun to be used effectively. Only by such use can organizations of any size hope to adapt and learn as rapidly as is required by the changes to which they are being subjected.

PROBLEM IDENTIFICATION

Actual and potential problems can be identified once symptoms and omens (presymptoms) have been identified. A symptom is a deviation of a system's behavior from what is considered to be normal behavior. For example, a fever is abnormally high body temperature. High and low blood pressure, costs, absenteeism, frequency of defects—in fact, high and low measures of any index of performance—can be used as symptoms. Symptoms may indicate either threats or opportunities; high costs, for example, may indicate a threat, but abnormally low costs may signal an opportunity.

Well-developed statistical procedures are available for defining "normal behavior" and for detecting significant deviations from it. These involve analysis of past and current performance of the system being controlled, other systems like it (for sake of comparison), and its environment. The selection of performance measures and indices to be used in symptom surveillance cannot presently be automated. It requires enlightened human judgment.

Information about performance indicators and measures can be provided routinely by an information system and computers can be used to detect symptoms using the information provided. But there is always a need for humans to look for symptoms in areas not previously scanned.

Omens are presymptoms, predictors of future symptoms. For example, when a person thinks he is catching a cold but does not yet have it, he has observed a presymptom. These are not mysterious premonitions but explainable phenomena. They are *nonrandom* normal behavior. Let me explain. Normal behavior is not absolutely constant but varies within a specifiable range. For example, normal body temperature may vary within 1 degree Farenheit around 98.6 degrees. Fluctuations within this range are usually random, that is, show no detectable pattern. Therefore, if we observe an increasing or decreasing sequence of temperatures within the normal range, we can predict a fever or lower-than-normal temperature. A trend is only one type of nonrandom behavior; a cycle is another. These and many other types of nonrandom behavior are detectable by use of statistical procedures which are subject to automation. Doing so enables us to anticipate future threats and opportunities earlier than would otherwise be possible. For example, detection of an increasing trend of unemployment rates each of which is within the normal range, may enable us to prevent abnormally high unemployment before it occurs.

Symptoms and presymptoms require explanation, diagnosis, before anything can be done about them. Diagnosis is the search for producers of abnormal and nonrandom normal behavior. Effective diagnostic procedures have been developed in science. This does not imply that symptom- and presymptom-producers are always easy to find and identify. This is an area in which human skill, imagination, and creativity has a major role to play. But significant progress has been made in automating diagnosis in medicine and in detecting causes of malfunctioning of machines. Although extensions to social systems seem inevitable, they are not imminent.

Once a diagnosis has been made, one can determine whether or not action is required. Diagnosis may reveal a self-correcting situation or one about which nothing can be done. If, however, a problem is revealed, then it can be fed into the decision-making subsystem.

DECISION MAKING

An adaptive-learning control system must be able to use information in solving its problems, in decision making. Decision making is a process that converts information into instructions. Instructions are messages that are intended to affect the behavior of the system that is controlled in such a way as to improve its performance.

Decision making requires thought and thought requires mental manipulation of a representation, a concept, of that which is to be decided about. Through manipulation of such representations a decision maker can determine what alternatives are available to him and what the consequences of each are likely to be.

One of the major intellectual developments of the Systems Age consists of the growing ability to formulate explicit, quantitative, and accurate representations of problem situations. These representations are usually expressed in symbolic form, hence are called *symbolic models*. The use of symbolic models to represent things other than problems is old hat in science. Children are taught that πr^2 represents the area of a circle and that $y = a + bx$ represents any straight line that can be drawn on a plane. Successful symbolic modeling of problems, however, has developed only recently. This development has made it possible (1) to improve significantly the quality of decision making, (2) to increase the rate at which it can be improved, and (3) to reduce the time it requires. Automation has helped make these things possible. Let us see how.

A symbolic model of a problem has two parts. The first is an equation that relates a measure of system performance to those aspects of the problem situation, both controlled and uncontrolled, that can affect it. The performance equation has the following form:

performance of the system = a specified relationship between controlled variables and uncontrolled variables

Measures of performance may include such quantities as the number of houses built per year, expected life, cost of a project, or net profit. Controlled variables may include such factors as the number of people employed, the amount of money spent on material, the kind of material used, and the location and size of a facility to be built. Uncontrolled variables may include such things as the weather, national economic conditions, the cost of labor, competitive behavior, and consumer preferences.

The second part of the model expresses the limits within which each of the controlled variables can be manipulated. For example, suppose that a specified amount of money is available and it must be allocated to several activities. Then the sum of the amounts cannot exceed the amount available, and the amount allocated to each cannot be less than zero. Such constraints can also be expressed in symbolic form.

The solution to a modeled problem consists of those values of the controlled variables that, within the specified constraints and under the relevant uncontrolled conditions, yield the best performance of the system. A solution that does so is said to be *optimal*.

A procedure for manipulating the symbols in a model that yields an optimal, or approximately optimal, solution is called an *algorithm*. When we have a model of a problem and an algorithm for extracting a solution from it, the decision process can either be automated or be carried out by researchers serving the decision makers. Clearly, the availability of a model and an algorithm reduces or eliminates the need for reliance on experience—trial and error—in the real world, hence greatly accelerates the process of learning.

Models and algorithms are usually developed and applied by operations researchers and management scientists. Their development often requires a considerable amount of research—research that usually provides new and deeper understanding of the operations of the system. Model building also reveals and makes explicit what generally is not, but should be, understood about the system's operations. Hence it directs an important learning process. Because the models developed are explicitly formulated, they are open to examination and criticism by the decision makers and other researchers. This also accelerates the improvement of decision making.

In many cases models are constructed for which algorithms cannot be found; that is, no systematic way of extracting optimal solutions from them is available. Such models, however, can be put to effective use. They can be used to *compare* alternative solutions that are proposed by the decision maker. Thus a manager and a model can engage in a dialogue through which the decision maker can systematically improve a proposed solution to a problem even if he cannot find the best one possible. The decision maker can try and err or experiment using the model rather than the real world, thereby accelerating and reducing the cost of the learning process.

Models of different problems can be linked together in such a way as to make explicit the relationships between the problems they represent. Therefore, by combining problem models into a system of models, a problematic situation or a mess can be modeled. Such complex model-systems can be used in the planning process.

The problems for which both models and algorithms are available, or can easily be produced, tend to be ones that are repetitive, routine, and operation oriented. They tend to be ones in which human behavior is not important and ones in which means rather than ends are to be selected. Strategic problems and those involving human behavior in a central role are more difficult to model and solve. The use of models and algorithms on simpler problems can and does free decision makers so that they can spend more time on more important, more complex, longer-range problems that normally are put aside under the pressure of daily short-run crises.

Automation of decision making does not diminish the manager's job; to the contrary, it enlarges it and makes it more difficult. The number of problems confronting him is not reduced because, recall, the solution to most problems almost always creates several new and more important ones. If a management system is to learn how to be more effective, then the managers within it must also learn how to cope effectively with problems of increasing complexity. In the Systems Age learning will become an increasing part of work of all types, particularly managerial.

CONTROL: ADAPTATION AND LEARNING

If a controlled system is to learn and adapt more effectively, then its controlling subsystem (management) must carry out the following four operations.

1. Specifying the expected effects of every, or almost every, decision.

The improvement expected to be brought about by a decision should be explicitly formulated by the decision maker (man or machine) and the time by which it is expected should be specified and recorded. In addition, a complete record of how the decision was made should be stored in an inactive memory along with the expectations. The memory should be inactive in the sense that it will not modify what is put into it in light of subsequent experience. Computers and filing systems can usually provide less active memories than can human decision makers.

If, for example, a program is initiated for the purpose of reducing unemployment, then the reduction expected and the time by which it is expected should be made a matter of record along with a complete description of how the program was arrived at. Unless this is done, the possibility of learning from subsequent experience is significantly reduced.

2. The information system should generate information about the actual state of affairs at the time at which a predicted improvement is expected, and the actual and expected state of affairs should be compared.

If the actual state of affairs meets expectations, then the decision and related systems have operated effectively. If not, the difference between them is a symptom of malfunctioning of the control system. Diagnosis is required.

3. Mismatches of expectations and actual outcomes should be explained.

Such deviations may be due to any one or combination of four reasons.

(*a*) The information used in making the decision was in error. If this is found to be the case the information system requires modification so that such errors are not made again. This enables the information system to learn.

(*b*) The conception or model of the problem on which the decision was based, or the way a solution was derived from it, was deficient. If this is the case then the decision system requires modification. This facilitates its learning.

(*c*) The instructions issued by the decision maker were not carried out properly. Implementation was defective. This requires appropriate changes in the controlled system, changes that enable it to learn.

(*d*) Unanticipated changes in the controlled system or its environment occurred. If these are permanent changes then any one or all of the management subsystems and the system controlled may have to be modified appropriately. If the deviant-producing changes are found to be temporary but subject to repetition, then the management system should be adjusted to take this possibility into account. In either case, the deviant-induced changes in the control and controlled system constitute adaptation.

4. Corrective action should be taken.

The ability to take the corrective action required to learn and adapt depends on the flexibility and changeability of the control and controlled systems. Most goal-seeking and purposeful systems, including private organizations and public institutions, seek stability and therefore resist change. The procedures by which they do so were accurately and humorously described by C. N. Parkinson and are reflected in the law that bears his name. We can design flexibility into mechanical (hence passive) systems but it is much more difficult to design it into purposeful systems. The problems associated with so doing, and possible solutions to them, are the subject of a growing interdisciplinary effort frequently referred to as "Organizational Development." This area was recently covered very effectively by Donald Schon.

REFERENCES

1. Advisory Commission on Intergovernmental Relations, *Metropolitan Social and Economic Disparities*, Superintendent of Documents, U. S. Printing Office, Washington, D. C., January 1965.
2. Ansoff, H. Igor, *Corporate Strategy*, McGraw-Hill Book Co., New York, 1965.
3. Anthony, R. N., "The Trouble with Profit Maximization," *Harvard Business Review*, 38 (November-December 1960), 126–134.
4. Balakrishnan, T. R., and G. D. Camp, *Family Planning and Old Age Security in India*, India Institute of Management, Calcutta, 1965.
5. Baumol, W. J., *Business Behavior, Value and Growth*, The Macmillan Co., New York, 1959.
6. ____, "Enlightened Self-Interest and Corporate Philanthrophy," in *A New Rationale for Corporate Social Policy*, Committee for Economic Development, New York, 1970, pp. 3–19.
7. Beranek, W., *Analysis of Financial Decisions*, Richard D. Irwin, Homewood, Ill., 1963.
8. Berry, Donald S., G. W. Blomme, P. W. Shuldiner, and J. H. Jones, *The Technology of Urban Transportation, Transportation Center*, Northwestern University Press, Chicago, 1963.
9. Bierce, Ambrose, *The Devil's Dictionary*, The World Publishing Co., Cleveland, 1911.
10. Blackett, P. M. S., "The Scientist and Underdeveloped Countries," in *The Science of Science*, Maurice Goldsmith and Alan Mackay, Eds., Pelican Books, Harmondsworth, Middlesex, England, 1966, pp. 47–64.
11. Blumberg, Paul, *Industrial Democracy*, Schocken Books, New York, 1969.
12. Brown, Wilfred, *Participation*, Management Decision Monograph, MCB Limited, 200 Keighley Road, Bradford, Yorkshire, England, 1972.
13. Cassell, Frank H., "The Corporation and Community: Realities and Myths," *Michigan State University Business Topics*, (Autumn, 1970), 11–19.
14. Chesbro, George C., "Short Circuit," *Alfred Hitchcock's Mystery Magazine*, October 1971, pp. 137–159.
15. Churchman, C. West, *Prediction and Optimal Decision*, Prentice-Hall, Englewood Cliffs, N.J., 1961.
16. Clark, Ramsey, *Crime in America*, Pocket Books, New York, 1971.
17. Clibbon, Sheila, and Marvin L. Sachs, "Creating Consolidated Clinical Spaces for an Expanding Role in Health Care," *Architectural Record*, 149 (February 1971), 105–112.
18. Commoner, Barry, *Science and Survival*, The Viking Press, New York, 1967.

19. Cyert, R. M., and J. G. March, *A Behavioral Theory of the Firm*, Prentice-Hall, Englewood Cliffs, N.J., 1963, Chapter 3.

20. Department of Housing and Urban Development, *Tomorrow's Transportation: New Systems for the Urban Future*, Washington, D.C., 1968.

21. Dewey, John, *The Quest for Certainty*, George Allen and Unwin, London, 1930.

22. ——, *Logic: The Theory of Inquiry*, Henry Holt and Co., New York, 1938.

23. Drucker, P. F., "Business Objectives and Survival Needs: Notes on a Discipline of Business Enterprise," *The Journal of Business*, 31 (1958), 81–90.

24. Dubos, René, *Mirage of Health*, Anchor Books, Garden City, N.Y., 1959.

25. ——, *Man Adapting*, Yale University Press, New Haven, 1965.

26. Dunlop, John T., "The Capacity of the U.S. to Provide and Finance Expanding Health Services," in *Closing the Gaps in Availability and Accessibility of Health Services*, New York Academy of Medicine, 1965, pp. 1326–1327.

27. Dykeman, Wilma, *Look to this Day*, Holt, Rinehart and Winston, New York, 1968.

28. Ellul, Jacques, *The Technological Society*, Vintage Books, New York, 1967.

29. Emery, F. E., and Einar Thorsund, *Form and Content in Industrial Democracy*, Tavistock Publications, London, 1969.

30. Fanshel, S., and J. W. Busch, "A Health-Status Index and Its Application to Health-Service Outcomes," *Operations Research*, 18 (1970), 1021–1066.

31. Field, Mark G., "Medicine and Industrial Society," in *Systems and Medical Care*, Alan Sheldon, Frank Baker, and Curtis P. McLaughlin, Eds., The M.I.T. Press, Cambridge, Mass., 1970.

32. Finnie, William C., *Towards a Systems Analysis of Racial Equality*, a Ph.D. dissertation in operations research, University of Pennsylvania, Philadelphia, 1970.

33. ——, "Field Experiments in Litter Control," mimeographed paper, Anheuser-Busch, Inc., St. Louis, June 12, 1972.

34. Fitch, Lyle C., et al, *Urban Transportation and Public Policy*, Chandler, San Francisco, 1964.

35. Flory, L. E., "Automated Highway," in *Proceedings of the Urban Transportation Alternatives Symposium*, Stanford Research Institute, Menlo Park, Calif., 1964, pp. 65–79.

36. Forbes, R. J., *The Conquest of Nature*, Mentor Books, New York, 1969.

37. Friedenberg, Edgar Z., "How to Survive in Your Native Land," book review in *The New York Times Book Review*, April 11, 1971, p. 19.

38. Friedman, Milton, *Capitalism and Freedom*, University of Chicago Press, Chicago, 1962.

39. Gabor, Dennis, *Inventing the Future*, Penguin Books, Harmondsworth, Middlesex, England, 1964.

40. Garfield, Sidney R., "The Delivery of Medical Care," *Scientific American*, April 1970, pp. 15–23.

41. Hall, John R., et al. *A Systems Approach to the Problems of Solid Waste and Litter*, a report of the Management and Behavioral Science Center, University of Pennsylvania, Philadelphia, September 1971.

42. Hauser, Philip M., "Wither the Urban Society," in *Is There an Optimal Level of Population*, S. Fred Singer, Ed., McGraw-Hill Book Co., New York, 1971, pp. 246–250.

43. Henderson, Hazel, "The Computer in Social Planning: A Chance for the Little Man to Be Heard," *MBA*, 6 (December 1971), 14–18.

44. Henry, J., *Culture against Man*, Random House, New York, 1963.

45. Herndon, James, *How to Survive in Your Native Land*, Simon & Shuster, New York, 1971.

46. Hirschman, A. O., and C. E. Lindblom, "Economic Development, Research and Development, Policy Making: Some Converging Views," in *Systems Thinking*, F. E. Emery, Ed., Penguin Books, Harmondsworth, Middlesex, England, 1969, pp. 351–371.
47. Howard, Ronald A., "Free for All." *Management Science*, 13 (1967), B-681–B-685.
48. Illich, Ivan, *Deschooling Society*, Harrow Books, New York, 1972.
49. Ireson, W. G., "Preparation for Business in Engineering Schools," in *The Education of American Businessmen*, F. C. Pierson et al, McGraw-Hill Book Co., New York, 1959.
50. Jackson, J. B., "Notes and Comments," *Landscape*, 17 (1968), 1–2.
51. Jennings, E. E., "The Worlds of the Executive," *TWA Ambassador*, 4 (1971), 28–30.
52. Laing, R. D., *The Politics of Experience*, Ballantine Books, New York, 1967.
53. Langer, S. K., *Philosophy in a New Key*, Penguin Books, New York, 1948.
54. Likert, Rensis, "The Influence of Social Research on Corporate Responsibility," in *A New Rationale for Corporate Social Policy*, Committee for Economic Development, New York, 1970, pp. 2–38.
55. McClenehan, J. W., and H. J. Simkowitz, "The Effect of Short Cars on Flow and Speed in Downtown Traffic: A Simulation Model and Some Results," *Transportation Science*, 3 (1969), 126–139.
56. McLuhan, Marshall, *Understanding Media: The Extensions of Man*, Signet Books, New York, 1964.
57. Morris, Charles, *Signs, Language and Behavior*, George Braziller, New York, 1955.
58. Morrisey, William R., "Nixon Anti-Crime Plan Undermines Crime Statistics," *Justice Magazine*, June/July, 1972, pp. 8–11.
59. Ortega y Gasset, José, *Mission of the University*, W. W. Norton & Co., New York, 1966.
60. Parkinson, C. N., *Parkinson's Law*, Houghton Mifflin, New York, 1957.
61. Penn-Jersey Transportation Study, Vol. 1, *The State of the Region*, 1964.
62. (N. V.) Philips' Gloeilampenfabrieken, *Work Structuring: A Summary of Experiments at Philips — 1963 to 1968*, Eindoven, Holland.
63. Piel, Gerald, "For the Living Generation," in *The Science of Science*, Maurice Goldsmith and Alan Mackay, Eds., Pelican Books, Harmondsworth, Middlesex, England, 1966, pp. 65–84.
64. Polgar, Steven, "Health," in *International Encyclopedia of the Social Sciences*, David L. Sills, Ed., Macmillan Co. and The Free Press, New York, 1968.
65. Porter, J. C., M. W. Sasieni, E. S. Marks, and R. L. Ackoff, "The Use of Simulation as a Pedagogical Device," *Management Science*, 12 (February 1966), B-170–B-179.
66. Powell, C. F., "Priorities in Science and Technology for Developing Countries," in *The Science of Science*, Maurice Goldsmith and Alan Mackay, Eds., Pelican Books, Harmondsworth, Middlesex, England, 1966, pp. 85–112.
67. Quittenton, R. C., "Forum," *University Affairs*, October 1972, p. 9.
68. Rapoport, Anatol, *Fights, Games, and Debates*, The University of Michigan Press, Ann Arbor, 1960.
69. Reagan, Thomas, B., *The Inside-Out Hoist*, The Detective Book Club, Roslyn, N.Y., 1971.
70. Rosenblueth, A., and N. Wiener, "Purposeful and Non-Purposeful Systems," *Philosophy of Science*, 17 (1950), 318–326.
71. ——————, and J. Bigelow, "Behavior, Purpose, and Teleology," *Philosophy of Science*, 11 (1943), 18–24.
72. Sagasti, Francisco, and Russell L. Ackoff, "Possible and Likely Futures on Urban Transportation," *Socio-Economic Planning*, 5 (1971), 413–428.

73. Saunders, Robert O., "Curbing the Corporations: Incentive and 'Pay-to-Pollute' Taxes," *MBA*, February 1972, pp. 57–58.
74. Schon, Donald, *Beyond the Stable State*, Random House, New York, 1971.
75. Shannon, C. E., and Warren Weaver, *The Mathematical Theory of Communication*, The University of Illinois Press, Urbana, 1949.
76. Silberman, Charles E., *Crisis in the Classroom*, Random House, New York, 1970.
77. Singer, E. A., Jr., *Experience and Reflection*, C. West Churchman, Ed., University of Pennsylvania Press, Philadelphia, 1959.
78. Snow, C. P., *The Two Cultures: A Second Look*, Mentor Books, New York, 1964.
79. Solomon, E., *The Theory of Financial Management*, Columbia University Press, New York, 1963.
80. Sommerhoff, G., *Analytical Biology*, Oxford University Press, London, 1950.
81. Stokes, B. R., "Status Report — BARTS," in *Proceedings of the Urban Transportation Alternatives Symposium*, Stanford Research Institute, Menlo Park, Calif., 1964.
82. Stone, Tabor R., *Beyond the Automobile: Reshaping the Environment*, Prentice-Hall, Englewood Cliffs, N.J., 1971.
83. Toffler, Alvin, *Future Shock*, Bantam Books, New York, 1971.
84. Vickers, Goeffrey, "Ecology, Planning and the American Dream," in *The Urban Condition*, L. J. Dahl, Ed., Basic Books, New York, 1963, pp. 374–395.
85. Von Bertalanffy, Ludwig, *General Systems Theory*, George Braziller, New York, 1968.
86. Wald, George, "A Generation in Search of a Future," *The Boston Globe*, March 8, 1969.
87. Wallich, Henry C., and John J. McGowan, "Stockholder Interest and the Corporation's Role in Social Policy," in *A New Rationale for Corporate Social Policy*, Committee for Economic Development, New York, 1970, pp. 39–59.
88. Ward, Barbara, *The Lopsided World*, W. W. Norton, New York, 1968.
89. ————, and René Dubos, *Only One Earth*, Pelican Books, Harmondsworth, Middlesex, England, 1972.
90. Wibberly, Leonard, *The Mouse that Roared*, Little and Co., Boston, 1955.
91. Wiener, Norbert, *Cybernetics*, John Wiley & Sons, New York, 1948.
92. Wilcox, Francis O., "Preface," to Barbara Ward [88].
93. Wofle, Dael, "Editorial," *Science*, 173 (July 9, 1971), 109.
94. Zandi, Iraj, "Design of Mixed Solid Waste Systems," presented at the Colloquim on Urbanism, University of Pennsylvania, Philadelphia, April 1971.

NOTES

vii   Ortega y Gasset quote from [59], p. 1.

4   Ellul reference is [28].
Forbes quotes from [36], p. 110.
Toffler quote from [83], p. 432.
Snow quote from [78], p. 45.

4-5   Vickers quote from [84], p. 374.

5   Schon quote from [74], pp. 227–228.
McCluhan reference is [56].

6   Wald reference is [86].
Toffler quote from [83], p. 477.

7   Chesbro quote from [14], p. 157.

12   Langer reference is [53].
Morris reference is [57].
Shannon reference is [75].
Wiener reference is [91].

13   von Bertalanffy reference is [85].

16   Singer reference is [77].
Sommerhoff reference is [80].
Rosenblueth et al. reference is [70] and [71].

20   Hauser quote from [42], pp. 249–250. Used with permission of McGraw-Hill Book Company

20-21   Dewey reference is [22].

23-24   Hirschman-Lindblom quotes from [46], p. 358.

31   Dewey reference is [21].

34   Mantua Community Planners is a neighborhood self-development group from Philadelphia.
Jennings quote from [51], p. 29.

35   *Newsweek* quote from May 17, 1971 issue, p. 80. Copyright Newsweek, Inc., 1971, reprinted by permission.

35-36   *The New York Times* quote from a report by Philip Shakecoff in December 22, 1973 issue, p. 1. © 1973 by the New York Times Company. Reprinted by permission.

36   Jennings quote from [51], p. 29.

37   Clark quote from [16], p. 14. Copyright © 1970, by Ramsey Clark. Reprinted by permission of Simon and Schuster.

37   *Look* quote of Abzug from July 13, 1971 issue, p. 61.

41   Brown quote from [12], p. 5, with permission by *Management Decision*.

42   If a platform receives more votes than is necessary for *n* constituencies (for example, 2) but less than is necessary for *n* + 1 (for example, 3), then *n* equal and oversized constituencies would be formed. The representative elected for each would have his vote in the legislature weighted to reflect this characteristic of his constituency. For example, if his constituency was 1.4 times the average size, he would have 1.4 votes.

44   Henderson quote from [43], p. 15.
Advisory Commission reference is [1].

48   Blumberg quote from [11], p. 123. Reprinted by permission of Schocken Books Inc. Copyright © 1968 by Paul Blumberg.
Philips quote from [62], pp. 7 and 27.
Nation's Business quote from November 1971 issue, p. 22.

49   *The New York Times* quote from a report by Agis Salpukas in February 2, 1973 issue, pp. 1 and 47. © 1973 by the New York Times Company. Reprinted by permission.
Fortune quote from September 1970 issue, p. 167.
Blumberg quote from [11], p. 3. Reprinted by permission of Schocken Books Inc. Copyright © 1968 by Paul Blumberg.

49-50   Brown quote from [12], p. 18, with permission of *Management Decision*.

50   Emery-Thorsund quote from [29], p. 86.

53   *The New York Times* quote from a report by Agis Salpukas in February 5, 1973 issue, p. 1. © 1973 by The New York Times Company. Reprinted by permission.

54   Rockefeller quote from his article, "Social Audit," which appeared in the May 1, 1972 issue of *The New York Times*. © 1972 by The New York Times Company. Reprinted by permission.

56   Friedman quotes from [38], p. 133.

57-58   Toffler quote from [83], p. 453.

58   *The New York Times* quote from a report by Terry Robards in April 14, 1972 issue, p. 1. © 1972 by The New York Times Company. Reprinted by permission.

58-59   Wallich-McGowan quotes from [87], pp. 55 and 44.

59   Baumol quote from [5], p. 17.
Likert quote from [54], p. 22.

59-60   *The Wall Street Journal* quote from a report by Frederick Andrews in the December 9, 1971 issue, p. 1. Reprinted with the permission of *The Wall Street Journal*, © Dow Jones & Company Inc. 1971.

61   Churchman quote from [15], p. 56. Reprinted by permission of Prentice-Hall, Inc., Englewood Cliffs, New Jersey.
Ansoff quote from [2], p. 31. Used with permission of McGraw-Hill Book Company.
Anthony reference is [3].
Solomon reference is [79].
Beranek reference is [7].
Baumol reference is [6].

61-62   Drucker quote from [25], p. 87.

62   Ansoff quote from [2], p. 34. Used with permission of McGraw-Hill Book Company.
Cyert-March reference is [19].
Bierce quote from [9].

64   Toffler quote from [83], p. 454.

65   National Center for Resource Recovery, Inc., 1211 Connecticut Ave., N.W., Washington, D.C., 20036.

71   *Newsweek* quotes from February 16, 1970 issue, pp. 69 and 65. Copyright Newsweek, Inc. 1970, reprinted by permission.

71-72   Silberman quote from [76], p. 10.

72   Sparer quote from September 30, 1972 issue of *The Washington Post.*
Herndon quote from [45], p. 19.

72-73   Friedenberg quote from [37], pp. 19-20.

73   Illich quote from [48], pp. 1–2.

76   *The New York Times* quote from April 3, 1971 issue, p. 1. © 1971 by The New York Times Company. Reprinted by permission.

77   Friedenberg quote from [37], p. 20.

80   Ireson quote from [49], p. 507. Used with permission of McGraw-Hill Book Company.
Wolfle reference is [93].

81   Henry quote from [44], p. 288.
Laing reference is [52], pp. 71-72.

82   Quittenton quote from [67], p. 9.

83   Farber quotes from April 2, 1971 issue of *The New York Times*. © 1971 by The New York Times Company. Reprinted by permission.

87   Porter reference is [65].

94   Macrae quote from January 22, 1972 issue of the *Economist*, p. x.

97   Dykeman quote from [27], p. 112.

97-98   Reagan quote from [69], pp. 66–67.

99-100   Laing quotes from [52], pp. 57 and 58.

100   Laing quotes from [52], pp. 71–72.
Clark quote from [16], p. 17. Copyright © 1970, by Ramsey Clark. Reprinted by permission of Simon and Schuster.

102   Densen-Gerber quote from January 11, 1972 Issue of *The New York Times.* © 1972 by The New York Times Company. Reprinted by permission.

103-104   Laing quotes from [52], pp. 87–88 and 94.

109   Rapoport reference is [68].

115   Cassell quote from [13], p. 12.

118   *The Evening Bulletin* (Philadelphia) quote is from January 22, 1971 issue.

118-119   Cassell quotes from [13].

120-121   Finnie reference is [32].

121   Cassell quote from [13], p. 14.

124   Story of MIDC in January 16, 1971 issue of *Business Week*, pp. 96–102.

127   Write-up of education program appears in "Businessmen Go to the Ghetto to Learn," in June 19, 1971 issue of *Business Week.*

134   Morrissey quote from [58], p. 8.

135   Clark quotes from [16], pp. 38 and 75. Copyright© 1970, by Ramsey Clark. Reprinted by permission.
Newsweek quote from p. 51, March 2, 1970. Copyright Newsweek, Inc. 1970, reprinted by permission.
Clark quote from [16], p. 39. Copyright © 1970, by Ramsey Clark. Reprinted by permission.
Wicker quote from September 16, 1971 issue of *The New York Times.* © 1971 by The New York Times Company. Reprinted by permission.
National Commission quote from p. 585.

135-136   *The Guardian* quote from August 28, 1971 issue.

136   Clark quote from [16], pp. 6 and 34. Copyright © 1970, by Ramsey Clark. Reprinted by permission.

        Dunne quote from March 2, 1970 issue of *Newsweek*, p. 52. Copyright Newsweek, Inc. 1970, reprinted by permission.

137   *The New York Times* account was by Tom Wicker in the September 15, 1971 issue.

137-138 Clark quotes from [16] pp. 17, 41, 28, and 6. Copyright © 1970, by Ramsey Clark. Reprinted by permission.

138   Clark quotes from [16], pp. 107, 197, and 217. Copyright © 1970, by Ramsey Clark. Reprinted by permission.

139   Clark quotes from [16], pp. 193, 199, 194, and 183. Copyright © 1970, by Ramsey Clark. Reprinted by permission.

139-140 Clark quote from [16], p. 206. Copyright©1970, by Ramsey Clark. Reprinted by permission.

140   Clark quote from [16]. p. 326. Copyright©1970, by Ramsey Clark. Reprinted by permission.

144-145 *The Evening Bulletin* (Philadelphia) quote from January 18, 1972 issue, p. 24.

145-146 *Parade* quote from July 23, 1972 issue, p. 14.

146-147 *Parade* quote from December 12, 1971 issue, pp. 6–8.

147   *The New York Times* quote from article by B. Drummond Ayers, Jr., in December 21, 1971 issue, p. 19. © 1971 by The New York Times Company. Reprinted by permission.

150   Howard quote from [47], p. B-684.

155   Dunlop quote from [26], pp. 1326–1327.

156   Polgar quotes from [64], Vol. 6, pp. 330 and 332.

157   Dubos reference is [24].

        Fanshel-Busch reference is [30].

160-161 Dubos quote from [25], p. 405.

161   Field quote from [31], p. 157.

161-162 Garfield quote from [40], p. 16.

163   Garfield quote from [40], p. 18.

164   Garfield quote from [40], p. 19.

        Laing quote from [52], p. 109.

164-165 Garfield quote from [40], p. 20.

165   Clibbon-Sachs reference is [17].

165-166 *The New York Times* quote from a report by John Sibley in December 18, 1971 issue. © 1971 by The New York Times Company. Reprinted by permission.

167-168 Garfield quotes from [40], p. 23.

169   Carhart quote from March 25, 1972 issue of *The New York Times.* © 1972 by The New York Times Company. Reprinted by permission.

172   Dubos quote from [24], pp. 227–228.

173   Ward-Dubos quote from [89], p. 47, by permission of Barbara Ward, René Dubos, Penguin Books Ltd., and André Deutsch, Ltd.

174   Commoner reference is [18].

175   Ward-Dubos quote from [89], p. 129, by permission of Barbara Ward, René Dubos, Penguin Books Ltd., and André Deutsch Ltd.

179   Finnie reference is [33].

181   Zandi quote from [94].

182   Lesher quote from June 1972 issue of *Nation's Cities.* Reprinted with

permission from NATION'S CITIES, magazine of the National League of Cities, Copyright 1972.

186   The procedure presented here is the product of a study reported in detail in [41].

189   Report of Management and Behavioral Science Center is [41].

190   *Metropolis* quote from June 1972 issue, p. 1.

190-191   Saunders quotes from [73], p. 58.

191   Ward-Dubos quote from [89]. pp. 102–103, by permission of Barbara Ward, René Dubos, Penguin Books Ltd., and André Deutsch Ltd.

192   Saunders quote from [73], p. 58.

193   Stone quote from [82], p. 98.
         Life quote from December 11, 1970 issue, p. 77. Copyright: LIFE Magazine, © 1970 Time, Inc.

194   Sagasti-Ackoff reference is [72].

195   Fitch quote from [34], p. 170.

196   First *The New York Times* quote is from a report by Paul Hoffman in March 30, 1972 issue, p. 6. © 1972 by The New York Times Company. Reprinted by permission.
         Second *The New York Times* quote is from a report by John H. Hess in November 14, 1971 issue. © 1971 by The New York Times Company. Reprinted by permission.

197-198   Jackson quote from [50], p. 2.

198   Stone quote from [82], pp. 98–99.

200   Stokes quote from [81], p. 13.
         Department of Housing and Urban Development quote from [20], p. 59.

201   Flory quote from [35], p. 69.
         Department of Housing and Urban Development reference is [20].

202   Berry quote from [8], p. 124.

203   Department of Housing and Urban Development quote from [20], p. 41.
         Occupancy figures from *Penn-Jersey Transportation Study*, 1964, p. 91.

204   McClenehan-Simkowitz reference is [55].
         Reference to *Mechanics Illustrated* is to October 1969 issue, p. 76. *Life* quote from December 11, 1970 issue, p. 77. Copyright: LIFE Magazine, © 1970 Time, Inc.

210   Toffler quote from [83], p. 37.
         Ward quote from [88], p. 11.
         The Mouse that Roared is [89].

211   Snow quotes from [78], p. 45.

212   Wilcox quote from [92], pp. 9–10.
         Ward quote from [88], p. 73.

213   Ward quote from [88], p. 75.
         Piel quote from [63], p. 68.
         Herzen quoted by Piel [63], p. 66.

214   Herzen quoted by Piel [63], p. 83.

215   Gabor quote from [39], p. 35.

216   Snow quote from [78], p. 48.
         Powell quote from [66], pp. 88–89.

216-217   U Thant quoted by Forbes [36], p. vii.

217   Wilcox quote from [92], p. 10.
         Ward suggestions appear in [88], pp. 121–128.

218	Lewis quoted by Powell [66], p. 101.
220	Forbes quotes from [36], pp. 88–89.
221	Balakrishnan-Camp reference is to an unpublished paper [4].
224	Ward reference is [88], pp. 106–110.
225	Schon quote from [73], p. 56.
236	Schon reference is [73].

In addition to those permissions explicitly acknowledged in the Notes I express appreciation for permissions also received from Alfred A. Knopf, Inc.; Basic Books; *Behavioral Science;* Cambridge University Press; Eugene E. Jennings; George C. Chesbro; Harper & Row Publishers, Inc.; John Wiley & Sons, Inc.; Judson Gooding; Macmillan Publishing Co., Inc.; *Management Science;* MBA Communications, Inc.; N. V. Philip's Gloeilampenfabrieken; Parade Publications, Inc.; Random House, Inc.; R. C. Quittenton; Simon & Schuster, Inc.; Stanford Research Institute; The Chase Manhattan Bank; *The Economist; The Guardian;* The New American Library, Inc.; The New York Academy of Medicine; The Transportation Center of Northwestern University; Walter J. Black, Inc.; W. H. Freeman and Company; and W. W. Norton.

NAME INDEX

SUBJECT INDEX